"Edwards and Mathews provide an excellent resource for readers eager to learn more about interpretations regarding women in ministry. Based on extensive research, the authors present various viewpoints fairly and clearly, and offer concise explanations to equip readers to draw their own conclusions on these pressing questions. I commend them for including a chapter on a topic that is not debatable, namely the importance of making churches and ministries safe for women."

—Lynn Cohick
Provost/Dean of Academic Affairs, Professor of New Testament,
Northern Seminary

"This is amazing! I get these questions every week and have for decades! I want everyone I know to have a copy. Edwards and Mathews offer the church one of the most charitable, accessible, and thorough surveys of the issue of women in ministry. Once you have this book, you'll pull it off the shelf time and time again for reference."

—Kat Armstrong
Author of *No More Holding Back, The In-Between Place,* and The Storyline Bible Studies

"What a gift Mathews and Edwards have given us in this accessible introduction to and evaluation of the two evangelical views on women and leadership in the church and home! If you care about the important contribution from this half of the body of Christ, and want to make a difference for the good of the church, this book is a great place to start."

—Ron Pierce
Editor, *Discovering Biblical Equality;*
Author, *Partners in Marriage and Ministry,*
Biola University

"*40 Questions About Women in Ministry* provides invaluable information that enables readers to make informed conclusions about God's purpose for women in ministry. Edwards and Mathews examine an important but contentious topic with humility and thoughtfulness, all the while promoting unity. Today's church can learn much from their respectful approach."

—Paul Lanum
Vice President of Publishing, RightNow Media

"Raise the topic of women in the church and the roles they have and you better be prepared to have your blood pressure checked along with the person you are talking to about the topic. Here is a book that calmly lays out the view's pro and con for the array of options the topic yields. It does so evenhandedly. 40 Questions lets you hear and consider the arguments from all sides, nuances included. I can think of no other work that does this and gives you what you need to consider how to see the topic and why. This is a much-needed work that supplies the up-to-date takes on what people discuss and deliberate on when the issue of women and the church is raised. Well done."

—Darrell Bock
Senior Research Professor of New Testament Studies,
Executive Director for Cultural Engagement for The Hendricks Center,
Dallas Theological Seminary

T0273881

"For too long, ignorance and shallow theology about women in ministry have caused harm and division in the church. So, with this book, Edwards and Mathews have provided a resource that the church desperately needs. Using language that is clear and accessible, they tackle the most common questions about complementarianism and egalitarianism. But, rather than elevating one position over the other, Edwards and Mathews provide a side-by-side analysis that allows the reader to make an informed decision on their own. If you are looking for a resource that will equip you to think critically about women in ministry with grace and love, this book is for you."

—Elizabeth Woodson
Bible teacher and author of *Embrace Your Life* and *From Beginning to Forever*

"Women are necessary for the mission of the church, full stop. Mathews and Edwards do a phenomenal job at navigating almost all the questions I ask and are asked by women (and men) as we seek to embody our beliefs on the value women bring to ministry, flourish in kingdom community, and pursue Jesus."

—Christian Williams
Director of Women's Discipleship,
Christ Community Church

"This is the book I was looking for years ago when I started asking my questions! With depth, relevance, and a fair representation of opposing sides, *40 Questions About Women in Ministry* will be a faithful companion to anyone exploring the breadth of this conversation for years to come."

—Aaron Armstrong
Lead Pastor,
Dallas Bible Church

"I am beyond thrilled to recommend this resource to you! Finally, questions are answered in a clear, biblical way that gives complete understanding of the calling and work of women to ministry and in the church. Edwards and Mathews have provided a unique tool and comprehensive study of Scripture as it relates to women, men, ministry, leadership, biblical times, current issues, and church history. In our complicated, ever-changing world with a variety of beliefs and misconceptions, this resource provides truth and explanation which builds health and unity—and is honoring to the Lord. A must-read for every woman (and man) who desires to do the will of God."

—Debbie Stuart
Women's Minister,
Green Acres Baptist Church

"I have never read a more comprehensive work on women in ministry in a single volume. It offers a clear understanding of key passages that help us understand women's roles in God's redemptive plan. Biblical, scholarly, and engaging, Edwards and Mathews write with a heart for Jesus and his church. This book is a gift to Christians everywhere."

—Jeff Warren
Senior Pastor,
Park Cities Baptist Church

40 QUESTIONS ABOUT
Women in Ministry

Sue Edwards
Kelley Mathews

Benjamin L. Merkle, Series Editor

40 Questions About Women in Ministry
© 2022 Sue Edwards and Kelley Mathews

Published by Kregel Academic, an imprint of Kregel Publications, 2450 Oak Industrial Dr. NE, Grand Rapids, MI 49505-6020.

This book is a title in the 40 Questions Series edited by Benjamin L. Merkle.

The Greek font GraecaU and the Hebrew font New JerusalemU are from www.linguistsoftware.com/lgku.htm, +1-425-775-1130.

ISBN 978-0-8254-4725-9

Printed in the United States of America

22 23 24 25 26 / 5 4 3 2 1

A prayer for us and our sacred siblings:
Help us, Lord Jesus, to fulfill your last request
before you went to the cross,
so that we may be brought to complete unity.
Then the world will know that God the Father
sent you and loves them even as he loves you.
(from John 17:20–23)

Contents

Preface

While our names are on the cover, this book came together through the efforts of a dedicated team. Cynthia Hester, Misty Hedrick, and Nandi Cozart collaborated with us, mostly via countless video chats during the pandemic of 2020–2021, to evaluate and question each step in the process. As part of their studies at Dallas Theological Seminary, Cynthia and Misty also led the writing of several chapters. We are grateful to each of these fine scholars and ministers for their contributions to this work.

We also thank Dr. Sandra Glahn, Dr. Ronald Pierce, and Dr. Darrell Bock for lending us their time and expertise as we consulted them for valuable insights in their areas of scholarly focus.

We are indebted to our series editor, Dr. Benjamin Merkle, for his eagle eye and broad knowledge of who's who in the world of evangelical scholars writing on the topic of women in ministry. He is a gift to the academy and church. Thank you, Kregel Academic, for inviting us to contribute to the 40 Questions series. We trust this volume will serve the church well.

Sue: I'm grateful for the men in my life—without them this book would not exist. First to my husband, David, for his sacrificial love, support, and care for me through more than half a century. When I was buried in this demanding writing project, he picked up the slack with a smile. I bless the day the Lord brought us together. To my seminary colleagues Mike Lawson, Jay Sedwick, and Phil Humphries, thank you for valuing my voice and contributions to our department and cheerleading me every step of the way. And to the dear women who have shared this journey with me: Dr. Joye Baker, my daughters, Heather and Rachel, granddaughter Becca, and a plethora of other cherished women.

Kelley: Writing the bulk of this book during the pandemic meant that I was constantly hiding in my home office, begging for someone to take the barking dogs away during our team video calls, and regaling my family with random facts I learned in my research. I am blessed with tolerant children who love me! Also, I have the best cheerleaders: a husband who supports and encourages me, knowing it will mean more work for him while I'm burrowed among my books, and a group of girlfriends who never fail to applaud, comfort, and counsel me as needed.

Abbreviations

DBE   *Discovering Biblical Equality: Biblical, Theological, Cultural, and Practical Perspectives.* 3rd ed. Edited by Ronald W. Pierce, Cynthia Long Westfall, and Christa L. McKirland. Downers Grove, IL: IVP Academic, 2021.

EFBT   Wayne Grudem, *Evangelical Feminism and Biblical Truth: An Analysis of More Than 100 Disputed Questions.* Wheaton, IL: Crossway, 2012.

MWOC   Philip B. Payne, *Man and Woman: One in Christ: An Exegetical and Theological Study of Paul's Letters.* Grand Rapids: Zondervan, 2009.

RBMW   *Recovering Biblical Manhood and Womanhood: A Response to Evangelical Feminism.* Edited by John Piper and Wayne Grudem. Wheaton, IL: Crossway, 2021.

Foreword

For the past eighteen years, I have taught a course at Dallas Theological Seminary that covers the same subject matter you will find in this book. And honestly, talking about what the Scriptures say regarding women in public ministry is a subject I wanted to avoid making "my issue." But eventually I had no choice. You see, I am Sandra, daughter of Ann, daughter of Velma, daughter of Ella. But the line back to Eve stops with me.

The fourth of five children, I loved belonging to a large family. And I wanted to be just like my mom—and not only her person. I saw in her vocation as wife and mother a woman's highest calling. Some of that perspective came from evangelical church teachings. But some of it came from a subculture that made *Fascinating Womanhood* a best seller and aspired for its young women to become like Amelia, Thackeray's "domestic goddess" (yes, they used that phrase).

I went to Bible college to give my future husband the best wife possible. And after my sophomore and his junior year of college, I married my high-school sweetheart, Gary. At that time, I had a few vocational aspirations: to be a pastor's wife, birth four kids, and homeschool them. I talked of dropping out of college, but Gary wanted me to finish. So he taught high school science, math, and biology until my commencement. Then we moved south for him to attend seminary.

In Texas, with the rest of the student families we knew, I ragged on Betty Friedan and loathed all things "feminist."

I took a job to support my husband—who always had broader views about what I could do than I had for myself. I made clear to everyone that I had no aspirations to continue as a "career woman." I was employed with a financial services corporation only to "put hubby through." Some felt my being the primary breadwinner undermined manhood. And I wondered that too (though Gary didn't). But I also noticed that the support of women didn't seem to undermine Jesus's manhood (Luke 8:3).

A few weeks after Gary graduated, we decided it was time to expand our family. But a year passed. And then another. I went to the doctor. Nothing. A third year passed. And then it happened—a positive pregnancy test! But cheers turned to sobs when I miscarried. And this scene repeated itself seven times—ending with a final ectopic pregnancy that required emergency surgery. This was followed by three failed adoptions.

The spiritual crisis during our decade of losses laid me lower than the emotional one. What did God want me to do? The wound struck at the core of my womanhood. Wasn't a woman designed to complete a man? Wasn't raising kids the proper channel for a woman with the gift of teaching? Isn't that what Bible-believing scholars said 1 Timothy 2 meant by "women will be saved through childbearing" (v. 15)?

I'd always heard (thanks to Augustine, I now know) that a female images God indirectly, as in via a man—when she's married. Following that logic, I assumed she would even more fully image God by bearing and rearing children. But where did I fit into this "biblical" anthropology?

As I write this, I marvel at the narrowness of my perspective. In God's pattern book, I now see a wide array of options for women serving him. And I wonder, where would my views have left those whom Paul encouraged to remain single (1 Cor. 7:8)? And what about the virtuous wife who bought and sold real estate, stretched forth her hand to the needy, sold belts in the marketplace, and—most shocking of all—taught the *torah* of *hesed* (Prov. 31:26)? Also, there was tentmaking Priscilla, who partnered with her husband to teach the orator Apollos—what about her? And the merchant of the Thyatira Purple Company, Lydia? I couldn't see then what I see now— that godly womanhood cuts its fabric from a wide swath, and its garments are not "one size fits all."

But I'm getting ahead of myself.

As I prayed about what I should do, my husband and my pastor's wife urged me to go to seminary. So I applied and was accepted. Yet, I still wondered if I was being a "feminist" by even going. Was I entering into a male vocational world? On the way out the door to my first class, I dropped to my knees in front of my couch (something I had never done), and I begged God to stop me if I was doing wrong. But to my surprise, these words from Jesus came to mind: "Mary has chosen what is better" (Luke 10:42). While Martha was accusing her sister of wrongly prioritizing theological seminary over domesticity, Jesus was saying, "Leave her alone."

I stood with confidence that day, and I walked out my door and into the classroom.

While at seminary, as I translated the New Testament, I saw many places where the Bible writers had women in view, but I had missed them. For example, I had memorized Paul's instruction to Timothy about discipleship, and I had thought Paul had only men in view: "And the things that thou hast heard of me among many witnesses, the same commit thou to faithful *men*, who shall be able to teach others also" (2 Tim. 2:2 KJV). But seeing the Greek, I realized Paul had in mind not males, but "people." And in the passage where it says that men who fail to provide for their families are worse than unbelievers, I was surprised to find the language was similarly inclusive (1 Tim. 5:8, 16).

Seeing these words and how translators rendered them told me that those who were saying, "women are in view in those texts too" were not radical feminists after all. They were right about what the Scriptures said.

I saw similar issues when translating the Old Testament. I also looked afresh at some broad themes. And I wondered, "How should I interpret that Adam was first? If birth order translates to authority, why is Jesus the *second* Adam?" And when I shared with others what I was learning, I saw how freeing my observations were, for men and women alike. I found many who didn't see themselves represented in the Bible—only to find that they were there all along.

After earning my ThM, I went on to get my PhD with a focus on first-century backgrounds, especially as they relate to women. And I also looked at history, tracing women and their contributions to the church for two thousand years. I found the order of widows and of women deacons referenced in the church fathers and ecumenical council records. I found the wives of male Reformers baptizing, preaching, and burying the dead as expressions of "the priesthood of all believers." So, Betty had not started some of that, after all.

As I mentioned earlier, for the past eighteen years, I've been teaching about what I found. Now, I realize that a drawback to telling about my life is that readers might think, "Your experience has led you to see the text a certain way." Of course it has! As has everyone's.

It is worth the risk for me to share my story, then. Because the upside is that perhaps my journey will help you put a human face on the questions being explored in the pages to follow. C. S. Lewis wrote to Sheldon Vanauken that "every disability conceals a vocation, if only we can find it, which will 'turn the necessity to glorious gain.'"[1] And the "glorious gain" of my own disability is that it has led me back to Scripture to discover that my body was not the only thing that needed the help of experts. My interpretation needed help, too.

Some have said that the dividing line in views about women's involvement in home, church, and society is biblical inerrancy. For example, some in positions of great influence have said that those who believe women can minister publicly, especially if they speak, hold a low view of the Bible. Meanwhile, some of those on the front lines self-identifying as egalitarians are also on the front lines defending inerrancy.

However, the key differences are for the most part about interpretation, not inerrancy. And the wideness in the range of interpretive options among those who love Scripture is exactly why my journey took me where it did. And it's why a "40 Questions" book on this topic is so needed. While many divide the views about women in public ministry into two camps—complementarian and egalitarian—I've actually found about eight different views on

---

1. Sheldon Vanauken, *A Severe Mercy* (San Francisco: HarperOne, 2009), 146–48. The letter is dated May 14, 1954.

how inerrantists interpret these verses. So, in the pages to follow, you will find a range of interpretive options in each answer rather than one definitive one.

The coauthors of this book, Dr. Sue Edwards and Kelley Mathews, are a terrific team to serve as your guides. They have already coauthored a number of books relating to ministry. And they bring to their task decades of experience from a variety of church and parachurch settings. Dr. Sue Edwards teaches on the subject at the doctor of ministry level at Dallas Theological Seminary. And Kelley Mathews holds a master's in theology, which included multiple semesters immersed in Greek and Hebrew. These scholars have been exploring this topic for years and years, and they bring to it some deep wisdom.

Woman was made to image God. And in creation, woman was necessary as man's indispensable companion before God could pronounce the world to be "very good." Whether she is single or married, divorced, or widowed, with or without biological or adopted children, a woman's highest calling—as is every human's—is to glorify God and multiply worshippers. This is what she was made for. This is a biblical anthropology. And this is the grid through which interpretation can begin.

—Dr. Sandra Glahn
Dallas Theological Seminary

Introduction

For more than forty years, I (Sue) have ministered to women in the church, parachurch, and academy. During this time, I've planted and implemented ministries to women in two megachurches; taught the Bible to thousands of women in various contexts; trained women leaders in Russia, Africa, and Germany; and for the last two decades have taught, advised, and counseled both men and women at Dallas Theological Seminary, where I now serve as Professor of Educational Ministries and Leadership. The consistent thread that I've observed through these years is the confusion and angst, from both men and women, regarding what women can and can't do in ministry. And the bewildering pitch grows louder and louder.

So when the opportunity arose to write a book tackling forty questions about this topic, I felt compelled to comply. I knew I needed a team, so I recruited my long-time writing partner, Kelley Mathews, two seminary student interns, and a doctoral student. I knew their varied ages and perspectives would enrich the project, and I believe it has. The first thing we did was send out a social media request for questions on the topic, and we received more than eighty questions in two days. Obviously, we struck a nerve! After combining and weeding out similar questions, and with the help of our editor, we chose the forty that comprise this book.

Our Goal

We hope to present the primary views clearly in everyday language, representing each fairly. When possible, we've attempted to eliminate theological jargon and arguments that require seminary-style academic background to understand. In our limited space, and to create a resource that's helpful but not overwhelming, we have attempted to draw from a variety of well-known and respected scholars who represent their constituencies. No doubt we've overlooked some, but it was not intentional.

One challenge has been to capture the essence of the differing ideas, especially on the "complementarian" side. This is because complementarians fall within a wide spectrum of perspectives, differing from one another in many ways. For example, complementarian churches today typically apply their convictions regarding what women can and can't do very differently. In one complementarian church, women can teach mixed Sunday school classes or lead mixed small groups. In another, they can't. In some, women can pass Communion, while in others, only ordained male leaders may oversee this sacred practice. The variety is legion and one of the reasons people are so confused.

In looking at our book as a whole, you will notice that more space is given to the views of the hetararchs than those of the hierarchs. This is because the hierarch's view is generally more well-known, and often heterarchs are responding to hierarchs. Heterarchs bring forward newer elements in the discussion that take more space to explain but need to be understood to evaluate the conversation between the two sides.

Our Approach

What does the Bible really teach about these issues? What pleases God? What will glorify him and result in health and unity in the home and church? We desire to give readers enough information to make an informed decision for themselves. And we will do our best to present these views honestly and clearly. We agree with Mark Twain when he said, "The difference between the *almost right* word and the *right* word is really a large matter. 'Tis the difference between the lightning bug and the lightning."[1] We cannot promise we'll choose the right word every time, but we promise to try. Also, we will do our best not to let our own views (we all have them) overshadow a fair representation of the varied primary voices out there today.

Our Hesitation to Align with Warring Factions

We grieve over the divisive nature of this "war." Some of our friends who have adopted extreme views on the spectrum related to this topic have chosen to withdraw from Christian organizations designed to promote unity because other members did not line up exactly with their spot on the spectrum.

The American Worldview Inventory 2020 found that the culture is influencing many churches to become more and more secular,[2] leading to less unity and more contentious disagreement. Divisive groups ignore Jesus's final request before he went to the cross:

> My prayer is not for them alone. I pray also for those who will
> believe in me through their message, that all of them may be
> one, Father, just as you are in me and I am in you. May they
> also be in us so that the world may believe that you have sent
> me. I have given them the glory that you gave me, that they

1.   Mark Twain, quoted by Caroline Thomas Harnsberger, *Everyone's Mark Twain* (New York: A. S. Barnes, 1972), 669.
2.   See Cultural Research Center at Arizona Christian University, *American Worldview Inventory 2020*, Release #11, "American Christians Are Redefining the Faith: Adherents Creating New Worldviews Loosely Tied to Biblical Teaching," www.arizonachristian.edu.

> may be one as we are one—I in them and you in me—so that
> they may be brought to complete unity. Then the world will
> know that you sent me and have loved them even as you have
> loved me. (John 17:20–23)

Some may argue that the issues around what women can and can't do in the church and home are so critical that those who do not align with their views hold heretical doctrines or are not even Christians. We disagree. As we have studied, taught, and discussed these ideas with men and women over many years, we have come to the conclusion that there is truth and error and unrighteous actions on both sides. Additionally, we believe the church would be better served by more light and less heat, by more honest dialogue and less presumption of ulterior motives. In a society that's becoming more and more hateful and enraged, Christians dare not follow the same destructive path.

However, we are not advocating abandoning the essentials of the faith or a high view of Scripture. As we examine the Bible and the amount of space dedicated to what women can and can't do in the home and church compared to other doctrines, we simply cannot include this issue as an "essential of the faith." May we all find ways to answer Jesus's final request together.

PART 1

Introductory Issues

What Terms Best Describe the Various Views on Women in Ministry?

Sometimes we use the same words, but speak a different language. This statement applies to many *word warriors* engaged in the ongoing battle over what Christian women can and cannot do in ministry and in the home. Words matter. They empower and convince, but when unclear, they easily result in confusion, stereotyping, and misunderstanding.

Sometimes we use the same words in conversation with a person believing that each of us means the same thing when often we don't. This misunderstanding results in many relational conflicts. Thus when we teach the Bible, we never say words like "submission" or "head of the home"[1] without explaining them in depth. We call these "trigger" words. They might trigger emotional reactions in listeners that raise resistant attitudes to whatever else we have to say. Without explanation, what our audience hears may not be what we meant.

The Problems with Current Terminology

We experience the same complications and misconceptions when we talk about women and the Bible. If we want to understand the current issues, we'll need clear terms that accentuate the real differences between the views. We need to boil down the core perspectives and not be satisfied with terms the factions have chosen for themselves, especially since some of these terms don't accurately communicate their differences. Sometimes those who define the terms control the arguments. Right now, the terminology in this debate is fraught with confusion.

---

1. The term "head of the home" isn't in Scripture. Instead the Bible says the husband is "head of the woman" (1 Cor. 11:3). See Question 21.

For example, two main groups have organized and taken up battle stations against one another. Each claims their own label that they insist best describes their views. They call themselves "complementarians" and "egalitarians." However, both groups adhere to doctrines that reflect the other group's label. For example:

- Like egalitarians, complementarians believe that men and women are equal in their dignity and worth in the sight of God.
- Like complementarians, egalitarians believe that men and women complement one another in their service in the church and family.

Yet, without unbiased study, one could easily assume otherwise because of the labels these groups give themselves.

Other similar beliefs include:

- Both groups hold a high view of Scripture.
- Both groups believe that men and women experience the same path to a saving faith, and will enjoy eternal life together.
- Both groups believe God gives men and women the same spiritual gifts.
- Both groups believe that God created men and women with gender differences and those differences are good.[2]

At face value, the labels complementarians and egalitarians give themselves are misleading and reductionistic, and they don't reflect their real, distinct differences. The uninformed pilgrims could easily jump to quick, incorrect assumptions in favor of or against a position simply because they like or don't like the meaning of the label. They may do this without realizing the issue is far more complex than the labels suggest and far more significant since the outcome affects not only women—at least half of the Christian population— but the whole church and its ministry and witness in the world.

Michelle Lee-Barnewall identifies the limitations of using the terminology of "complementarian" and "egalitarian":

> There is a growing sense among many that neither position quite encapsulates what they sense is the biblical view, along with the desire to explore the topic beyond the bounds of the

---

2. Although egalitarians and complementarians believe God created men and women with gender differences, egalitarians tend to limit those differences to related research results (i.e., brain physicality and functioning, decision-making, driving preferences, etc.; see Leonard Sax, *Why Gender Matters* [New York: Broadway, 2005], chaps. 1–6 for examples), while many complementarians assume stereotypes of gender qualities that have little or no research evidence (e.g., men are rational, women are emotional; men lead, women follow).

current positions. . . . I have come to believe that the topic cannot be completely defined by either the complementarian or the egalitarian viewpoint, and that there is room, perhaps even a necessity, for an alternative way of conceptualizing gender issues.[3]

Lucy Peppiatt also rejects the terms "complementarian" and "egalitarian" as the clearest terms to describe the two current organized camps. Instead, she prefers the terms "hierarchicalists" and "mutualists." She writes,

The term *complementarian* should describe a view where two different entities enhance one another in a reciprocal, harmonious, and interdependent fashion. Although complementarians claim to hold a view that describes the relation of men to women as such, my opinion is that this represents a sleight of hand. . . . Complementarians believe that men and women stand before God as equally saved, but their view of the relations of men and women sociologically is predicated on the subordination of women to men, where men hold positions of authority and women do not unless they are under male authority.[4]

Peppiatt argues that "mutualists" is a better term for egalitarians because it connotes what they actually promote—that interactions between men and women are characterized by equally shared power for the mutual benefit of both.[5]

We understand Peppiatt's arguments but find her terms a mouthful to say, and we don't want to communicate that complementarians reject *any* mutuality or mutual benefit in their relationships between men and women. We've worked with some complementarians who are mutualists in many respects.

In conclusion, both groups say men and women are truly equal in their humanity and value. Both believe gender differences exist and see the benefit of men and women working together. Thus their current labels are misleading. So what are the *real* differences between them?

---

3. Michelle Lee-Barnewall, *Neither Complementarian nor Egalitarian: A Kingdom Corrective to the Evangelical Gender Debate* (Grand Rapids: Baker Academic, 2016), 1.

4. Lucy Peppiatt, *Rediscovering Scripture's Vision for Women: Fresh Perspectives on Disputed Texts* (Downers Grove, IL: IVP Academic, 2019), 6.

5. Peppiatt, *Rediscovering Scripture's Vision*, 8.

Real Differences Between the Two Views

The clear distinction that separates the two groups relates to how each group believes God has ordered men and women's relationships and opportunities for service.

Complementarians insist God has ordained an order in the home and church that is hierarchical, or layered, where men lead women and where men hold the highest leadership positions. Most hold that this order benefits the church, the family, and society at large.

Egalitarians believe the Bible does not reveal this hierarchical system but instead that it has been imposed on the Christian faith by interpreters influenced by a patriarchal culture and sometimes by interpreters' personal dispositions. They believe God's Word reveals a flat organizational structure in the home and church based on mutual respect and merit. We will explain how these groups come to these conclusions in the following chapters.

Each group looks to the Bible to support their views, focusing on particular passages and ignoring others or deriving different "truths" from the same passages. Each plays up the passages they like and plays down those they don't. Both groups include extreme elements that interpret the Bible *evangelastically*[6]—*they stretch the text to give credence to what they want it to say.*

We have found Andrew Bartlett's explanations of the differences helpful.[7] Here is a brief synopsis of his opinion:

Egalitarianism

- God created men and women to be truly equal, but since the fall, women have been oppressed by men. Historically, patriarchal cultures unjustly kept women under male control.
- Jesus came to redeem the world from the effects of sin, including women's liberation from male domination, but after a short-lived good start, the church accommodated itself to patriarchal culture.
- It is only recently that churches have begun to treat women as equals of men; there is more work yet to be done.
- Complementarianism must be opposed. It is a misguided attempt to cling to misinterpretations of the Bible that arose from the sinfulness of patriarchal culture.

---

6. I (Sue) have used this word for many years to communicate stretching the meaning of the text to fit one's view, although I believe I first heard it from a seminary friend, JoAnn Hummel.
7. For the full treatment of this topic, see Andrew Bartlett, *Men and Women in Christ: Fresh Light from the Biblical Texts* (London: InterVarsity, 2019), 11–12.

Complementarianism

- God created men and women to be truly equal. It is right to acknowledge men's bad behavior toward women, which conflicts with God's design. The modern controversy over a woman's place has had the good effect of highlighting and correcting wrong attitudes.
- The concern for equality does not justify departing from the "plain" teaching of the Bible, which is for our good and for God's glory.
- There is an important distinction to be drawn between equality of worth and sameness of role. God has called men and women to different roles. Men are called to lead in the family and in the church.
- Egalitarianism must be opposed. It fails to distinguish correctly between God's Word and cultural misinterpretations of God's Word.

Clearly, each side views the issue through different lenses.

Fresh Terminology Reflecting the Core Differences

To present varied views clearly and fairly, we need accurate terms. In light of the current confusion and to avoid aligning with any factions, we have chosen not to use the terms "complementarian" and "egalitarian" in this project.[8] Nor do we believe either group has an absolute corner on biblical truth related to this issue. In reality, significant differences exist within each group, resulting in a wide spectrum of beliefs and practices.

Hierarchy

Instead of "complementarian," we will use the term *hierarch*. Some complementarians may resist this term, but we believe it communicates the true contrast. Complementarians would be honest to own it. They insist that men and women have different "roles" in life that cannot change because these roles are based on one's biological sex. They argue that these roles are good and result in an order in the church, family, and society that ultimately benefits everyone. Families will be healthy when involved and caring men lead them. The church will function better if men make the final decisions. And healthy families and churches lead to thriving societies. Role distinctions are permanent, based on a hierarchical system where men possess authority over women.

---

8. Use of caution when there is great difficulty in applying a clear and concise meaning to a term is one option. However, robust discussion and careful consideration of the language is crucial. Clarifying, standardizing, or abandoning the use of terminology that is confusing and/or not helpful in furthering communication across disciplines should all be carefully considered.

In many other contexts, roles are temporary. Doctors may make their living in the medical profession, but as doctors age, they should retire if they can no longer perform their duties well. Their role as doctors is temporary. Even if we take on the role of a father or a son, a daughter or a mother, that role changes over time in the ways we live out that role, in both responsibilities and authority. The military is arranged in a hierarchical structure, but even there everyone has the opportunity to advance up the ranks.

But the complementarian holds that when a person is born a man or a woman, they are locked into that "role" for life, regardless of how much they learn, mature, serve, or accomplish. As I'm a woman, I will always be under the authority of a man, and that's the way God wants it. Complementarians believe that God has ordained a permanent, role-related hierarchy. Therefore, we believe the word "hierarch" instead of "complementarian" is a more honest word to label this view because it reflects the core distinction that everyone on the complementarian spectrum agrees with.

English dictionaries generally agree on the meaning of *hierarchy*:

- A group of persons or things arranged in order of rank, grade, class, etc.[9]
- A system that organizes or ranks things . . . a formalized or simply implied understanding of who's on top or what's most important.[10]
- A system or organization in which people or groups are ranked one above the other according to status or authority.[11]

Thus, a "hierarch" is a person who believes that God created men and women to live according to a divine order based on their biological sex, and that each role is permanent, creating a hierarchy.

Heterarchy

Instead of "egalitarian," we will use the term *heterarch*. This term may take some getting used to. It's not a common word, but we believe it's the most accurate word to express the core difference between this group and hierarchs (aka complementarians).

English dictionaries generally define *heterarchy* this way:

- A system of organization where the elements of the organization are unranked. . . . In social and information sciences, heterarchies are networks of elements in which each element shares the same

---

9. Yourdictionary.com, s.v. "hierarchy."
10. Vocabulary.com, s.v. "hierarchy."
11. Lexico.com, s.v. "hierarchy."

"horizontal" position of power and authority, each playing a theoretically equal role.[12]

- A form of management or rule in which any unit can govern or be governed by others, depending on circumstances, and, hence, no one unit dominates the rest. Authority within a heterarchy is distributed.[13]
- Generally, the word "hierarchy," the elements of which are ranked relative to one another, is contrasted with "heterarchy," the elements of which are unranked, or possess the potential for being ranked in a number of different ways.[14]

Thus, a "heterarch" is a person who believes that God has not ordained permanent roles, but instead wants men and women to function in the world according to merit, preferences, spiritual gifts, abilities, and experience. Heterarchs refute that the Bible teaches a permanent divine order where men always lead women in the home, church, or society at large. Opportunities to lead are not based on gender ranking or biology, but rather on preferences and merit according to spiritual gifts, abilities, and experience.

For example, if a female heterarch has been trained as a certified public accountant and has an acumen for numbers and her heterarch husband does not, they may decide that she should oversee their family's finances despite the appearance that she may be "leading" the family related to their finances. But a hierarch couple who believes the Bible teaches that men should lead their families in the area of finances may not be comfortable with such an arrangement.

Multiply these kinds of decisions by the millions of divergent choices in the Christian home and church and, as you can see, whatever view people embrace has tremendous ramifications for marriage, church, and society.

We believe the word "heterarch" instead of "egalitarian" is a more honest word to label this view because it reflects the core distinction that everyone on the egalitarian spectrum agrees with.

Summary

Scholars holding two opposing perspectives on what women can and can't do in ministry chose the terms "complementarian" and "egalitarian" to represent themselves. However, we believe that neither term accurately reflects the core difference between these two groups. Both groups believe that men and women should work together in ministry in complementary ways and that men and women experience the same path to a saving faith and will enjoy eternal life together. Both groups believe the Bible is true and both use

12. Educalingo.com, s.v. "heterarchy."
13. Britannica.com, s.v. "heterarchy."
14. Encyclopedia.com, s.v. "heterarchy."

Scripture, interpreted differently, to back up their claims. Both groups believe God gives men and women the same spiritual gifts and that God created men and women with gender differences.

The core difference between these two groups is how they believe God has ordered men and women's relationships and opportunities for service. Complementarians insist God has ordained an order in the home and church which is hierarchical, or layered, where men lead women and where men hold the highest leadership positions. Egalitarians believe God's Word reveals a flat organizational structure in the home and church based on mutual respect and merit. As a result, we have chosen the term "hierarch," a layered authority structure, instead of "complementarian," and the term "heterarch," a flat authority structure, instead of "egalitarian."

REFLECTION QUESTIONS

1. What do the terms "complementarian" and "egalitarian" mean to you?

2. What assumptions do you naturally make regarding each term?

3. Why do the authors want to change the terms to "hierarch" and "heterarch"?

4. What is the main idea that unites all hierarchs?

5. What is the main idea that unites all heterarchs?

What Do Different Groups Believe About the Bible and Feminism?

On what basis do these different groups base their arguments? Do they appeal to culture, reason, tradition, history, or Scripture to make their points? You'll see that, throughout this book, these scholars primarily use the Bible to attempt to persuade Christians that their arguments are the most "biblical." Have any of them been so influenced by secular feminists that these Christians are acclimating to or reacting against what's going on in society today? We don't see valid evidence to make that accusation concerning either group.

The Bible

The websites of two organizations, one representing hierarchs, the Council on Biblical Manhood and Womanhood (CBMW), and one representing heterarchs, Christians for Biblical Equality (CBE), contain statements of faith that affirm a high view of the Bible.

Hierarchs (CBMW) say: "We believe that the Scriptures of the Old and New Testaments are inspired by God and inerrant in the original writings, and that they alone are of supreme and final authority in faith and life."[1] Heterarchs (CBE) say: "We believe the Bible is the inspired word of God, is reliable, and is the final authority for faith and practice." CBE's first core value reads: "Scripture is our authoritative guide for faith, life, and practice."[2]

However, both accuse the other of misreading and misinterpreting Scripture. CBE's home page reads, "Families and churches thrive when both women and men are free to use their gifts to lead and serve. All of us are

---

1. The Council on Biblical Manhood and Womanhood, "Statement of Faith," https://cbmw. org/about/statement-of-faith.
2. CBE International, "CBE's Mission and Values," https://www.cbeinternational.org/content/ cbes-mission.

gifted. Right now, women aren't free to use their leadership gifts due to mis-reading Scripture." CBE gives this as one of four reasons they believe their views are correct. The other reasons subtly leveled against hierarchs, but without naming them, are "strict gender roles, sexist religious beliefs, and Christian patriarchy."

Wayne Grudem in *Evangelical Feminism and Biblical Truth* accuses het-erarchs by name ("egalitarians")[3] of "incorrect interpretations of Scripture, reading into Scripture things that aren't there, incorrect statements about the meanings of words in the Bible and methods of interpretation that reject the authority of Scripture and lead toward liberalism."[4] He also says that heter-archs effectively "place personal experience higher than Scripture" and sup-press relevant information.[5]

Grudem makes some strong predictions about the direction that heter-archs will ultimately take Christianity should their views prevail. He bases these claims on "the hints we now have of the doctrinal direction in which evangelical feminism is moving."[6] He predicts that heterarchs will destroy the idea of distinct masculinity, and they will create an androgynous Adam who isn't male or female and a Jesus whose masculinity means nothing. He accuses them of moving toward the idea that God is both Father and Mother, and fi-nally just Mother. He also insists that their methods of interpreting Scripture will ultimately be used by those who argue for homosexuality as morally right. He claims that all this will come about because heterarchs consistently undermine the authority of Scripture.[7]

As you can see, the battle is heated and based on accusations that the other group doesn't hold the Bible in high esteem, yet both clearly and force-fully claim they themselves do. Who is right? Do both these groups believe that the Bible is true but simply interpret the text differently? Are both groups supported by the work of godly and respected biblical scholars? Do one or both groups sometimes read and interpret *evangelistically*? In the chapters ahead, you'll need to evaluate the strengths and approaches of hierarchs and heterarchs to answer those questions for yourself.

Feminism

Some words bring with them associated assumptions in the mind of the hearer. When I teach the Bible, I'm careful not to use words like that without thoroughly explaining them—for example, the word "submission." To some women this word conjures up a picture in their mind's eye of a doormat or a

---

3. Egalitarians are the group we call "heterarchs." See Question 1 on terms for a further expla-nation of our reasoning.
4. Grudem, *EFBT*, 527–28.
5. Grudem, *EFBT*, 529.
6. Grudem, *EFBT*, 517.
7. Grudem, *EFBT*, 517.

woman without a voice. These kinds of words might trigger strong gut reactions that color meaning and may easily distort what the speaker attempts to communicate.

Also, if I want to discredit a person or group, I might connect a trigger word with that person or group. When I do, I've automatically attached nuances of meaning that may further my cause. But I also risk skewing, instead of leveling, the playing field when I interact with those whom I disagree, and that usually breeds ill will and distrust.

Like "submission," "feminism" is a trigger word. Why? Because although twelve different kinds of secular feminisms exist today,[8] most Christians don't know that. They believe all feminists are "radical feminists." The quote below from a secular book, *Feminist Thought*, summarizes the secular radical feminist platform.

> They [radical feminists] claim that power, dominance, hierarchy, and competition characterize the patriarchal system. It cannot be reformed but only ripped out, root and branch. Radical feminists insist that it is not enough for us to overturn patriarchy's legal and political structures on the way to women's liberation; we must also thoroughly transform its social and cultural institutions (especially the family and organized religion).[9]

Understandably, when the radical feminist movement gained a powerful hold on culture in the 1960s, Christianity reacted with a backlash of extreme concern and fear. Since heterarchs, like secular feminists, seemed to be "for women," it was easy to mistakenly think they were in the same camp, and some hierarchs continue to link them together today.

In a footnote in the preface of his book *Evangelical Feminism and Biblical Truth*, Grudem writes, "Throughout this book I use *egalitarian* and *evangelical feminist* as synonyms."[10] A synonym is a word with the same or similar meaning. Why might some people consider the partnering of these two groups, egalitarian and feminist, a sleight of hand? Because when most Christians think of feminists, they associate them with radical, bra-burning, male-hating women leading a crusade against God, the church, and the home. Do heterarchs share the same goals?

---

8. Rosemarie Tong and Tina Fernandes Botts, *Feminist Thought: A More Comprehensive Introduction*, 5th ed. (New York: Westview, 2018).

9. Tong and Botts, *Feminist Thought*, 2.

10. Grudem, *EFBT*, 17n2.

Similarly, if heterarchs label hierarchs using loaded terms like "sexist, power-mongering, male chauvinist woman-haters," they'll be guilty of the same kinds of rhetoric.

Are these word associations fair? Exhibiting these kinds of tactics or rhetoric, including name-calling, unjust labeling, and unfair association, is never helpful; nor is it wise to assume uncharitable motivation in those who disagree with us because we can't know their inner thoughts and heart attitudes. These kinds of strategies don't further the likelihood that Christians will promote the peace, charity, and unity that's commanded among fellow believers in the Bible.

Summary

From our studies over the last three decades and our experience interacting with godly men and women from both camps, we don't believe that either side rejects a high view of Scripture. However, some on both sides have been guilty of *evangelastic* interpretation, stretching the truth to fit their views.[11] We've also observed respected scholars representing both camps who contribute thoughtful, well-documented arguments to support their ideas.

Heterarchs are not secular radical feminists in disguise. Their ultimate goal isn't to destroy the home and the church. They aren't man-haters. Likewise, hierarchs' priority of male authority in the church and in the home doesn't mean they hate women and their views automatically lead to abuse. We don't believe that either group has a corner on the truth.

REFLECTION QUESTIONS

1. How important is it that scholars attempt to interpret Scripture as honestly as possible, without hidden agendas?

2. What examples can you think of where godly scholars interpret a passage in the Bible differently from each other?

3. What is your first reaction to the term "feminism"?

4. What is a "trigger" word?

5. Why is it important to take the time to define "trigger words" carefully?

---

11. I (Sue) have used this word for many years to communicate stretching the meaning of the text to fit one's view, although I believe I first heard it from a seminary friend, JoAnn Hummel.

What Are the Best Methods for Interpreting the Bible?

The way we interpret the Bible determines how we believe God wants men and women to relate to one another. If people insist the Bible only means what they want it to mean, in the end, God's Word is meaningless. One scholar explains,

> Bible interpretation begins by acknowledging the biblical text as the written expression of an authority, and that we must submit to this authority. In other words, we are subject to the text, not the other way around. . . . When it comes to interpretation of Scripture, a seminary professor absolutely believes that personal passions and individual proclivities must be set aside in favor of dependable rules of interpretation.[1]

But, even for seminary professors, gender issues are hot-wired. Who we are as men and women and how we relate to the "other" touches our deepest core, our identity, our affections, and our attitudes about power. Our personalities, parents, mentors, church backgrounds, education, spiritual gifts, and many other factors color how we interpret biblical passages related to men and women—often in ways we aren't even aware of.

As a result, some tend to interpret the Bible *evangelastically*.[2] They stretch the meaning to fit their personal perspectives and assumptions. Don't be one

---

1. Mark M. Yarbrough, *How to Read the Bible Like a Seminary Professor: A Practical and Entertaining Exploration of the World's Most Famous Book* (New York: FaithWords, 2015), xiii–xiv.
2. I (Sue) have used this word for many years to communicate stretching the meaning of the text to fit one's view, although I believe I first heard it from a seminary friend, JoAnn Hummel.

of them! We will point out these tendencies as we go along. And, as we warn you of this danger, we caution ourselves. We are *all* subject to seeing God's Word through our own tinted lenses.

To read the Bible responsibly, you should do the following:

- Evaluate our arguments carefully.
- Humbly ask God to show you if you are being influenced by your own biases as you interpret these passages.
- Do your part by familiarizing yourself with the following tried-and-true principles to help you personally guard against interpreting *evangelastically* and to help you recognize this tendency in others.

Tried-and-True Interpretive Principles[3]

Observation—What Does the Text Say?

Observe the text like a detective. If you are already acquainted with the passage, try to read it as if for the first time. Ask questions and seek answers that enable you to discern how to live out God's best plan for men and women. Ask questions like the following:

- What did the text mean to the original audience?
- What words seem especially important to understand?
- What would that word have meant to someone reading it who lived whenever it was written?
- Where were they?
- What was the situation?
- Can you observe anything in the text that gives you a clue concerning how men and women related in that context?
- What social norms related to gender were common at the time that might have a bearing?
- Am I imposing any ideas on the text that aren't explicitly there?

Also, biblical authors, under the guidance of the Holy Spirit, created many different kinds of literary structures that can be clues to help us understand what they are talking about. Thus, additional questions might include these:

---

3. These principles have been taught at a variety of respected seminaries around the world, including Dallas Theological Seminary, based on the works of scholars like Robert A. Traina, Howard G. Hendricks, and Mark M. Yarbrough, among others. This chapter is based on what we learned in our seminary courses and what we personally attempt to apply today as we teach and write.

- How did the author structure the passage?
- Are there obvious relationships between parts of the text, like cause and effect?
- Is the author using past, present, or future tense words? That will determine if he's talking about something that already happened before that time, something related to the present, or something that will happen in the future for the original readers. Once we've observed how the passage related to the original context, then we can begin to figure out how the timing relates to us today.

First, we must observe the passage thoroughly and carefully!

Interpretation—What Does the Text Mean?

How do you discern the meaning? Different experts suggest different ways. Some are below.

Bombard the text with more questions and find as many answers as you can. Become familiar with the customs, geography, history, and any other related information that will shed light on what the text meant for those first readers. This kind of information can be found in commentaries and in online resources. These commentaries provide the author's verse-by-verse opinion on what each verse means, and their in-depth insight, experience, and scholarly study is often extremely helpful. But as you search for answers, you'll soon see that different commentators voice different opinions. Just remember what my seminary professor said to our class: "Commentators are just common taters." They're people with tinted lenses too. Thus, when researching gender issues, wisdom dictates you hear from scholars who hold varied views and, ultimately, you'll need to make up your own mind.

If you want to go even deeper, delve into the meanings of words in the original languages. Since few have the opportunity to learn these languages, locate several reliable experts who can provide insight. Again, when attempting to understand passages related to men and women, find experts who believe differently and set out to discover why they come to divergent conclusions.

Sometimes words in Greek or Hebrew can legitimately be translated several different ways into English. Thus, the choice is up to the interpreter. But often the everyday reader is unaware of these options. This decision impacts millions of relationships, churches, and homes. That's a lot of pressure for one little word—we better take the time to get it right!

These days, more women have had the opportunity to study the original languages as they work on advanced academic degrees. As a result, more female scholars have a voice in these interpretive decisions. They often bring perspectives that reveal a fresh but equally valid interpretation that dramatically changes what the text reveals about how God wants men and women to relate. When several meanings are possible for a given Hebrew or Greek word, scholars should examine the context as thoroughly and neutrally as possible, hoping to determine what God really meant.

If you want to research the meanings of these important words for yourself, learn to use tools like an interlinear Bible that shows you both the English and the original language. Also, you'll need a Bible dictionary that contains precise English meanings of the original language.[4]

After we've observed the text like a detective and discerned what we honestly believe the passage meant, then we're ready to apply what we've learned to life today—but not before! Otherwise, we may apply an assumption that's actually not based on God's Word at all. We may distort the Bible—and that's dangerous.

Application—What Does God Want Me to Do?

What are the implications this text has for us regarding how we live as men and women? How do we treat people of the opposite sex? How does God want men and women to relate in the church, community, and home?

The ultimate goal of knowing the Bible is *living* the Bible, involving transformation of our character, attitudes, and actions. Once we've observed and interpreted God's Word, we are ready to live it out. As faithful sons and daughters of our heavenly Father, we are obliged to treat the opposite sex as God instructs, serve him together in ways he reveals, create healthy homes and churches, and represent God to the world. We are obliged to humbly lay down our preconceptions, assumptions, and even our traditions if we find they really don't line up with his Word, regardless of the reasons we hold them and no matter how uncomfortable that might feel.

What Kind of Literature Is It?

We've said that for accuracy in determining what God says about men and women, we employ the investigative process of observation, interpretation, and application. In addition, we must consider the kind of divine literature before us. God has written the most exquisite literature of all time. To understand its true meaning, we must determine what kind of literature it is and know the guiding interpretive principles related to each. Failure here can lead to wrong conclusions about God's desires for men and women—with drastic consequences!

---

4.   We recommend Moisés Silva, *New International Dictionary of New Testament Theology and Exegesis*, rev. ed., 5 vols. (Grand Rapids: Zondervan, 2014), for New Testament study. For the Old Testament, a proven resource is Ludwig Köhler, Walter Baumgartner, M. E. J. Richardson, and Johann Jakob Stamm, *The Hebrew and Aramaic Lexicon of the Old Testament* (Leiden/ New York: E. J. Brill, 1994–2000).

Another term for these various kinds of literature is *genre*. Below are two of the genres you'll see most in this book.

Narrative

Another word for narrative is story. The Bible is full of true stories about God's words and works, as well as accounts of individual people who, under the influence of the Holy Spirit, wrote about their experiences. Examples include Genesis, Exodus, the Gospels, and the book of Acts. As Mark Yarbrough explains,

> The narrative genre is an organized presentation of a historical event artistically advanced to recount God's working in His creation and through His people. Narrative is simply storytelling, and it's the most common genre in the Bible. . . . Approximately 40 percent of the Old Testament and 60 percent of the New Testament is narrative.[5]

Narrative can be tricky. When my husband and I watch a movie or read a book of fiction, we sometimes draw different conclusions from a situation that arises in the story. Something happens, and we are left to determine what it means. There's really no way to prove who is correct because the conclusion is inferred and not directly or clearly stated. We must discern between what is explicitly taught and what is implicit. Gordon Fee and Douglas Stuart define implicit teaching as "that which is clearly present in the story but not stated in so many words."[6] They write:

> Being able to distinguish what is explicitly taught can be fairly easy. Being able to distinguish what is implicitly taught can be more difficult. It requires skill, hard work, caution, and a prayerful respect for the Holy Spirit's care in inspiring the text. After all, you want to read things *out of* the narrative rather than *into* it.[7]

We must be careful to hold inferred assumptions in biblical narrative loosely.

Initially, read and attempt to understand a narrative by observing the story carefully, without any outside influence, including other parts of the Bible. If you ignore the warnings below, you may believe, say, or communicate to others that the Bible teaches something it doesn't teach at all.

---

5. Yarbrough, *How to Read the Bible*, 175.
6. Gordon D. Fee and Douglas Stuart, *How to Read the Bible for All Its Worth: A Guide to Understanding the Bible*, 4th ed. (Grand Rapids: Zondervan Academic, 2014), 103.
7. Fee and Stuart, *How to Read the Bible*, 104.

The narrative itself must be the starting point for understanding it, not elements imported into the story from outside, unless they are directly part of the setting.[8] Fee and Stuart in their classic book *How to Read the Bible for All Its Worth* give us additional helpful guidance to read narrative literature correctly:[9]

1. Narratives are not written to answer all our theological questions. They have particular, specific, limited purposes and deal with certain issues, leaving others to be dealt with elsewhere in other ways.[10]
2. Don't decontextualize by ignoring the full historical and literary context. If you concentrate on small units or details, you can miss the main concepts the author emphasizes.[11] Fee writes, "If you take things out of context enough, you can make almost any part of Scripture say anything you want it to. But at that moment you are no longer reading the Bible, you are abusing it."[12]
3. Narratives record what happened—not necessarily what should have happened or what ought to happen every time. Therefore, not every narrative has an individual moral application.[13]
4. All narratives are incomplete. Not all relevant details are always given. What does appear in the narrative is everything that the inspired author thought important for us to know.[14]
5. Narratives may teach explicitly (by clearly stating something) or implicitly (by clearly implying something without actually saying it).[15]
6. Don't allegorize. That means don't try to think of meanings beyond the clear intended message of the text.[16]
7. Don't be selective. Don't pick and choose specific words and phrases to concentrate on, while ignoring others, and don't ignore the overall sweep of the story.[17]

Fee and Stuart conclude:

> Narratives are precious to us because they so vividly *demonstrate* God's involvement in the world and *illustrate* his

---

8. See *The Old Testament Narratives: Their Proper Use*, a series on the website of Redeemer Church, Bellingham, WA, July 26, 2010, redeemernw.org.
9. These seven concepts are synthesized from Fee and Stuart, *How to Read the Bible*, 93–111. Some in this list are reworded and some are direct quotes.
10. Fee and Stuart, *How to Read the Bible*, 111.
11. Fee and Stuart, *How to Read the Bible*, 111.
12. Fee and Stuart, *How to Read the Bible*, 108.
13. Fee and Stuart, *How to Read the Bible*, 111.
14. Fee and Stuart, *How to Read the Bible*, 111.
15. Fee and Stuart, *How to Read the Bible*, 111.
16. Fee and Stuart, *How to Read the Bible*, 108.
17. Fee and Stuart, *How to Read the Bible*, 108.

principles and calling. They thus teach us a lot—but what they directly teach us does not systematically include personal ethics. For this area of life, we must turn elsewhere in the Scriptures—to the various places where personal ethics are actually taught categorically and explicitly.[18]

Keep in mind that, if a box with a crystal chandelier shows up on your front porch without a sticker reading "handle with care," you may open a container full of sharp glass shards. The same precautions apply to God's divine genres.

Epistles

Epistles are another genre of biblical literature we will deal with a lot in this book. This category goes by several other names: exposition, discourse, and letters. About this genre Hendricks and Hendricks write, "An exposition is a straightforward argument or explanation of a body of objective truth. It is a form of writing that appeals primarily to the mind. The argument usually has a tight structure that moves from point to point in logical fashion."[19]

Often epistles teach a truth *explicitly*, by clearly stating that truth outright. Prominent examples include Paul's, Peter's, and John's letters in the New Testament to churches and individuals. However, Fee and Stuart warn, finding the true meanings isn't always easy:

> There is one item that all of the Epistles have in common, and this is *the* crucial item to note in reading and interpreting them: They are all what are technically called *occasional documents* (i.e., arising out of and intended for a specific occasion) and they are *all* from the *first century*. . . . Their *occasional* nature must be taken seriously. . . . Usually the occasion was some kind of behavior that needed correcting, or a doctrinal error that needed setting right, or a misunderstanding that needed further light.[20]

Epistles are like hearing one end of a telephone conversation and trying to figure out who is talking on the other end and what they are saying. Theology is implied, but Fee and Stuart call it "task theology," meaning that it's being written to respond to the "task at hand."[21] It is theology "applied to or directed toward a particular need."[22]

---

18. Fee and Stuart, *How to Read the Bible*, 110.
19. Howard G. Hendricks and William D. Hendricks, *Living by the Book: The Art and Science of Reading the Bible* (Chicago: Moody, 1991), 210.
20. Fee and Stuart, *How to Read the Bible*, 60.
21. Fee and Stuart, *How to Read the Bible*, 60.
22. Fee and Stuart, *How to Read the Bible*, 61.

Other genres are parables, poetry, proverbs and wisdom literature, and prophecy. For further insight into biblical genres, read and digest Yarbrough, Hendricks and Hendricks, Fee and Stuart, Robert Traina, and Robert Plummer, all cited in the footnotes.

Also, we must figure out when a biblical issue is cultural and when it is unchanging. We devote the next chapter to this important and thorny question because it's so crucial in discerning how God wants men and women to interact and treat one another.

Summary

It's vital that we learn to use sound interpretive principles when attempting to evaluate biblical truth, and it's also important that we leave our assumptions, biases, and preconceptions at the door. Come to these passages asking questions, with open hearts and minds, and with a passion to follow what God teaches in his Word; do so regardless of whether it supports what you've always thought and done, regardless of whether your personality moves you toward one view or another, regardless of what your cherished mentor or favorite author told you, and regardless of what you yearn for the Bible to say. Remember God always has your best interests at heart; you can trust him, and you can trust his Word—when it's handled with care and correctly interpreted.

REFLECTION QUESTIONS

1. How have you attempted to know what the Bible means in the past?

2. Can you summarize the three-step interpretive process presented in this chapter to help you correctly understand the Bible?

3. What do you need to consider when attempting to understand what a narrative passage of Scripture means?

4. How is interpreting an epistle different from interpreting narrative literature?

5. Why is it important that you consider the kind of literature when attempting to honestly understand the meaning of a passage?

When Is a Biblical Issue Cultural and When Is It Unchanging?

Some people struggle to believe that an ancient book like the Bible can still be true or even helpful today, particularly concerning the interaction between men and women in the church, the home, and the community. Their concern is understandable, especially if interpreters fail to discern whether a biblical issue is cultural or unchanging. What do we mean by this? We are asking if the application is different in a different culture or whether it's true just the way it's written on the page for all cultures for all time. To answer this question, first we must know what the original author meant as he was writing to the original audience. Andrew Bartlett explains,

> Paul and Peter were not modern Western thinkers. We must enter into the thought-world of the biblical writers in order to gain an accurate understanding of their meaning, rather than peering through the distorting spectacles of our own times and imposing on it our own concerns. This is very difficult for all of us, because our own culture is so familiar to us that we are often unaware of it.[1]

Wise interpreters realize that some biblical statements should be applied in the exact way they are stated on the page while others should be sifted to discover the principle that can be lifted out of that cultural setting and applied to the contemporary setting. For example, Paul concludes one of his letters to the Corinthian church like this: "The churches in the province of Asia send you greetings. Aquila and Priscilla greet you warmly in the Lord, and so does

---

1. Andrew Bartlett, *Men and Women in Christ: Fresh Light from the Biblical Texts* (London: InterVarsity, 2019), 360.

the church that meets at their house. All the brothers and sisters here send you greetings. Greet one another with a holy kiss" (1 Cor. 16:19–20). In many ancient cultures, people greeted friends by grabbing their shoulders, leaning forward, and planting a kiss or multiple kisses on their cheeks or lips. Imagine if we trained our male greeters in North American churches to welcome everyone this way, even guests. Regardless of how often church leaders preached sermons or taught Sunday school lessons on the correctness of this practice because "that's what the Bible teaches," we're pretty certain its awkwardness would hinder it becoming a "best practice" for greeters today. No, instead we practice what communicates the intent of the original author: warmth and friendliness, expressed today in Western cultures by a hearty verbal welcome and possibly a handshake.

If Paul attended a service now where we made every effort to "obey" these instructions as written on the page, he would be appalled and undoubtedly exclaim, "But that's not what I intended. I meant for this practice to communicate friendliness and warmth. Do what communicates that principle wherever you are. That's what's true and helpful." What passages related to gender issues are only true and helpful today when the related principle is lifted out of the ancient culture and applied correctly to the current culture? On the other hand, what passages should be applied as written on the page for all time?

The Complexity of Cultural Correctness

As men and women who love God's Word and want to apply it correctly, we must identify, learn, and use sound interpretive principles to address this complex issue. If we honestly believe the application would be distorted if we apply it as written on the page, we must discern the intent and underlying principle and purpose of the passage. Then we must lift that principle out of the text with care, and attempt to apply it so that it communicates the same principle, purpose, and intent as the original author had in mind but in the new cultural setting.

This process can be challenging and requires us to set aside agendas and biases. For this reason, after we've studied a passage on our own, it's wise to go to trusted scholarly experts and read what they say in articles or commentaries. However, these scholars sometimes disagree. Welcome to the complex world of this book's topic.

Therefore, you'll need to listen to all sides, think deeply and carefully, and make up your own mind. In an attempt to help you, we'll provide a basic method and additional resources.

A Basic Method

Here is a basic method of four steps to help you discern whether a text is cultural or unchanging.

1. Discover the cultural background of the text. Mark Yarbrough suggests that we ask six questions of the text:

- Who was in authority?
- What did the people believe?
- When did they live?
- Where did they reside?
- Why did they act?
- How did they work?[2]

Through answering these kinds of questions, we should gather various social, spiritual, geographic, legal, and economic insights that clarify what was going on in that culture. Without that information, we might easily distort the author's original meaning for the first audience and then misapply that meaning in our world today.

For example, without an understanding of the Old Testament practice of gleaning, parts of the book of Ruth won't make much sense. Without knowing why eating meat sacrificed to idols was so important to the Corinthians, we'll miss key mandates that help us love and guide those newer to the faith. Without some understanding of what women's hairstyles communicated in the early church, we'll likely miss what Paul was teaching them regarding modesty and interaction with men in the congregation. As a result, we could easily impose a practice or teaching on people today that distorts the original intent of the author and the text.

2. If the cultural context is essentially different from your cultural context, determine the underlying principle the original author is communicating to the original audience. State that principle clearly.

3. Ascertain what might be an equivalent practice or teaching of that principle in the culture where you are applying the passage. Teach the equivalent principle.

4. If the application isn't impacted by differences in the original culture and the culture where you are, the application is probably universal, the same in all cultures for all time.

---

2. Mark M. Yarbrough, *How to Read the Bible Like a Seminary Professor: A Practical and Entertaining Exploration of the World's Most Famous Book* (New York: FaithWords, 2015), 146–63.

Trusted Resources

These trusted resources can help you discern whether a text is cultural or unchanging:

- Mark Yarborough, *How to Read the Bible like a Seminary Professor: A Practical and Entertaining Exploration of the World's Most Famous Book*. New York: FaithWords, 2015.
- Howard G. Hendricks and William D. Hendricks, *Living by the Book: The Art and Science of Reading the Bible*. Chicago: Moody, 1991.
- Robert A. Traina, *Methodical Bible Study: A New Approach to Hermeneutics*. Grand Rapids: Francis Asbury, 1980.
- Henry A. Virkler and Karelynne Ayayo, *Hermeneutics: Principles and Processes of Biblical Interpretation*. 2nd ed. Grand Rapids: Baker, 2007.
- Gordon D. Fee and Douglas Stuart, *How to Read the Bible for All Its Worth: A Guide to Understanding the Bible*. 4th ed. Grand Rapids: Zondervan Academic, 2014.
- William J. Webb. *Slaves, Women and Homosexuals: Exploring the Hermeneutics of Cultural Analysis*. Downers Grove, IL: InterVarsity, 2001.
- Robert L. Plummer, *40 Questions About Interpreting the Bible*. 2nd ed. Grand Rapids: Kregel Academic, 2021.

Summary

As you can see, it's important to answer the question of whether the application of any given passage is unchanging or not. Without deep thinking and clear understanding, today women might be covering their faces with veils when they attend church, and men might be planting big kisses on guests as they arrive. Imagine the impact of those practices on present-day Christianity! In future chapters, we'll do our best to explain different scholarly opinions when cultural issues are a factor. But if you want to be a fair-minded and knowledgeable Bible student, you would do well to make it a goal to learn all you can about the ancient cultures of the books of the Bible.

REFLECTION QUESTIONS

1. How important has understanding the culture of the biblical setting been to you in the past?

2. Why don't we "greet one another with a holy kiss" as Paul instructs in 1 Corinthians 16:20?

3. How do you discern whether a passage applies just to the original audience or to all people for all time?

4. Why is "cultural correctness" important in assessing what the Bible actually teaches about how God wants men and women to relate to one another?

5. How might you prepare yourself to be more biblically culturally literate?

PART 2

Questions Related to
the Old Testament

Foundations in Genesis

What Does It Mean That God Is Imaged as Both Male and Female?

Are women made in the image of God in the same way men are, and how does the answer influence the discussion on women's place in ministry? The concept of humans made in God's image first appears in Scripture in Genesis 1:26–27:

> Then God said, "Let us make mankind in our image, in our likeness, so that they may rule over the fish in the sea and the birds in the sky, over the livestock and all the wild animals, and over all the creatures that move along the ground."
> So God created mankind in his own image, in the image of God he created them; male and female he created them.

Then God evaluated his creation of man and woman and declared that it was not just "good," the words he used about the rest of creation, but "very good" (1:31). He assigned a special worth and value to those he made in his own image that he did not ascribe to anything else.

"Imaged" Descriptively

"Descriptively, to bear God's image means to bear God's likeness," writes Ali Zimmerman.[1] Jen Wilkin elaborates by listing God's incommunicable attributes, which God alone possesses, and his communicable attributes, which human beings also have the potential to possess:

---

1. Ali Zimmerman, "Bearing His Image Together," *Voice*, Dallas Theological Seminary, July 30, 2021, https://voice.dts.edu/article/bearing-his-image-together.

Incommunicable: infinite, incomprehensible, self-existent, eternal, immutable, omnipresent, omniscient, omnipotent,[2] and sovereign.

Communicable: holy, loving, just, good, merciful, gracious, faithful, truthful, patient, and wise.[3]

The apostle Paul assured Christians that it's possible and expected for men and women to reflect God's communicable attributes in the following passages:

> Do not lie to each other, since you have taken off your old self with its practices and have put on the new self, which is being renewed in knowledge in the image of its Creator. Here there is no Gentile or Jew, circumcised or uncircumcised, barbarian, Scythian, slave or free, but Christ is all, and is in all. (Col. 3:9–11)

> And we all, with unveiled faces reflecting the glory of the Lord, are being transformed into the same image from one degree of glory to another, which is from the Lord, who is the Spirit. (2 Cor. 3:18 NET)

> For those God foreknew he also predestined to be conformed to the image of his Son, that he might be the firstborn among many brothers and sisters. (Rom. 8:29)

At the fall, however, sin hindered the potential for humans to reflect God's character well. But Jesus came to redeem us from our sin and to model the image of God to us, challenging us to become more and more like him as we grow in our faith.

> The Son is the image of the invisible God. . . . Once you were alienated from God and were enemies in your minds because of your evil behavior. But now he has reconciled you by Christ's physical body through death to present you holy in his sight . . . if you continue in your faith, established and firm, and do not move from the hope held out in the gospel. (Col. 1:15, 21–23)

---

2. "Omnipresent" means God is present everywhere at the same time, "omniscient" means he knows everything, and "omnipotent" means he is all-powerful.
3. Jen Wilkin, *In His Image: 10 Ways God Calls Us to Reflect His Character* (Wheaton, IL: Crossway, 2018), 21–22.

So, God desires that both Christian men and women look more like the image of Jesus as they mature in their faith. But there's more.

"Imaged" Functionally

Zimmerman continues, "Functionally, it [bearing the image of God] means to represent Him and to rule on His behalf."[4] Genesis 1:26 and 27 clearly call both men and women to be his representatives and to rule over the rest of his creation. Nothing in the text infers that God gives this responsibility differently to men than to women. What is God actually asking men and women to do?

J. Richard Middleton argues that God is delegating rule over the earth and its creatures to human beings created in his image. But to understand the phrase "image of God" (in the Hebrew, *tsalem elohim*), we must understand what that phrase meant to people in the ancient world. "The image [*eikon*] of a god was a statue placed in a temple, and people believed that the deity they worshipped somehow channeled his or her power and presence through the statue to the worshippers. The primary function of an image, therefore, is *mediation*."[5]

The first command God gave his followers was not to make any carved images of him like the pagans made of their gods, and for good reason. Middleton contends that this is because men and women are the "authorized mediators of God's presence," and "it is the human task to fill the earth not just with progeny but ultimately with God's presence, a task accomplished by faithful representation of the divine King, who rules from heaven."[6]

Thus, the creation of men and women as *imago Dei* in Genesis 1 means that God's people are mediating divine presence from heaven to earth. This responsibility isn't automatic but is missional because it can be furthered or hindered by how men and women exercise their delegated authority on behalf of Almighty God.[7]

In his book *Cultural Intelligence: Living for God in a Diverse, Pluralistic World*, Darrell Bock writes that this mission has never been more important than it is today:

> Still, none of these challenges or changes alters the need for the church to image God in the world. That is the assignment God gave those he calls to him. It is why the church bears the description "the body of Christ." We are called to be an

---

4. Zimmerman, "Bearing His Image Together."
5. J. Richard Middleton, "The Genesis Creation Accounts," in *T&T Clark Handbook of Christian Theology and the Modern Sciences*, ed. John P. Slattery (London: Bloomsbury, 2020), 23.
6. Middleton, "Genesis Creation Accounts," 23.
7. Middleton, "Genesis Creation Accounts," 24.

incarnation of God's presence in the world, his audiovisual in a unique set of individuals and a special community. How we engage in showing God's grace and character matters.[8]

Divergent Views

Traditional View

For centuries, theologians taught that women were not made in the image of God in the same way as men. For example, Augustine states, "The woman together with her own husband is the image of God, so that that whole substance may be one image; but when she is referred separately to her quality of help-meet, which regards the woman herself alone, then she is not the image of God; but as regards the man alone, he is the image of God as fully and completely as when the woman too is joined with him in one."[9] In the fifth century, Theodoret of Cyrus, bishop of Cyrrhus and influential theologian of the School of Antioch, saw the creation order as grounds for women's inferiority.[10] In the eighteenth century, English Baptist pastor and theologian John Gill explained his view of Genesis 1:26–27: "Man was first originally and immediately the image and glory of God, the woman only secondarily and mediately through man. The man is more perfectly and conspicuously the image and glory of God, on account of his more extensive dominion and authority."[11]

Hierarchs

Wayne Grudem admits that men and women are "equal in value and dignity" and that "to be in the image of God is an incredible privilege."[12] However, Grudem also argues that women do not reflect God's image related to authority in the way that men do, based on the authority differences in the Trinity, nor are both men and women needed to reflect the full expression of the image of God.[13]

Thomas Finley makes a similar argument. He insists that God created both men and women to bear God's image but states that "in his headship man images God in a way that woman does not. Woman is the 'glory' of man in responding to his headship even as man is the 'glory of God' in responding

8. Darrell L. Bock, *Cultural Intelligence: Living for God in a Diverse, Pluralistic World* (Nashville: B&H Academic, 2020), 6–7.

9. Augustine, *On the Trinity* 12.7.10.

10. Theodoret of Cyrus, *Commentary on 1 Timothy* (PG 82, 809A). Cited in Roger Gryson, *The Ministry of Women in the Early Church*, trans. Jean Laporte and Mary Louise Hall (Collegeville, MN: Liturgical, 1976), 8.

11. John Gill, *Exposition of the Entire Bible* [1746–1763], Internet Sacred Texts Archive, https://www.sacred-texts.com/bib/cmt/gill/index.htm.

12. Grudem, *EFBT*, 25–26.

13. Grudem, *EFBT*, 452–54.

to His headship." Then he cites Proverbs 12:4, "A wife of noble character is her husband's crown, but a disgraceful wife is like decay in his bones."[14]

Heterarchs

Aída Besançon Spencer claims that "the complete image of God will only be manifested in its full expression when men and women stand side by side in the church" and that both "men and women leaders are needed to fully reflect the image of God." Also, if we want to show the world what God's image looks like, as well as helping both men and women to mature into God's image, Spencer says, we must have both men and women modeling all the aspects of God's image.[15] Philip Payne writes:

> God's image is not restricted to the male [in Genesis 1:26–27] nor does the text imply any difference between the image of God in man and woman. . . . Nothing in the first chapter of Genesis grants man priority in status or authority over woman. Genesis 1–3 consistently depicts the unity of the man and the woman as equal partners, not woman under man.[16]

He goes on to offer support from the New Testament:

> All believers are created in God's image: their new self in Christ is "being renewed in knowledge in the image of its Creator" (Colossians 3:10). In Colossians 2:10 and 11, he affirms that all Christians, female as well as male, "have this fullness [of the Godhead] in Christ . . . in whom you were also circumcised." Paul depicts females as . . . being circumcised and males as the bride of Christ (Ephesians 5:22–27) because their gender is irrelevant to their being in the image of God and their being in Christ.[17]

Summary

Being made in the image of God means to reflect his likeness, to represent him on the earth, and to rule over his creation. Throughout history, many leaders taught that women were not made in the image of God in the same

---

14. Thomas Finley, "The Relationship of Woman and Man in the Old Testament," in *Women and Men in Ministry: A Complementary Perspective*, eds. Robert L. Saucy and Judith K. TenElshof (Chicago: Moody, 2001), 52.

15. Aída Besançon Spencer, *Beyond the Curse: Women Called to Ministry* (Peabody, MA: Hendrickson, 1997), 122.

16. Philip B. Payne, *Man and Woman, One in Christ: An Exegetical and Theological Study of Paul's Letters* (Grand Rapids: Zondervan, 2009), 42.

17. Payne, *Man and Woman*, 43.

way that men were. Today, many hierarchs argue that both men and women bear that image except related to authority, and that the Bible teaches that woman is the glory of man, particularly related to their relationship in marriage. Heterarchs counter that both men and women bear the image of God, and both are needed to fully reflect that image; thus, for Christian ministry to flourish, both are needed working side by side.

Wherever you land in regard to this beautiful picture of God creating all of us in his image, we hope you will agree with Elizabeth Garn in this related article. She concludes:

> This is a beautiful call to imitate the creative work God himself accomplished in creation. It's about *being* who he created you to be. Filling the earth is about filling the empty spaces with beauty and using your gifts and talents to show the world the creative nature of its God. Having dominion is about bringing order—ordered hearts, ordered relationships, ordered businesses, ordered homes—out of chaos. We must know him, be with him, and rest in him if we are going to reflect him to the world.[18]

REFLECTION QUESTIONS

1. What do you think being made in the image of God means?

2. What are the differences between incommunicable and communicable attributes?

3. Evaluate the statement that being made in the image of God means that we are God's representatives and we reflect God to the world.

4. Do you believe that single and married people reflect the image of God the same or differently, and why?

5. If you tend to agree with either hierarchs or heterarchs on this issue, explain why.

18. Elizabeth Garn, "What Women Need to Know about Being Image-Bearers of God," The Gospel Coalition, July 19, 2017, https://www.thegospelcoalition.org/article/what-women-need-to-know-about-being-image-bearers-of-god.

What Does Genesis 1–2 Reveal About Male and Female Relationships?

Almost all scholars agree that the first two chapters of the Bible give us an ideal pattern for how God intended and created men and women to relate to one another in marriage, the church, and in society. But hierarchs and heterarchs disagree on the nature of this perfect pattern. Our understanding of these chapters forms a foundation, a lens through which we will interpret the rest of the Bible concerning relationships between men and women. We cannot overstate the importance of getting this right.

Our charge is to discern what's clearly communicated in the text and what's speculation. What assumptions are lifted out of the story to support personal agendas or bias? Would the respective arguments convince someone who came to the text without any previous commitment to a particular view? Come with fresh eyes, asking for the Lord's guidance and the ability to release any preconceptions that might discolor what's clearly in the text.

The Genre of Genesis

Before we begin our journey through the relevant verses, we must consider the genres of these two chapters. In the first chapter of Genesis we hear the voice of the narrator generally explaining how God created the universe and everything in it. The second chapter is narrative literature, where we learn details.

In Genesis 1, the narrator tells us clearly what's going on, while Genesis 2 is written in story form. We must discern what truths can legitimately be lifted out of the situations in the story. In Question 3, we explained how some truths are explicit, stated directly and clearly, but in some kinds of divine literature, especially narrative, the truths are implicit. There may be clues or hints that easily lead to speculation and assumptions. Two people may look at what happens in the story and come away with two different opinions about what the text is really saying.

After we've done our best to study the story carefully with an eye to discerning truth, we can then look to see if other parts of the Bible clearly affirm our assessments. Here again we must guard against *evangelastic* thinking.[1]

Let's walk through Genesis 1 and 2 quickly, stopping at each verse used in arguments by hierarchs and heterarchs, comparing and contrasting their ideas. At each stop, attempt to discern whether or not the verses teach us a clear, direct truth about men and women, or whether or not the ideas are based on speculation or assumptions that should not hold nearly the weight of the former in our final analysis.

Genesis 1:26–28—Image and Ruling

Genesis 1 recounts God's creation of the earth, its inhabitants, and the first humans as his crowning event. Verses 26–28 supply our first concept that shows us God's ideal for men and women. These verses are examples of direct, clear biblical truth. The narrator is speaking:

> Then God said, "Let us make mankind *in our image*, in our likeness, so that they may *rule over* the fish . . . the birds . . . the livestock and all the wild animals, and over all the creatures that move along the ground.
>
> So God created mankind in his own image, in the image of God he created them; male and female he created them.
>
> God blessed them and said to them, "*Be fruitful and increase in number*; fill the earth and *subdue* it. *Rule over* the fish . . . birds . . . and over every living creature that moves on the ground." (Gen. 1:26–28, emphasis added)

Being Made in the Image of God

Hierarchs and heterarchs agree that these verses clearly say that both men and women are generally made in the image of God, and this privileged status affirms their equal value and dignity.[2] Some hierarchs argue that the author uses the term "man" in verse 26 instead of "mankind" to hint at what's ahead, man's headship over women.[3] The translators of more than twenty-five English versions disagree, insisting the term refers here to humankind, comprised of both male and female.[4]

---

1. I (Sue) have used this word for many years to communicate stretching the meaning of the text to fit one's view, although I believe I first heard it from a seminary friend, JoAnn Hummel.
2. Grudem, *EFBT*, 25–27.
3. Raymond C. Ortlund Jr., "Male-Female Equality and Male Headship: Genesis 1–3," in *RBMW*, 97–99.
4. NET Bible, New English Translation (Dallas: Biblical Studies Press, 1996–2003), Genesis 1:26n48. See Question 5 for a more thorough treatment of what it means that men and women are made in the image of God.

Ruling Over, Subduing the Earth

Obviously, from 1:26–28, both men and women are made in the image of God and they are commanded to rule and subdue the earth together. Some hierarchs underplay this command. Others mention it briefly.[5] As expected, heterarchs tend to showcase these verses (see Question 5).

Genesis 2:7—The "Order of Creation" Debate

Much more information about men and women's relationships comes from the second chapter. "Then the LORD God formed a man from the dust of the ground and breathed into his nostrils the breath of life, and the man became a living being" (Gen. 2:7). God formed the man in verse 7 and the woman in verses 21 and 22. In many instances, being first has its benefits: the oldest child seems to enjoy greater freedoms and privileges, at least in the eyes of the younger; the winner of a race can boast of a superior ability; the CEO earns top dollar. Did Adam's creation before Eve's grant him—and, by extension, all males—any special benefits? And what's the significance of being first in Scripture?

Hierarchs

Wayne Grudem sums up this perspective: "Adam was created first, was put in the garden and given commands by God, and Eve was created as a helper for Adam; in that sequence of events God gave Adam a leadership role."[6] He goes on to argue that in the Hebrew family and in much of the ancient world, everyone would have understood this. He believes this pattern preserves a certain order, is for all time, and will result in God's best for everyone.

The term for the privileges of the firstborn is called "primogeniture." The resulting hierarch argument is called "the order of creation" and many of the later arguments begin with this basic foundation and scaffold from there. Because Adam was first, he is logically the leader of the couple.[7]

Heterarchs

In the Bible, primogeniture, the automatic rights of the firstborn, is turned on its head. Time after time, God chose a younger brother to rule over the elder.

---

5. Thomas Finley writes, "God makes them rulers over all life" ("The Relationship of Woman and Man in the Old Testament," in *Women and Men in Ministry: A Complementary Perspective*, eds. Robert L. Saucy and Judith K. TenElshof [Chicago: Moody, 2001], 50).
6. Grudem, *EFBT*, 68.
7. Grudem, *EFBT*, 68.

Jacob and Esau

In Genesis 25, Isaac's wife Rebecca was pregnant with twin boys. Before she gave birth, the Lord told her, "Two nations are in your womb, and two peoples from within you will be separated; one people will be stronger than the other, and the older will serve the younger" (Gen. 25:23). This prophecy came to fruition in the lives of Jacob and Esau, with Jacob, the younger, receiving God's favor as the son of the covenant and the one whose children would become Israel, God's chosen people.

The Choosing of King David

We also see this pattern when God instructed Samuel to find and anoint the next king (1 Samuel 16). David's father, Jesse, brought his sons to Samuel, all except the youngest, assuming that Samuel would choose from the older boys. But God didn't affirm any of the seven older sons; instead God said to Samuel, "Do not consider his appearance or his height, for I have rejected him. The LORD does not look at the things people look at. People look at the outward appearance, but the LORD looks at the heart" (1 Sam. 16:7). Then Samuel had Jesse bring up his youngest from the fields. When young David arrived, the Lord said to Samuel, "Rise and anoint him; this is the one" (16:12).

The Life and Teaching of Jesus

When Jesus's disciples were arguing about who was the greatest among them, Jesus said to them, "Anyone who wants to be first must be the very last, and the servant of all" (Mark 9:35). Then he took a little child in his arms as an object lesson. Later he told his disciples, "But many who are first will be last, and the last first" (Mark 10:31). Jesus was born into poverty. Many of the disciples were uneducated fishermen. Jesus didn't use cultural norms to measure God's best ways, and he praised servanthood above all else.

Heterarchs challenge Christians to decide whether being first reflects the tone of who God is, his attributes, his character, and what he values most. Heterarchs believe the "order of creation" argument to put males in a permanent leadership role in the family, church, and community is not in sync with the overall tone of the Scriptures and who God has revealed himself to be.

Genesis 2:18—The Meaning of "Helper"

"The LORD God said, 'It is not good for the man to be alone. I will make a helper suitable for him'" (Gen. 2:18). God declared every part of creation "good" until verse 18. Adam was lacking something significant. The Hebrew for the term translated here as "helper suitable" is *ezer kenegdo*. Is "helper" an accurate translation? The meaning of this critical term will help you discern what you believe God desires for men and women's relationships then and now (see Question 8 for a more thorough exploration of *ezer kenegdo*).

Genesis 2:23 and 3:20—Timing of the Naming of Eve

God created a woman from a part of the man's side (the Hebrew says nothing about a rib). Then God brought her to the man, and he exclaimed: "'This is now bone of my bones and flesh of my flesh; she shall be called "woman," for she was taken out of man.' That is why a man leaves his father and mother and is united to his wife, and they become one flesh" (Gen. 2:23–24). Was Adam giving the woman a new name that she would go by—"I am Man, you are Woman"? Or instead, when he called her "woman," was he making a point about their oneness—"I am man (*ish*), you are woman (*ish'ah*)"?

To complicate the issue, after sin and its consequences are described in the narrative, Genesis 3:20 says, "Adam named his wife Eve, because she would become the mother of all the living." So, did the first man name the first woman in the garden before sin entered the world or after God laid out their consequences for sinning? And what is the significance of him naming her?

The timing of the naming, *before* or *after* the fall, is significant because hierarchs believe that naming something implies authority over it. Therefore, if the pattern of male headship and authority over the female was ordained *before* the fall, it denoted God's all-time best for everyone.

Heterarchs maintain that naming does not imply authority, and even if it did, Adam named the woman *after* the fall, and men's authority over women began as a consequence of the couple's rebellion as expressed in 3:16, "Your desire will be for your husband, and he will rule over you." They believe that Genesis 2 emphasizes oneness and unity, a better foundation for healthy relationships between men and women (see Question 9 for an in-depth exploration of different views on the naming of Eve).

Summary

Genesis 1 and 2 are the foundation for understanding the rest of the Bible's discussion on how God wants men and women to relate to one another. Both hierarchs and heterarchs build on the concepts in these chapters. In light of sound interpretive principles, what can you rely on as clearly true? What ideas seem more like speculations and assumptions? Build carefully, since your answers profoundly affect your ultimate conclusions.

What do you believe about these basic foundational issues?

- Being made in the image of God
- Ruling over, subduing the earth

- The "order of creation" debate
- The meaning of "helper" (*ezer kenegdo*)
- The naming of Eve—the nature of their relationship

We've provided additional chapters on several of these important aspects of Genesis 1 and 2, indicated throughout the text. We hope this chapter has provided a foundation for digging deeper into the details.

REFLECTION QUESTIONS

1. What are the primary themes and differences between the first two chapters of the Bible?

2. Why is it important to consider the genre of Genesis 2 before we begin to try to discern what God wants to communicate?

3. What preconceptions do you bring to the meaning of Genesis 1 and 2?

4. How do hierarchs and heterarchs generally disagree about the "order of creation" argument?

5. What do you find most interesting about this chapter?

How Do Both Men and Women "Exercise Dominion over the Earth"?

In the great story of creation found in Genesis 1, God fashions humanity and gives them a purpose: to be his representatives and regents in the land. As he announces his intention, he describes what they will be and do:

> Then God said, "Let us make mankind in our image, in our likeness, so that they may rule over the fish in the sea and the birds in the sky, over the livestock and all the wild animals, and over all the creatures that move along the ground." . . . God blessed them and said to them, "Be fruitful and increase in number; fill the earth and subdue it. Rule over the fish in the sea and the birds in the sky and over every living creature that moves on the ground." (Gen. 1:26–28)

Our English Bibles translate the Hebrew word *radah* in these verses as "rule." This term is strong, meaning "rule over, dominate, direct, lead, control, subdue, i.e., manage or govern an entity, people or government with considerable or forceful authority."[1] In verses 26 and 28, it appears as a plural verb, modifying "them" or "they."

In verse 28, we read that God also commanded the couple to "subdue" creation. This word, *kabash*, includes the connotation of dominating, bringing into submission. Together, the Hebrew terms show clearly that God's human representatives—both of them—were commanded to take charge of the creation and steward it. In Genesis 1, dominion is not given to humans over one another—only over the rest of creation.

---

1. James Strong, *Enhanced Strong's Lexicon* (Woodside Bible Fellowship, 1995), n7287.

The creation story in Genesis 2 employs a different viewpoint. The man is created first, and while no commands to rule are given, God does put the man "in the Garden of Eden to work it and take care of it" (2:15). He then says it is not good for the man to be alone and announces his intention to create an *ezer kenegdo* for him (see Question 8). But first, he brings the animals to the man so that he could name them and notice that, while each animal had a partner, he did not.

In this chapter, we explore what God's command in Genesis 1:28 means for male and female relationships. Both are told to rule and subdue the earth. Does Genesis 2 provide more guidance on exactly how that calling should look? If so, what might it look like today for a man, or for a woman? Let's look at the hierarchs' thoughts first.

Hierarchs

At first glance, hierarchs and heterarchs agree that God meant humans—male and female—to rule. Raymond Ortlund states, "Man stands between God above and the animals below as God's ruling representative. . . . This is consistent with God's intention, stated in verse 26, that both sexes should rule: '. . . and let *them* rule.'"[2]

Denny Burk, in his lengthy article that summarizes the theology of complementarianism, says, "In essence, God appoints male and female as his vice-regents on earth—the ones who would extend God's dominion over creation by extending their own dominion over the whole earth. God addresses this command not only to the man but to the woman as well. That means that the mandate to rule over creation extends to men and women equally."[3]

Hierarchs affirm women in their role as mothers—a necessary element for humanity to "be fruitful and increase in number; fill the earth and subdue it" (Gen. 1:28). They also affirm women using their natural skills and spiritual gifts to benefit their homes and the church in many ways.

However, after describing man and woman as co-regents, both Ortlund and Burk qualify the equality of the couple by turning to male headship, which looks something like this: Adam, as the first created, names the animals, then names the woman, all of which hint at a God-instituted hierarchy in the garden.[4] Ortlund never specifically addresses dominion itself; rather, he focuses on Adam as the authority of the couple and the woman as his helper/assistant.

John MacArthur, in his book *Divine Design*, approaches the issue from a different angle. He seems to assert male authority as a result of the fall (see

2. Raymond C. Ortlund Jr., "Male-Female Equality and Male Headship: Genesis 1–3," in *RBMW*, 96–97.
3. Denny Burk, "Mere Complementarianism," Council on Biblical Manhood and Womanhood, Nov. 20, 2019, https://cbmw.org/2019/11/20/mere-complementarianism/#_ftnref12.
4. Ortlund, "Equality and Male Headship," 101.

Gen. 3:16): "As part of the curse, God in effect said to the woman, 'You were once co-regents, wonderfully ruling together as a team, but from now on the man is installed over you.' That was a new kind of ruling—an authority that had never been known before."[5]

In MacArthur's view, God stripped from the woman her original status as a co-regent during his confrontation with the first couple after they sinned. From that point, instead of the man and woman ruling creation together, the man now rules the woman as well as creation. And according to God's complete statement in Genesis 3:16–19, the effects of sin would make their mandate grow more difficult.

Today, hierarchs generally relegate male authority to the home and church. Men are to lead, reflecting the common understanding of their status as "head" of the wife and, by extension, the church. Little is said regarding a woman's permission to exercise dominion outside of those spheres of influence.

Heterarchs

Heterarchs take Genesis 1:26 and 28 at face value, with no qualifications. When God told the man and woman to rule and subdue the earth, he was establishing humanity as his regents over creation. Both male and female, together. And because heterarchs do not recognize male headship in the garden, they maintain that God's ideal plan was for humanity, as his image-bearers male and female, to steward his creation.

In this, heterarchs agree with hierarch MacArthur when they acknowledge that sin marred both the image of God in humanity and their ability to carry out their mandate to rule. Did sin change the dynamic between men and women? Yes, of course. But MacArthur believes God prescribed the new reality, instituting a new paradigm in which men would rule women. Heterarchs believe God was describing the natural consequences of sin—that relationships between men and women would falter, making their calling to rule and subdue the earth more difficult.

What else would degrade? Read God's warning in Genesis 3:17–19:

> Cursed is the ground because of you;
> through painful toil you will eat food from it
> all the days of your life.
> It will produce thorns and thistles for you,
> and you will eat the plants of the field.
> By the sweat of your brow
> you will eat your food

---

5. John MacArthur, *Divine Design: God's Complementary Roles for Men and Women* (Colorado Springs: David C. Cook, 2011), 22.

until you return to the ground,
since from it you were taken;
for dust you are
and to dust you will return.

Heterarchs react to the curse by pointing to Jesus. He came to show a better way, to redeem what was broken. Christians, as part of our mission to make the world a better place, are to pursue renewal, holiness, and freedom from sin. In the context of the creation mandate, men and women can steward the world together, overcoming the challenges wrought by sin. Sandra Glahn writes:

> We don't say it's wrong to buy weed killer, even though weeds were part of the fall. And we don't tell students learning Greek that they're out of God's will to take language courses because God confused languages at Babel. We're to fight the effects of sin, not embrace them. In the same way, we should embrace rather than re-craft the story about women having dominion in partnership with men—sisters and brothers shouldering the load together.[6]

Heterarchs reject an artificial delineation between home and work, church and office. They maintain that God gave humanity a holy identity and a critical purpose without a gender qualification. This perspective acknowledges that women, singles, and childless people are invited to participate in the creation mandate beyond the roles of spouse or parent.

They point out that in earlier decades and centuries, women's work was in the gardens and fields, vital to a family's sustenance. The husband and wife together labored to feed and support their family. We see this in the Bible as well: Rachel and Zipporah herded sheep, Ruth gleaned grain, Abigail managed her household, the Proverbs 31 woman did everything from oversee servants to real estate to clothing manufacturing. These women worked hard.

Heterarchs contend that women work hard today, as well, in all spheres of influence. Christian women can be found in the kitchen, the boardroom, the pulpit, the halls of Congress, and everywhere in between. As their gifts and talents enable them to serve and lead effectively, most societies offer them the opportunities.

---

6. Sandra Glahn, "Women Rule," *Engage* (blog), Bible.org, Sept. 6, 2011, https://blogs.bible .org/women-rule.

Summary

Today, men and women alike work in professional fields of science, environmental care, farming, research, forestry, animal husbandry . . . virtually every category of work that cultivates harmony between humans and the world. Creation care manifests in ways as varied as the places and times in which people live. It can look like building a magnificent cathedral, but it also can look like protecting the natural magnificence of the Grand Tetons. It can look like a wild, uninhabited island, but it can also look like the sheep-scattered, stone-walled landscape of rural England.

Whether the hierarchs are right, and wives act under the auspices of husbands, or the heterarchs' understanding of continuing co-regency is more accurate, men and women alike continue to have the opportunity and responsibility to steward this earth for its thriving, as representatives of our common Creator.[7]

> When I look up at your skies,
> at what your fingers made—
> the moon and the stars
> that you set firmly in place—
> what are human beings
> that you think about them;
> what are human beings
> that you pay attention to them?
> You've made them only slightly less than divine,
> crowning them with glory and grandeur.
> You've let them rule over your handiwork,
> putting everything under their feet—
> all sheep and all cattle,
> the wild animals too. (Ps. 8:3–7 CEB)

REFLECTION QUESTIONS

1. How have you interpreted God's command for both men and women to "rule" the earth in the past?

---

7. It is beyond the scope of this book to include a thorough theology of stewardship and details on what it can look like on a practical level. We recommend Sandra Richter's *Stewards of Eden* (Downers Grove, IL: InterVarsity, 2020), which explores a biblical theology of creation care and offers tangible ways for believers to connect biblical mandates to current environmental issues.

2. What part do you think women have in "ruling" the earth today, and is it different for men?

3. Do you tend to agree with hierarchs' or heterarchs' ideas on men and women ruling together? Why?

4. How do you steward the earth in your everyday life?

5. How might you do a better job of living out this important command?

What Does It Mean That Woman Was Man's "Helper Corresponding to Him"?

The Genesis 2 creation story focuses on how humankind, specifically, originated. The author tells us, "Then the LORD God formed a man [Adam] from the dust of the ground and breathed into his nostrils the breath of life, and the man became a living being" (2:7). This living being was then put in the garden to work and take care of it. God instructs him concerning what he's allowed and not allowed to eat. Then we hear, for the first time, God declare that something in his creation is not good.[1] God says, "It is not good for the man to be alone. I will make an *ezer kenegdo* for him" (2:18). We'll come back to that phrase shortly.

How do we know he's alone? The writer gives us a short flashback in verses 19–20. Animals had been created and brought before Adam, each with its partner like it. He named them, and, during this process, the man became aware that he had no partner. While every animal had a mate, a creature like itself, of its same nature, there was no corresponding human. Only Adam.

The writer of Genesis pronounces the problem, "But for Adam [the man] no *ezer kenegdo* was found" (2:20), and a solution: "So the LORD God caused the man to fall into a deep sleep; and while he was sleeping, he took one of the man's ribs and then closed up the place with flesh. Then the LORD God made a woman from the rib he had taken out of the man, and he brought her to the man" (2:21–22).

What is the meaning of the Hebrew words *ezer kenegdo?* They describe the person who would satisfy what was missing in the man's life: a companion unlike the animals but rather like himself.

---

1. Genesis 1:9–25 describes God's reaction to each stage of creation: "God saw that it was good." When humankind is created, male and female (vv. 27–31), "it was very good."

Various English Bible versions translate *ezer kenegdo* in different ways:

- "A helper fit" (RSV, ESV)
- "A help meet" (KJV, ASV, Webster, Jubilee 2000)
- "A helper as his counterpart" (LEB, YLT)
- "A helper suitable" (NASB, NIV)
- "A helper comparable" (NKJV, WEB)
- "A helper as his partner" (NRSV)
- "A helper as his complement" (HCSB)
- "A helper corresponding to him" (CSB)

These translations have contributed to the confusion around the nature of women, particularly as they relate to men. What do the terms mean? To determine that, we turn to the Hebrew. First we will explore the definitions of each term separately, then connect them to discover the intent of the phrase as a whole.

Terms to Define

Ezer

The Hebrew word *ezer* is a combination of two roots, one meaning "to rescue," "to save," and the other meaning "to be strong." Both meanings can be seen in the way the word is used in different Old Testament contexts.

As a noun, *ezer* appears twenty-one times in the Hebrew Scriptures, translated into various words, always with the connotation of assisting, empowering, or serving another with what is needed.[2] Two of those occurrences appear here in Genesis 2 identifying the woman. Sixteen times the word refers to God as Israel's helper (Exod. 18:4; Deut. 33:7, 26, 29; Pss. 20:2; 33:20; 70:5; 89:19; 115:9, 10, 11; 121:1–2; 124:8; 146:5; Hos. 13:9), and three times it identifies military powers (Isa. 30:5; Ezek. 12:14; Dan. 11:34).

The verb form of *ezer* is *azer* ("to rescue or save"), cited eighty-one times in the Hebrew Scriptures. The word refers mostly to military assistance, often from God himself (see 2 Chron. 14:10; 25:8; 26:7, 13; Isa. 41:13, 14; 44:2; 49:8; 59:7, 9). We find more personal, nonmilitary assistance in Psalms (10:14; 22:11; 28:7; 54:4; 72:12; 86:17; 107:12; 119:173; 119:175).

In the case of Genesis 2, the translation question is complicated (or simplified?) by a second word. *Ezer* is combined with a modifying term that sheds light on how to understand its connotation.

---

2. James Swanson, *Dictionary of Biblical Languages with Semantic Domains: Hebrew* (Oak Harbor, WA: Logos Research Systems, 1997), 6469.

Kenegdo

This Hebrew word that modifies *ezer* is actually a conjunction, a primary word merged with two prepositions: *k-neged-o*. Together, they function as a short phrase: "according to what is in front of—corresponding to."

Interestingly, *kenegdo* occurs only this one time in the Bible.[3] We must rely on context, root words, and usages in other ancient literature to help us gain the clearest understanding of the term. Rabbinic texts use the word to describe "things which are like one another."[4] In rabbinic texts, the word means "similar."[5]

Kenegdo tells us that Eve was a person who was similar to Adam, who corresponded to him, who was his equal counterpart. Because she is introduced to him in the context of the animals, each of which had a similar partner, the writer is saying that she is fully human, like Adam in all the ways that the animals were not. He now has a partner, a being like himself.

R. David Freedman, in his exploration of the linguistic origins of *ezer* and *kenegdo*, says:

> When God creates Eve from Adam's rib, his intent is that she will be—unlike the animals—"a power (or strength) equal to him." I think that there is no other way of understanding the phrase *ezer kenegdo* that can be defended philologically [relating to the study of literary texts and languages].[6]

When Adam saw the woman, he reacted with the first recorded poem:

> This one, at last, is bone of my bone
> and flesh of my flesh;
> this one will be called "woman,"
> for she was taken from man. (Gen. 2:23 CSB)

Implications for Translating *Ezer Kenegdo*

The practice of Bible translation combines scholarship with a bit of art: we must know the meaning of the original language yet put the words together so that their meanings make sense in context. Depending on the context, *ezer* can be translated as either "help," "helper," "power," or as "strength,"

---

3. This situation is called a *hapax legomenon*.
4. Heinrich Friedrich Wilhelm Gesenius, *Gesenius' Hebrew-Chaldee Lexicon to the Old Testament Scriptures*, trans. Samuel Prideaux Tregelles (London: Samuel Bagster & Sons, 1857), https://www.blueletterbible.org/lexicon/h5048/niv/wlc/0-1.
5. Gesenius, *Gesenius' Hebrew-Chaldee Lexicon to the Old Testament Scriptures*, https://www.blueletterbible.org/study/lexica/gesenius/index.cfm.
6. R. David Freedman, "Woman, a Power Equal to Man: Translation of Woman a 'Fit Helpmate' for Man Is Questioned," *Biblical Archaeology Review* 9, no. 1 (Jan./Feb. 1983): 58.

"deliverer," "savior," depending on the context. Such decisions are somewhat subjective, though hopefully always true to context, hence the variety of any given verse across translations.

Translation is also an exercise in losing some connotation of a word by choosing only one of its linguistic options. For instance, in Genesis 2, should *ezer* be translated as "helper" or "savior" or "power"? Each term communicates a primary meaning of *ezer*—but not all of its implications. In English, a helper is an assistant, usually lesser in rank. A savior, however, has the ability and authority to deliver a lesser being from some sort of danger. A power, or strength, holds no connotation of over or under, lesser or greater, but implies a neutral position of force. Translators must decide which English word—any of which is indeed an aspect of the definition of *ezer*—to use wherever the term shows up.

Given the overwhelming biblical usage of *ezer* as military and divine help—all from positions of strength—the *ezer kenegdo* of Genesis 2 is a strong character, one created to fill a need in Adam, to come alongside in strength to alleviate any lack. But scholars emphasize different qualities in the *ezer kenegdo* by choosing one definition over another.

The *Theological Wordbook of the Old Testament* defines *ezer kenegdo* as "a help corresponding to him, i.e., equal and adequate to himself."[7] Likewise, all major English translations use "helper" for *ezer* in Genesis 2 with differing phrasing to reflect the meaning of *kenegdo*.[8]

Hierarchs

John Piper and Wayne Grudem lead the position that argues for male hierarchy. They assert that Adam was looking for a helper among the animals but could not find one suitable. They define *ezer kenegdo* as a helper who shared the man's human nature, was equal to him in "Godlike personhood," and much different from any animal. "Yet in passing through 'helpful' animals to woman, God teaches us that the woman is a man's 'helper' in the sense of a loyal and suitable assistant in the life of the garden."[9]

---

7. R. Laird Harris, Gleason L. Archer, and Bruce K. Waltke, eds., *Theological Wordbook of the Old Testament* (Chicago: Moody, 1980), 1289a.
8. For additional insight into the term *ezer* and Christian marriage, see Darrell Bock, "The Foundational Language of Marriage in Scripture," in Curt Hamner, John Trent, Rebekah J. Byrd, Eric L. Johnson, and Eric Thoennes *Marriage: Its Foundation, Theology, and Mission in a Changing World* (Chicago: Moody, 2018), 70–71.
9. John Piper and Wayne Grudem, "An Overview of Central Concerns: Questions and Answers," in *RBMW*, 87. The opening argument is not supported in the biblical text: nowhere does it state or infer that Adam was looking for a helper when he was naming the animals. This perspective understands the woman's value in the man's life as primarily an assistant to the work he was given to do. It ignores the declaration of God that "it is not good for man to be alone," as well as the Genesis 1:28 command to both the man and woman to "fill the earth and subdue it."

Raymond Ortlund believes that maleness and femaleness, being born one sex or the other, defines a person's role in God's kingdom and in relation to the opposite sex: "So, was Eve Adam's equal? Yes and no. She was his spiritual equal and, unlike the animals, 'suitable for him.' But she was not his equal in that she was his helper. . . . A man, just by virtue of his manhood, is called to lead for God. A woman, just by virtue of her womanhood, is called to help for God."[10]

Some hierarchs understand "help" in Genesis 2 as work someone offers from an inferior position, whether the helper has a higher, equal, or lower rank. David Clines explains, "Though superiors may help inferiors, strong may help weak, gods may help humans, in the act of helping they are being 'inferior.' That is to say, they are subjecting themselves to a secondary, subordinate position. Their help may be necessary or crucial, but they are assisting some task that is already someone else's responsibility. They are not actually doing the task themselves, or even in cooperation, for there is different language for that."[11]

Heterarchs

Heterarchs lean more toward the correspondence of man to the woman, emphasizing their similarities over differences. Freedman goes so far as to define *ezer kenegdo* as "a power equal to . . . whose strength was equal to man's. Woman was not intended to be merely man's helper. She was to be instead his partner."[12]

Walter Kaiser explains how "helpmate" erroneously became associated with *ezer*:

> The woman was never meant to be an assistant or "help-mate" to the man. The word *mate* slipped into English since it was so close to Old English *meet*, which means "fit to" or "corresponding to" the man. . . . What God had intended then was to make a "power" or "strength" [i.e., *ezer*] for the man who would in every way "correspond to him" or even "be his equal."[13]

John Walton reminds readers that "helper" is a common and neutral term describing someone who comes to the aid of or provides a service for someone:

10. Raymond C. Ortlund Jr., "Male-Female Equality and Male Headship: Genesis 1–3," in *RBMW*, 102.
11. David Clines, *What Does Eve Do to Help? And Other Readerly Questions to the Old Testament*, JSOTSup 94 (Sheffield: JSOT, 1990), 25–48.
12. Freedman, "Woman, a Power Equal to Man," 56–58.
13. Walter C. Kaiser Jr., Peter H. Davids, F. F. Bruce, and Manfred Brauch, "Genesis," in *Hard Sayings of the Bible* (Downers Grove, IL: InterVarsity, 1996), 94.

"In fact, the noun form of the word found in this verse as used elsewhere refers almost exclusively to God as the One who helps his people."[14] He maintains that "helper" cannot be understood as the opposite/complement of "leader."

A Modern Illustration

Since *ezer* appears predominantly in military situations throughout the Old Testament, let's imagine the Allies of World War II: Britain has stood up against the Nazis, fighting for her life as the rest of Europe has fallen. She is a strong nation but her enemy is steadily overwhelming her. Enter the Americans, her own former colonies turned allies, arriving just in time to reinforce the British and forge a new alliance stronger than their enemy. Together they beat back the Nazi attacks and begin their strategy to defeat their enemy.

America was Britain's *ezer kenegdo*.

The Americans provided what the British could not. Only together could they stand, side by side, united, working in harmony to accomplish their mission. In the cosmic spiritual war, men and women need each other as allies to stand firm against their common enemy, the devil. Having an *ezer kenegdo*, or being an *ezer kenegdo*, can only strengthen humanity's striving to bring the kingdom of God into preeminence.

Summary

When God declared that it was not good that Adam was alone, with no one like himself to share life with, God said he would create someone like him but also different from him, someone who corresponded to him—an *ezer kenegdo*. Those two words begin the foundation for us to build how we determine how God wants men and women to relate to and treat one another. Different groups translate these two words in various ways, focusing on different emphases. Hierarchs generally emphasize that the man is the leader, and the woman is his "helper" in the sense of a loyal and suitable assistant. Heterarchs insist that the woman is not an assistant but instead supplies what the man lacks, providing qualities that he needs to thrive as they work together to fill and subdue the earth. They insist that she in every way corresponds to him and is his equal.

REFLECTION QUESTIONS

1. What do you think of when you hear the word "helper"?

---

14. John H. Walton, *Genesis: The NIV Application Commentary* (Grand Rapids: Zondervan, 2001), 176.

2. How has the term "helper" in Genesis 2:20 influenced your view of who you are as a man or a woman?

3. Do you tend to agree more with hierarchs or heterarchs concerning Genesis 2:20? Why?

4. Considering the Hebrew meaning of the words usually translated as Adam's "helper," what do you think might be a better way to express the relationship God desires between men and women?

5. How might you live out your convictions concerning Genesis 2:20 as you relate to people of the opposite sex?

What Does Genesis 3 Reveal About Male and Female Relationships?

Bible-believing scholars agree that the sin of Adam and Eve in Genesis 3, known as "the fall," resulted in horrific consequences for people and the earth. But they disagree as to the effect of those consequences on relationships between men and women. Their varied conclusions and the ramifications color how Christians view the rest of the Scriptures pertaining to gender issues, and how they believe God desires men and women to function in both the family and the church.

The Effect of the Fall According to Early Christian Thinking

Genesis 3 influenced what the majority of Christians thought about relationships between men and women for most of church history, what we call the "traditional" view. Here is a sampling of quotes from early church fathers:

> And do you not know that you are (each) an Eve? The sentence of God on this sex of yours lives in this age: the guilt must of necessity live too. You are the devil's gateway: you are the un-sealer of that (forbidden) tree: you are the first deserter of the divine law: you are she who persuaded him whom the devil was not valiant enough to attack. You destroyed so easily God's image, man. On account of your desert—that is, death—even the Son of God had to die. (Tertullian, AD 155–220)[1]

> For nothing disgraceful is proper for man, who is endowed with reason; much less for woman, to whom it brings shame

---

1. Tertullian, *On the Apparel of Women* 1.1, The Tertullian Project, https://www.tertullian.org/anf/anf04/anf04-06.htm#P331_68246.

to even reflect of what nature she is. (Clement of Alexandria, AD 190)[2]

Woman is a misbegotten man and has a faulty and defective nature in comparison to his. Therefore she is unsure in herself. What she cannot get, she seeks to obtain through lying and diabolical deceptions. And so, to put it briefly, one must be on one's guard with every woman, as if she were a poisonous snake and the horned devil. . . . Thus in evil and perverse doings woman is cleverer, that is, slyer, than man. Her feelings drive woman toward every evil, just as reason impels man toward all good. (Albert Magnus, AD 1258)[3]

Thankfully, both hierarchs and heterarchs reject these ideas today. However, neither can argue their own view is historical.

More Recent Views on Genesis 3

To explore current views on Genesis 3, let's walk through this passage quickly, stopping at each verse that is used in the arguments by hierarchs and heterarchs, comparing and contrasting. Remember that Genesis 3 is divine narrative literature, so we must interpret the text according to sound interpretive principles related to stories (see Question 3 on interpretive principles). At each stop, attempt to discern what's clear and what's speculation.

Most of us know something about this account in general terms. But how do hierarchs and heterarchs interpret what happened at the fall related to the following questions?

Why Did Satan Approach Eve First? (Gen. 3:1)

"Now the serpent was more crafty than any of the wild animals the LORD God had made. He said to the woman, 'Did God really say, "You must not eat from any tree in the garden"?'" (Gen. 3:1).

Hierarchs

Raymond Ortlund insists that Satan, in the form of a serpent, went to Eve first to strike a blow to Adam's authority.

2. Clement of Alexandria, *The Instructor* 2.2 , in *The Writings of Clement of Alexandria*, trans. William Wilson (London: Hamilton, 1867), 209.
3. *Quaestiones super de animalibus* 15.11, quoted in Vivian Phelips, *The Churches and Modern Thought* (Watts, 1911), 203.

What actually happened is full of meaning. Eve usurped Adam's headship and led the way into sin. And Adam, who (it seems) had stood by passively, allowing the deception to progress without decisive intervention—Adam, for his part, abandoned his post as head. Eve was deceived; Adam forsook his responsibility. Both were wrong and together they pulled the human race down into sin and death.[4]

Heterarchs

Andrew Bartlett responds that no basis for this idea exists in the text: "Nothing is said about Eve usurping Adam's headship or about Adam abandoning his headship; the story is not presented in those terms."[5]

After the Fall, Why Did God Address Adam First? (Gen. 3:10–13)

After Adam and Eve rebelled against God (3:6), God confronted the couple: "They hid from the LORD God among the trees of the garden. But the LORD God called to the man, 'Where are you?'" (Gen. 3:8–9).

Hierarchs

Thomas Finley speaks for many hierarchs when he argues that even though both Adam and Eve sinned, God held Adam primarily responsible:

> This is clear first from God's summons to Adam, "Where are you?" In the Hebrew, the word "you" has a form that is appropriate for addressing one individual who is also a male. It is also brought out through the fact that God issues an indictment only for the man. . . . "Because you listened to the voice of your wife."[6]

Heterarchs

Bartlett counters this way:

> Ortlund says that God calls out to Adam first (v. 9) because Adam is the head. Grudem says the same. But it is unclear how they know this. The text does not say that this is the

---

4. Raymond C. Ortlund Jr., "Male-Female Equality and Male Headship: Genesis 1–3" in *RBMW*, 107.
5. Andrew Bartlett, *Men and Women in Christ: Fresh Light from the Biblical Texts* (London: InterVarsity, 2019), 77–78.
6. Thomas Finley, "The Relationship of Woman and Man in the Old Testament," in *Women and Men in Ministry: A Complementary Perspective*, eds. Robert L. Saucy and Judith K. TenElshof (Chicago: Moody, 2001), 59.

reason. . . . The text does not state a reason. One could say, with as little justification, that Eve is the head because in verses 16–17 [laying out the consequences of the fall] God addresses Eve before Adam.[7]

Do the Consequences for Adam and Eve Imply They Have Different Roles? (Gen. 3:16–19)

> To the woman he said, "I will make your pains in childbearing very severe; with painful labor you will give birth to children. Your desire will be for your husband, and he will rule over you." To Adam, he said, "Because you listened to your wife and ate fruit from the tree about which I commanded you, 'You must not eat from it,' cursed is the ground because of you; through painful toil you will eat food from it all the days of your life. It will produce thorns and thistles for you, and you will eat the plants of the field. By the sweat of your brow you will eat your food until you return to the ground, since from it you were taken; for dust you are and to dust you will return." (Gen. 3:16–19)

Hierarchs

Dan Doriani writes, "When God announced his judgment, he applied it to the man in his work and to the women in her relationships."[8] Claus Westermann adds, "Just where the woman finds her fulfillment in life, her honor and her joy, namely in her relationship to her husband and as mother to her children, there too she finds that it is not pure bliss, but pain, burden, humiliation and subordination."[9]

Grudem comes to the same conclusions on Adam's consequence as he does Eve's: "One aspect of the curse was imposing *pain on Adam's particular area of responsibility*, raising food from the ground. . . . Another aspect of the curse was to impose *pain on Eve's particular area of responsibility*, the bearing of children."[10]

Much has been assumed about the different "roles" of men and women on the basis of his reasoning. Many hierarchs believe man's function is to provide and protect their families, and a woman's function is to keep house and take care of the children. In this view, men gain fulfillment from their careers while women gain fulfillment from relationships.

---

7. Bartlett, *Men and Women in Christ*, 78.
8. Dan Doriani, *Women and Ministry: What the Bible Teaches* (Wheaton, IL: Crossway, 2003), 62.
9. Claus Westermann, *Genesis 1–11: A Continental Commentary* (Minneapolis: Augsburg, 1984), 263.
10. Grudem, *EFBT*, 39, emphasis original.

Heterarchs

The Hebrew word for "labor pains" in verse 16 is the same word used to describe the man's consequence, "painful toil" (v. 17) working the reluctant ground. The text seems to show similar consequences for both women and men. The consequences spoken to Adam affect the entire human race, male and female. Eve and all future men and women have wrestled with life on an uncooperative planet.

Heterarchs reject the idea of particular "roles" for men and women. For example, they say that both men and women are assigned the joint task of bearing and raising children—to be fruitful and multiply (Gen. 1:28). Linda Belleville asks,

> Why then the pairings of the woman and childbearing and the man and toiling the land in Genesis 3:16–19? They certainly do make sense. Only women can bear children, and certain physical tasks are more readily accomplished by men. Yet this is a far cry from saying that the woman's divinely ordained role is inside (i.e., the domestic sphere) and the man's divinely ordained role is outside (i.e., the public sphere). Nothing in Genesis 1–3 explicitly supports this.[11]

What Is the Significance of the Man Naming the Woman Eve?

Immediately after God pronounces the man and woman's consequences for sin, the man turns to her and gives her the name "Eve": "*Adam named his wife Eve*, because she would become the mother of all the living" (Gen. 3:20, emphasis added). But earlier, in the garden, before sin entered the picture, God presented the woman to the man, who broke out into poetry upon meeting her: "Then the LORD God made a woman from the rib he had taken out of the man and he brought her to the man. The man said: 'This is now bone of my bones and flesh of my flesh; *she shall be called "woman" for she was taken out of man*,'" (Gen. 2:22–23, emphasis added). Questions central to the discussion include:

- When Eve first approached Adam in the garden, did he name her "woman" in his poetic response in 2:23?
- Or did Adam actually name her after the fall, when he called her "Eve" in 3:20?
- Does the timing of his naming her matter?
- What is the significance of naming someone?

---

11. Linda L. Belleville, *Women Leaders and the Church: Three Crucial Questions* (Grand Rapids: Baker, 2000), 100. See Question 10 to answer the question, "What did God mean that, 'Your desire will be for your husband, and he will rule over you'?"

Hierarchs

Genesis 2:23 is a foundational passage for hierarchs. Grudem argues that in his first greeting to Eve, Adam "is giving a name to her."[12] This is important, Grudem argues, because "in that context the original readers would have recognized that the person doing the 'naming' of created things is always the person who has authority over those things."[13] When the man named the animals before the woman was created, he did so as the one already given dominion over them (Gen. 1:26–29). Therefore, this line of reasoning goes, when the man named the woman, he did so in his God-given authority.

After the fall God confronts the disgraced couple and the man gives the woman the name "Eve" (3:20). Ortlund understands this event as the moment in which the couple experienced a breakdown in their relationship, which before the fall was an already-established, God-ordained hierarchy. In this view, the fall ruined what should have been the man's benevolent, agape-love service toward his wife, turning his role into "rule," described in Genesis 3:15 as "enmity."[14]

Heterarchs

Heterarchs understand Adam's earlier poetic welcome in 2:23 not as an actual naming but as a recognition that, finally, he is one of two, just as the animals were in pairs. He sees that she is a human, like himself. Glenn Kreider explains why this statement should not be understood as a naming declaration: The man calls her what she is: *ishah* (woman) to his *ish* (man), they share humanity. "That is the narrator's point, that there is unity and diversity; they are one but different. They are equal, but not the same."[15]

The Hebrew text reads: "of this one it will be said, 'woman.'"[16] This phrasing is echoed in other biblical passages (e.g., 1 Sam. 9:9; 2 Sam. 18:18; Prov. 16:21; Isa. 1:26), which use the same grammatical structure as Genesis 2:23. But in none of these other passages is the person, place, or thing understood to be in submission to the one calling it by name. To be *called* is to be *described* in a certain way based on a clue in the context.[17]

---

12. Wayne Grudem, "The Key Issues in the Manhood-Womanhood Controversy, and the Way Forward," in *Biblical Foundations for Manhood and Womanhood*, ed. Wayne Grudem (Wheaton, IL: Crossway, 2002), 26.

13. Grudem, "Key Issues," 26.

14. Ortlund, "Equality and Male Headship," 102–3.

15. Glenn Kreider, "Eve: The Mother of All Seducers?," in *Vindicating the Vixens: Revisiting Sexualized, Vilified, and Marginalized Women of the Bible*, ed. Sandra Glahn (Grand Rapids: Kregel, 2017), 137.

16. NET Bible notes, Gen. 2:23, note b.

17. The NET Bible explains for Genesis 2:23 (note b, emphasis original):

"Some argue that naming implies the man's authority or ownership over the woman here. Naming can indicate ownership or authority if one is calling someone or something *by* one's name and/or calling a name *over* someone or something (see 2 Sam. 12:28;

In Genesis 2, Adam himself says why he called the new human "woman": "because she was taken out of man" (v. 23b). As Kreider explains, *ish* and *ishah* are a play on words, one derived from the other, sharing an essence. Echoes of this wordplay are also seen in the English words "man" and "woman."

The Significance of Naming

Heterarchs argue that when Adam actually names the woman "Eve" in 3:20, he did so as an expression of her identity, whom she would become, "the mother of all the living." Was he exercising authority in naming her Eve? The context allows for that understanding but does not require it.

Naming exercises in the Bible reveal a variety of reasons, including occasions of authority being demonstrated (e.g., Num. 32:42, when the conquered city is renamed by the victors), but also occasions where the characteristics of a person are being recognized. For example, in Genesis 25:25–26, Esau was given the name "hairy" because the text described his whole body as looking like a hairy garment, and Jacob was given the name "heel grabber" because he grasped the heel of his brother who was born first. Sometimes a name merely described a person or object (e.g., Isaac naming his well in Gen. 26:22). The strongest example of naming that did not demonstrate authority but conveyed a description occurred when the slave Hagar named God El Roi, the God Who Sees (Gen. 16:13). Martin Shields states,

> It is perhaps the most remarkable aspect of most scholars' exegesis of this passage that they simply assume that name giving conveys this notion [authority]. The fact that names are often bestowed by those with authority over the recipient is insufficient basis for concluding that naming is, in every instance, an expression of authority.[18]

Lucy Peppiatt adds, "The fact that Adam names Eve signifies their intimate connection, not an unequal relationship of the ruler and the ruled."[19]

---

2 Chron. 7:14; Isa. 4:1; Jer. 7:14; 15:16), especially if one is conquering and renaming a site. But the idiomatic construction used here (the Niphal of קָרָא [*qara*'] with the preposition לְ [*lamed*]) does not suggest such an idea. In each case where it is used, the one naming discerns something about the object being named and gives it an appropriate name (see 1 Sam. 9:9; 2 Sam. 18:18; Prov. 16:21; Isa. 1:26; 32:5; 35:8; 62:4, 12; Jer. 19:6). Adam is not so much naming the woman as he is discerning her close relationship to him and referring to her accordingly. He may simply be anticipating that she will be given an appropriate name based on the discernible similarity."

18. Martin Shields, *Man and Woman in Genesis 1–3* (ThM thesis, Sydney College of Divinity, 1995), 43.

19. Lucy Peppiatt, *Rediscovering Scripture's Vision for Women: Fresh Perspectives on Disputed Texts* (Downers Grove, IL: IVP Academic, 2019), 51.

No matter why Adam named Eve, heterarchs contend, it is worth remembering that he named her after sin had entered their relationship. If he was exercising some sort of authority over her, we must consider that such an arrangement—which even hierarchs describe as harsh, sinful, and dominating—between man and woman, or husband and wife, was not God's original desire for them.

Summary

Libraries of books and articles have been written in an attempt to decipher the meaning of Genesis 1–3 regarding men and women's relationships. The task is especially difficult because Genesis 2 and 3 are divine narrative literature—story. Some Christians believe the story reveals a timeless principle that men have authority over women in the home and the church. Other Christians say they see nothing explicit about leadership, headship, or authority there. They argue that the words "head," "leader," or "authority" don't exist in the text. The word "rule" is there twice, referring to the privilege given to Adam and Eve to rule together, and once in 3:16 when it's used as a negative, overbearing kind of ruling.

Typically, hierarchs and heterarchs highlight different emphases. Heterarch Michelle Lee-Barnewall writes: "The story of Adam and Eve presents vital principles about obedience that will be carried into the rest of Scripture. Also, because of their failure to obey God, their intended unity is shattered. . . . The importance of the motif of unity between the first man and the first woman should not be underestimated."[20]

Hierarch Grudem admits, "Some arguments are not as forceful as others, though all have some force. Some of them whisper male headship and some shout it clearly. But they form a cumulative case showing that Adam and Eve had distinct roles before the Fall, and this was God's purpose in creating them."[21]

Heterarch Bartlett counters Grudem: "The argument depends entirely on supposed implications. . . . The Genesis writer's own conclusion focuses on the unity of man and woman (2:24). . . . The complementarian arguments from Genesis 2 cannot convince anyone who does not have a prior commitment to the idea of male leadership. . . . Debatable implications are not a sufficient basis for a doctrine."[22]

---

20. Michelle Lee-Barnewall, *Neither Complementarian nor Egalitarian: A Kingdom Corrective to the Evangelical Gender Debate* (Grand Rapids: Baker Academic, 2016), 141.
21. Grudem, *EFBT*, 42.
22. Bartlett, *Men and Women in Christ*, 84.

REFLECTION QUESTIONS

1. What do you think about the fact that for centuries Christians have been arguing about what the fall means for relationships between men and women?

2. What have you thought about these issues in the past and why?

3. What are your thoughts concerning the different consequences women and men received as a result of their disobedience?

4. After weighing the different perspectives presented in this chapter, what are your current thoughts?

5. What impact has Genesis 3 had overall on Christian theology?

QUESTION 10

What Did God Mean That "Your Desire Will Be for Your Husband, and He Will Rule Over You"?

A man gave a woman his seat on the subway; she fainted. When she revived, she thanked him, and he fainted." Although less and less politically correct, gender jokes almost always yield a smile, a snicker, or a belly laugh. They often reflect what's known as "the battle of the sexes," defined as the struggle for power between men and women.[1] Four related questions come to mind:

- Does this battle actually exist?
- If so, where did this battle originate?
- How do hierarchs and heterarchs differ in their perspectives?
- How does God want men and women to relate to one another?

Does the Battle of the Sexes Actually Exist?

This battle does indeed exist. We sometimes observe evidence of this tension in small ways when men and women interact in meetings. For example, I've attended committee meetings where a woman states an idea and it's ignored, but then a man comes up with the same suggestion stated a bit differently and the other men love it. God created men and women differently and beautifully, but sometimes these differences aren't appreciated. Throughout history, all over the world, and in extreme cases, gender domination, rivalry, manipulation, and opposition has progressed to practices

---

1. *Merriam-Webster*, s.v. "battle of the sexes," accessed Sept. 30, 2021, https://www.merriam-webster.com/dictionary/battle%20of%20the%20sexes.

like foot-binding, female genital mutilation, bride-burning, and other forms of rape, assault, and abuse.[2]

Hierarch Henry Morris writes: "Generally speaking, man has subjugated woman with little regard for her own personal feelings and needs. In non-Christian cultures and religions, such subjugation and humiliation have been almost universal, until very recent times her husband often having even the power of life and death over her."[3]

Although some of these attitudes toward women prevailed in the first century, Jesus broke with those social norms regarding women, as we'll see in later chapters. In response, women flocked to follow him. How would Jesus advise us today regarding the battle of the sexes? What is best for the family, the church, the society, and the world? Not all Christians agree on the answer.

Where Did the Battle of the Sexes Originate?

The battle of the sexes began early in humankind's history, right after the first man and woman disobeyed God. We find a devastating consequence of the fall for women in Genesis 3:16: "Your desire will be for your husband, and he will rule over you." Neither hierarchs nor heterarchs claim this statement is prescriptive; instead they both say this verse is descriptive. This means that neither camp claims that this consequence of the fall is good. They agree that God is not prescribing that men and women *should* relate this way. They both admit that this passage describes how men and women *actually have related* to one another since the fall, and neither side contends it's God's ideal.

Nevertheless, each side believes that the Bible teaches something different about the meaning of Genesis 3:16. And each side comes to a different conclusion concerning how God wants men and women to relate to one another in the home and the church.

Each side's view is colored by their presuppositions concerning the first couple's relationship *before* the fall. Hierarchs argue that the focus in Genesis 1 and 2 is on Adam's leadership and authority over Eve, while heterarchs see the focus on the couple's unity and one-flesh relationship (see Question 9 for a thorough discussion of this question).

As a result, how do hierarchs and heterarchs differ concerning Genesis 3:16? Let's look closer at these contrasting perspectives.

Hierarchs

Some hierarchs assume that the "desire" in this text refers to a woman's sexual desire for her husband. Wayne Grudem refutes that idea because God

---

2. For multiple examples, see Nicholas D. Kristof and Sheryl WuDunn, *Half the Sky: Turning Oppression into Opportunity for Women Worldwide* (New York: Random House, 2009).
3. Henry M. Morris, *The Genesis Record: A Scientific and Devotional Commentary on the Book of Beginnings* (Grand Rapids: Baker, 1976), 123.

told the first couple to "be fruitful and multiply" (Gen. 1:28 NET), and as a result he contends that sexual desire within marriage is good and would not be a consequence of the fall. Instead, he sees this as a woman's aggressive desire to come against her husband, to compete with him for power and domination, leading to the battle of the sexes.[4]

Fellow hierarchs who teamed up to produce the English Standard Version (ESV) believed so strongly that the woman's desire for her husband in 3:16 referred to a power struggle, rather than sexual desire, that they interpreted the Hebrew to match their belief: rather than translating the Hebrew preposition *el* as "to/toward/for," they chose to render it "contrary to."[5]

Hierarchs believe that God gave Adam and Eve distinct and permanent roles before the fall. Adam was given authority over Eve and his role was to lead, while her role was to support him in that benevolent leadership. They base this idea on the order of creation—because Adam was created first—as well as a number of other related interpretations that they believe support their view (see Question 6).[6]

Thus, "the curse brought a distortion of previous roles, not the introduction of new roles."[7] In other words, Genesis 3:16 did not change Adam's mandate to benevolent "ruling" but it did explain that because of the fall, men would experience and sometimes act on an urge to take advantage of women, and in extreme cases to dominate them through cruel abuse.

Heterarch Lucy Peppiatt writes regarding Genesis 3:16 that the hierarch "who believes that women are originally made to be under male authority sees a distortion of the God-intended roles of male leadership and female submission." She continues that, for the hierarch:

> In God's ordered society, men are destined to rule in a Christlike and loving fashion, and women are destined to follow in a Christlike submissive fashion. The fall, however, disrupts the benignly ordered relations of male and female, and God decrees that from then on women will have an aggressive desire to conquer their husbands and husbands will rule harshly. . . . It is a disordered picture of the God-given order.[8]

---

4. See Grudem, *EFBT*, 30–37.
5. For a detailed but clear explanation of how the Hebrew terms can be understood, and why heterarchs object to the ESV's choice of "contrary to" as biased, see Scot McKnight's blog post: "Why the ESV's 'Contrary to' in Genesis 3:16 Matters," Jesus Creed, Oct. 5, 2016, https://www.patheos.com/blogs/jesuscreed/2016/10/05/why-the-esvs-contrary-to-in-gen-316-matters.
6. See Grudem, *EFBT*, 30–37.
7. Grudem, *EFBT*, 37.
8. Lucy Peppiatt, *Rediscovering Scripture's Vision for Women: Fresh Perspectives on Disputed Texts* (Downers Grove, IL: IVP Academic, 2019), 52.

Henry Morris admits Genesis 3:16 has become reality since the fall but believes the problem brought about by the distortion of previous roles revealed in the garden has a simple solution:

> It is surely true that, in the Israelite economy outlined in the Mosaic Code, and even more in the Christian relationships enjoined in the New Testament, the role of the woman is eminently conducive to her highest happiness and fulfillment, as multitudes of Christian women have testified. In nominally Christian countries, of course, and even in many Christian homes and churches, the proper roles of husband and wife have often been distorted in one direction or another. This can best be corrected by simple obedience to God's revealed Word.[9]

Heterarchs

Heterarch Philip Payne agrees with Grudem and other hierarchs that Genesis 3:16 doesn't express God's will for the relationships of men and women, but he disagrees with Grudem that "the curse brought a distortion of previous roles, not the introduction of new roles."[10] Payne argues that all the consequences of the fall are something brand new, not preexisting. None of the other consequences are examples of distortions of what came before, and insisting that man's rule over woman has simply changed would be out of harmony with every other consequence of the fall.

For example, every other consequence is disastrous news for those addressed. Each one relates to what's going to happen in the future as a result of the fall. Payne writes: "Every other result of the fall for humankind is something people should try to overcome, such as pain in childbearing (through medical techniques) and removal of thorns and thistles (through weeding and farming). People should not foster, but rather alleviate, the consequences of the fall, including the husband's rule over his wife."[11]

Neither does heterarch David Freedman see a God-decreed order that men should lead and women follow before the fall. As a result, he sees Genesis 3:16 as a different kind of tragedy from hierarchs. "The first relationship of mutual support and strength, of equality and sharing, of recognition of the same and the difference in one's closest companion, has become horribly disordered and an emotionally unequal, power-based, unloving relationship. The woman will desire her husband, but he will dominate her. It is a chilling transition."[12]

---

9. Henry M. Morris, *The Genesis Record*, 123.
10. Grudem, *EFBT*, 130.
11. Morris, *Genesis Record*, 123.
12. David R. Freedman, "Woman, a Power Equal to a Man: Translation of Woman a 'Fit Helpmate' for Man Is Questioned," *Biblical Archaeology Review* 9, no. 1 (Jan./Feb. 1983): 56–58.

Summary

How does God want men and women to relate to one another? Does the hierarch's view or the heterarch's view of Genesis 3:16 ring true to you? You will be highly influenced by whether you think that in the garden and before the fall, God ordained a good and permanent order of men leading and women following, or God showed us that he desires for men and women to always work and lead together.

Regardless, God desires that as men and women, we defeat the urge to war against one another. There is only one winner in the battle of the sexes—and it isn't God, men, women, families, churches, or societies.

Paul exhorted us all, both men and women, both hierarchs and heterarchs:

> As a prisoner for the Lord, then, I urge you to live a life worthy of the calling you have received. Be completely humble and gentle; be patient, bearing with one another in love. Make every effort to keep the unity of the Spirit through the bond of peace. There is one body and one Spirit, just as you were called to one hope when you were called; one Lord, one faith, one baptism; one God and Father of all, who is over all and through all and in all. (Eph. 4:1–6)

REFLECTION QUESTIONS

1. What evidence have you seen of the "battle of the sexes" around the world?

2. Have you personally experienced these tendencies in yourself or others?

3. How can Christians overcome these tendencies and instead work together for the cause of Christ?

4. Do you believe that in the garden and before the fall, God ordained a good and permanent order of men leading and women following? If so, why?

5. Do you believe that in the garden and before the fall, God showed us that he desires for men and women to always work and lead together? If so, why?

Women in the Rest
of the Old Testament

What Can We Learn from Women Prophets of the Old Testament?

Before we begin to discern the answer, we must consider several preliminary questions. Then we'll delve into two biblical accounts of Old Testament women prophets, Deborah and Huldah.

What Is a Prophet, and What Is Prophecy?

A prophet was a man or woman God used to communicate his message to the people.

> For prophecy never had its origin in the human will, but prophets, though human, spoke from God as they were carried along by the Holy Spirit. (2 Peter 1:21)

> I will pour out my Spirit on all people. Your sons and daughters will prophesy, your young men will see visions, your old men will dream dreams. Even on my servants, both men and women, I will pour out my Spirit in those days and they will prophesy. (Acts 2:17–18, quoting Joel 2:28–29)

Prophets' communication consisted of both forthtelling (a moral message to that generation often warning of impending judgment unless they changed their ways) and foretelling (a prediction of future events).[1]

Most Old Testament prophets were male, but five women carried the title prophet: Miriam (Exod. 15:20), Deborah (Judg. 4:4), Huldah (2 Kings 22:14,

---

1. Nathan D. Holsteen and Michael J. Svigel, *Exploring Christian Theology*, vol. 1, *Revelation, Scripture, and the Triune God* (Minneapolis: Bethany House, 2014), 265–66.

2 Chron. 34:22), Noadiah, a false prophet (Neh. 6:14), and Isaiah's wife (Isa. 8:3). We will look at Deborah and Huldah briefly.

The Prophet Deborah (Judg. 4:4–5)

> Now Deborah, a prophet, the wife of Lappidoth, was leading Israel at that time. She held court under the Palm of Deborah between Ramah and Bethel in the hill country of Ephraim, and the Israelites went up to her to have their disputes decided. (Judg. 4:4–5)

After Israel settled in the Promised Land around 1250 BC, God raised up judges to lead them. Although in a general sense Israel conquered all of Canaan, pockets of enemy groups still existed, attacking, pillaging, and testing whether or not the Israelites would trust and obey God. When Israel did, God blessed them with victory in battle followed by times of peace and prosperity. But typically the nation waffled between times of blessing and periods when "everyone did as they saw fit" (Judg. 21:25). God called twelve judges to deliver God's people from these warring groups and then to rule them during the times of peace.[2]

Hierarchs

Obviously, Deborah led Israel at that time as the highest-ranking "judge" as well as a prophet. However, some hierarchs dispute whether she carried out her leadership positions as male judges did. Also, hierarchs try to understand why God raised up a woman to this high place of leadership because it doesn't fit their view of the created order. French sixteenth-century theologian John Calvin laid the foundation for the belief that female prophets in the Old Testament were "breakouts," extraordinary acts of God, exceptions that "do not overturn the patterns and rules that govern and bind us today."[3]

Some insist that God permitted women to lead during times when Israel experienced a vacuum of adequate male leaders. For example, they say, Moses's sister, Miriam, was allowed to lead because no qualified men were available after years of slavery in Egypt. During the period of the judges, God raised up Deborah as a female prophet and judge, exceptional measures, because of Israel's depravity when everyone did what was right in their own eyes. Wayne Grudem exclaims, "Something is abnormal, something is wrong—there are no men to function as judge!"[4]

---

2. Irving L. Jensen, *Judges & Ruth: A Self-Study Guide* (Chicago: Moody, 1987), 3–5.
3. John Calvin, *Commentaries on the Epistles to Timothy, Titus, and Philemon* (Grand Rapids: Baker, 1979), 67.
4. Grudem, *EFBT*, 134.

Verse 5 also challenges the hierarchical view of the created order. Typically, male leaders held court outdoors where the Israelites, both men and women, traveled from all over the country to meet with the judge, who would dispense justice. Verse 5 seems to fit with this custom but not with the hierarchs' "created order" presupposition. How do they reconcile this alleged contradiction?

John Piper attempts an answer by distinguishing between personal and directive influence versus nonpersonal and nondirective influence. He writes,

> To the degree that a woman's influence over man is personal and directive it will generally offend a man's good, God-given sense of responsibility and leadership, and thus controvert God's created order. A woman may design the traffic pattern of a city's streets and thus exert a kind of influence over all male drivers. But this influence will be non-personal and therefore not necessarily an offense against God's order.[5]

Piper and others in his camp argue that women prophets in the Old Testament only exhibited this nonpersonal and nondirective kind of influence. Thus, women prophets limited their speaking and teaching to private judgments, speaking, and teaching. They reason that although the function and office of a prophet was open to women, the offices of priest and king were not. She could speak for the Lord, but she didn't possess the personal authority to oversee, rule, or execute orders like a king or priest.[6] She could never teach or preach, and she could only prophesy in private, never publicly. Also, she could speak for God, but she had no authority to explain what she prophesied or apply it to her listeners. Only priests could teach God's message.[7]

Heterarchs

Heterarchs see Old Testament women prophets as evidence that God calls women into leadership roles. They say that the women prophets open the door for women to serve as senior pastors and elders. They point out that the biblical

---

5. John Piper, "A Vision of Biblical Complementarity: Manhood and Womanhood Defined according to the Bible," in *RBMW*, 51.
6. Thomas Finley provides a thorough discussion on women and leaders in ancient Israel in "The Ministry of Women in the Old Testament," in *Women and Men in Ministry: A Complementary Perspective*, eds. Robert L. Saucy and Judith K. TenElshof (Chicago: Moody, 2001), 73–88. The first section focuses on general insights followed by a section on four prominent women: Deborah, Miriam, Huldah, and the ideal wife in Proverbs 31:10–31. We find Finley's moderate views on the complementarian perspective helpful.
7. For more detail on this view, see Grudem, *EFBT*, 136–38, where Grudem refutes the egalitarian claim that Old Testament female prophets give precedents for women in leadership roles today.

text never states or hints that Deborah was lifted to the position of judge and prophet due to the lack of a qualified man. Therefore, they reject the presupposition that women cannot teach or lead both men and women. They believe that God can always identify, equip, and use leaders to carry out his will regardless of situational challenges, as he does so many other times in the Bible.

Heterarchs deem it impossible for Deborah to speak for God and judge Israel in a way that resulted in the land enjoying peace for forty years (Judg. 5:31) without judging and speaking publicly. These scholars believe that she presided over public gatherings outdoors at the Palm of Deborah within hearing distance of officials and bystanders, much as any other judge would. They reject any teaching that Deborah only taught or judged privately as an unsupported extrapolation of the text.

The Relationship Between Deborah and Barak (Judg. 4:6–10)

> [Deborah] sent for Barak son of Abinoam from Kedesh in Naphtali and said to him, "The LORD, the God of Israel, commands you: 'Go, take with you ten thousand men of Naphtali and Zebulun and lead them up to Mount Tabor. I will lead Sisera, the commander of Jabin's army, with his chariots and his troops to the Kishon River and give him into your hands.'"
>
> Barak said to her, "If you go with me, I will go; but if you don't go with me, I won't go."
>
> "Certainly I will go with you," said Deborah. "But because of the course you are taking, the honor will not be yours, for the LORD will deliver Sisera into the hands of a woman." So Deborah went with Barak to Kedesh. There Barak summoned Zebulun and Naphtali, and ten thousand men went up under his command. Deborah also went up with him. (Judg. 4:6–10)

In a nutshell, Jabin, king of Canaan, and his savage general, Sisera, had oppressed Israel for twenty years. God assured Deborah of deliverance, and she sent for Barak and gave him God's specific instructions. He agreed but wanted her to accompany him. But why, and did God approve or disapprove of Barak's response? Was he fearful to go by himself or determined it was wise to have God's prophet beside him to ensure success? Your answer will shed light on how and where you believe God wants women to lead.

Hierarchs

Piper and Grudem describe Barak as weak and timid on the basis of the rebuke implied when Deborah prophesied that the glory of victory would go to a woman because he refused to go into battle without her. Grudem writes, "Deborah did not summon the people of Israel to battle, but encouraged Barak to do this (Judg. 4:6–7, 14). Thus, rather than asserting leadership and authority for herself, she affirmed the rightness of male leadership." He argues, "Barak should not have insisted that Deborah come with him. He should have acted like a man and led on his own."[8] Piper and Grudem insist that "Deborah, a prophetess, judge, and mother in Israel . . . along with Jael . . . was a living indictment of the weakness of Barak and other men in Israel who should have been more courageous leaders."[9]

Scholars who limit women's leadership roles disagree about whether or not Deborah actually accompanied Barak to the battlefield. Thomas Schreiner says, "[Deborah] seems to be the only judge in Judges who has no military function,"[10] and Grudem downplays that she had any significant role there. However, other hierarchs like Dan Doriani and Thomas Finley suggest that Deborah accompanied Barak to the battlefield where she led beside him as a co-leader.[11] They contend she didn't actually fight during the battle but stayed close by as an observer and adviser. Her involvement and actions as God's spokesperson are reflected in Judges 4:9, 10, and 14.

Heterarchs

Heterarchs argue that Barak was neither weak nor timid when he asked Deborah to go with him. They hold this view because the New Testament book of Hebrews' "Hall of Faith" describes him as someone who was "powerful in battle and routed foreign armies" (Heb. 11:32–40). They see Barak's desire that Deborah go with him as a wise man choosing a strong partner, a faithful prophet, and a nationally recognized leader. Pierce writes, "Barak's insistence that she accompany him should be understood as no less than an appropriate plea for the presence of God."[12]

Other heterarchs suggest that Deborah either directed or fought in the battle against the Canaanites and use words like "warrior" and "military leader" to describe her. Two go so far as to interpret her role on the battlefield "evangelastically,"[13] saying, "The male general was afraid to lead the hosts of

---

8. Grudem, *EFBT*, 132.

9. John Piper and Wayne Grudem, "An Overview of Central Concerns: Questions and Answers," in *RBMW*, 72.

10. Thomas R. Schreiner, "The Valuable Ministries of Women in the Context of Male Leadership: A Survey of Old and New Testament Examples and Teaching," *RBMW*, 216.

11. See Dan Doriani, *Women and Ministry: What the Bible Teaches* (Wheaton, IL: Crossway, 2003), 33–38; and Finley, "The Ministry of Women," 78–81.

12. See Ron Pierce, "Deborah: Only When a Good Man Is Hard to Find?," in *Vindicating the Vixens: Revisiting Sexualized, Vilified, and Marginalized Women of the Bible*, ed. Sandra Glahn (Grand Rapids: Kregel, 2017), 191–210, for an explanation by those who believe women are free to serve as leaders in the church today.

13. I (Sue) have used this word for many years to communicate stretching the meaning of the text to fit one's view, although I believe I first heard it from a seminary friend, JoAnn Hummel.

Israel against so formidable a foe, and so Deborah marched with him at the head of the troops."[14]

Another reason some give for Deborah's prominence is evidenced in the Song of Deborah (Judges 5). Judges 5:7 reads, "Villagers in Israel would not fight; they held back until I, Deborah, arose, until I arose, a mother in Israel." Also, they assert her priority because of her stellar leadership.[15] For example, before her leadership "the highways were abandoned; travelers took to winding paths" (Judg. 5:6). Afterward, they no longer needed to travel the back roads to avoid the perilous highways full of thieves and marauders.

She brought peace and prosperity to the nation for forty years (Judg. 5:31). Pierce points out that Deborah is the only judge to function as both judge and prophet and the first judge to be given generous detailed coverage—two chapters. He doesn't differentiate between her role as judge and king because "both normally had sustained periods of recognized leadership that went beyond an immediate military crisis and extended over a time of peace."[16] He insists that "this is a biblical text to be celebrated—not qualified or lamented."[17]

The Prophet Huldah (2 Kings 22:14–20; 2 Chron. 34:22–28)

Huldah might stump most Christians in a Bible quiz, but she's an important figure in women's quest to know whether or not God limits their service to him. She ministered at a critical time in Judah's history, about 640 BC, during the reign of King Josiah, the last righteous king before the corrupt nation crumbled. The temple lay in shambles. The people mixed a tepid faith in Yahweh with Baal worship and idolatry. In the midst of temple repair ordered by the king, workmen discovered a scroll with some portion of God's Word on it. King Josiah sought a prophet to learn more. Although the prophets Jeremiah and Zephaniah were Huldah's contemporaries and neither were out of town, the king sent the high priest and his other top officials to the prophet Huldah.

Heterarchs surmise that "the delegation sought her out immediately. She must have had a reputation as a true prophetess of the Lord. . . . The Scripture gives no indication that anyone thought it strange that Josiah would seek a woman in order to hear from the Lord."[18] Alice Mathews suggests that she

14. Richard Clark Kroeger and Catherine Clark Kroeger, *I Suffer Not a Woman: Rethinking 1 Timothy 2:11-15 in Light of Ancient Evidence* (Grand Rapids: Baker, 1992), 18.

15. Linda L. Belleville, "Women Leaders in the Bible," in *Discovering Biblical Equality*, eds. Ronald Pierce and Cynthia Long Westfall, 3rd ed. (Downers Grove, IL: InterVarsity Press, 2021), 72–73.

16. Pierce, "Deborah," 195.

17. Pierce, "Deborah," 192.

18. Finley, "The Ministry of Women," 84. Finley is a hierarch but is more moderate than others, illustrating again the broad spectrum of views in the hierarchs' camp. For more on his ideas about Huldah, see 83–84.

must have been well known for her piety, wisdom, and trustworthiness.[19] Huldah prophesied severe judgment on Judah but mercy for her penitent and God-fearing king who would be spared witnessing the nation's destruction (2 Kings 22:15–20).[20]

Generally, hierarchs and heterarchs use the same arguments to support their views about Huldah as they do about Deborah. Hierarchs attempt to show similar reasons why Huldah's service to God limits women's service today, and heterarchs argue the opposite.

Summary

Hierarchs argue that Deborah and Huldah and other women prophets lived out their leadership roles in a more limited way than male leaders, illustrating that God continues to limit how women can serve him. But they differ greatly in their determination of how much God actually limits them. The spectrum spreads from no leadership roles all the way to any role except senior pastor and elder.

Heterarchs interpret Deborah's key role as prophet, judge, and the nation's top leader and military adviser and Huldah's role as prophet as God sanctioning women today to occupy any leadership role for which they are gifted, equipped, and called.

REFLECTION QUESTIONS

1. What was the role of prophets in the Old Testament?

2. Why was Deborah outstanding as a judge?

3. Why was Huldah outstanding as a prophet?

4. Do you agree more with hierarchs' views of female prophets? If so, why?

5. Do you agree more with heterarchs' views of female prophets? If so, why?

---

19. Alice Mathews, *A Woman God Can Lead: Lessons from Women of the Bible Help You Make Today's Choices* (Grand Rapids: Discovery House, 1998), 135.

20. For a well-researched treatment of this female prophet, see Christa L. McKirkland, "Huldah: Malfunction with the Wardrobe-Keeper's Wife," in *Vindicating the Vixens*, 213–32.

How Does Proverbs 31 Inform Us About God's Design for Women?

To some women, the Proverbs 31 woman reflects an impossible standard of perfection that breeds guilt and insecurity—she's Superwoman—the woman they love to hate. Our challenge is to set aside that assumption and delve into why God concluded the book of Proverbs with this portrait of a wise woman and what we can learn from her today. We suggest beginning this chapter by reading Proverbs 31:1–31.

The Context

Author

Verses 1–8 offer helpful insight before we jump ahead to the portrait of the Proverbs 31 woman in verses 10–31. These two sections should be seen in tandem. Verse 1 reveals that these words are "the sayings of King Lemuel—an inspired utterance his mother taught him." Thus, the portrait of the Proverbs 31 woman originated with the king's mother, although King Lemuel passed on what she taught him. We know nothing more about her or her son.

Audience

The king's mother crafted these words for the benefit of her son to teach him how to rule wisely: "Listen, my son! Listen, son of my womb! Listen, my son, the answer to my prayers!" (Prov. 31:2). The first audience was not women at all, but young men, specifically the future king who would need good judgment, a benevolent heart, and a wise queen by his side.

Structure

This poem is skillfully constructed as an acrostic. Each verse begins with a successive letter of the Hebrew alphabet, making it easier to memorize.

Purpose

The queen advised her son to shun strong drink and champion the defenseless (31:1–9), but first she warned him to avoid foolish women: "Do not spend your strength on women, your vigor on those who ruin kings" (v. 3). Then, knowing the necessity of a fitting royal wife, she instructed him on what to look for—*voilà*—the Proverbs 31 woman. She isn't Wonder Woman. She's not even a real person. This well-known passage is a beautiful poem, or hymn, describing the value, life, and character of wise, admirable women, the kind of women devoted mothers would want their sons to marry, the kind of women God praises and wants women to emulate. But God never expects them to be her perfectly, nor will every detail of her life fit women today who live in a different century, culture, and situation. Yet, the insights and principles remain the same. So, if you are a woman, disregard any guilt or insecurity and let's look together with our brothers to see what useful principles we can glean related to our topic (see Question 4 on sound interpretation related to culture).

Subject Matter

This poem actually describes the life of a married aristocratic woman with servants who has lived wisely and invested her time and energy in what matters. Now she's reaping the rewards of an accomplished husband who loves and trusts her and her grown children who rise up and bless her. Is God promising you that, if you live exactly as she did, you'll reap the same rewards? As men and women who desire to please God, how should we apply Proverbs 31? How do hierarchs and heterarchs differ on the answers?

Inferences on Gender Roles

Does this poem prove the Bible prescribes specific and rigid "roles" for men and women? Hierarch Wayne Grudem says "yes" and uses verses 15, 21, and 27 to argue for this perspective:

> She gets up while it is still night; she provides food for her family and portions for her female servants. (v. 15)

> When it snows, she has no fear for her household; for all of them are clothed in scarlet. (v. 21)

> She watches over the affairs of her household and does not eat the bread of idleness. (v. 27)

Grudem adds: "Two other aspects of a husband's headship in marriage are the responsibilities to provide for and to protect his wife and family. A corresponding responsibility for the wife is to have primary responsibility to care for home and children. Each can help the other, but there remains a primary responsibility that is not shared equally."[1] Also, Grudem asserts that these rigid roles are true because "there is the internal testimony from both men's and women's hearts" that says they are.[2]

Heterarch Andrew Bartlett counters Grudem's perspective:

> Grudem draws a stronger distinction than is justified. His reasoning is faulty, for he relies mainly on scriptures which are descriptive rather than prescriptive. Even where the scriptures give instructions, there is no instance where they explicitly allocate contrasting general responsibilities as between husbands and wives in the way he proposes. The Old Testament depicts both parents, not mothers alone, as responsible for teaching children how they should live. And the subjective testimony of men's and women's hearts is not a valid doctrinal argument.[3]

Not all hierarchs hold to such rigid gender roles, but most affirm the term "roles," even when they don't agree as to what they are. For example, Dan Doriani writes:

> The Bible never says women should stay at home, barefoot and pregnant. It never advocates the cloistering of women, common as it was in antiquity. . . . No Scripture says men must earn money while women stay home and spend it. Our culture, not Scripture, declares a man successful when he earns so much that his wife need work at nothing but carpool and décor. Still, at least during the childbearing and child-rearing years, Paul urges married women to work in the home. The Bible grants women freedom to work, but it also affirms their traditional roles.[4]

Inferences on Marriage and Singleness

Since the Proverbs 31 woman was a wife and mother, is this the most favored life for women? Since the Reformation in the 1500s, the Christian church has often insinuated that marriage is the preferred state. The Bible,

---

1. Grudem, *EFBT*, 44.
2. Grudem, *EFBT*, 45.
3. Andrew Bartlett, *Men and Women in Christ: Fresh Light from the Biblical Texts* (London: InterVarsity, 2019), 86.
4. Dan Doriani, *The Life of a God-Made Man: Becoming a Man after God's Heart* (Wheaton, IL: Crossway, 2001), 39.

however, refutes that assumption. Paul counseled the Corinthians regarding marriage and singleness:

> Now to the unmarried and the widows I say: It is good for them to stay unmarried, as I do. But if they cannot control themselves, they should marry, for it is better to marry than to burn with passion. (1 Cor. 7:8–9)
>
> I would like you to be free from concern. An unmarried man is concerned about the Lord's affairs—how he can please the Lord. But a married man is concerned about the affairs of this world—how he can please his wife—and his interests are divided. An unmarried woman or virgin is concerned about the Lord's affairs. (vv. 32–34)

Of course, God instructed the first man and woman to rule the world together and to increase in number, so we are free to marry. Both estates are honorable and please God.

Almost all women in Bible times were married out of necessity. Few could supply their own means to live, and most needed a male representative for legal protection and security. However, Paul's teaching in 1 Corinthians on marriage and singleness casts doubt on whether the Proverbs 31 woman sets forth a cookie-cutter pattern for all women for all time.

Inferences on Working Outside the Home

Since the Proverbs 31 woman seems to have overseen several money-making projects, can or should women work outside the home and help provide for the family? "She considers a field and buys it; out of her earnings she plants a vineyard. She sets about her work vigorously; her arms are strong for her tasks. She sees that her trading is profitable, and her lamp does not go out at night" (Prov. 31:16–18). Hierarch John MacArthur says that Proverbs 31 makes it clear that the Bible does not specifically forbid a woman from working outside the home but with a caveat:

> Whether or not a woman works outside the home, God's primary calling is for her to manage the home. That is the most exalted place for a wife. The world is calling many modern women out of the home, but not the Lord. His Word portrays the woman's role as one preoccupied with domestic duties. It is a high calling, far more crucial to the future of a woman's children than anything she might do in an outside job.
>
> The ultimate decision is a personal one that each woman must make in submission to her husband's authority. . . . A woman who is a mother obviously has primary responsibility

in the home and would therefore not be free to pursue outside employment to the detriment of the home. . . . However, her children and her husband will rise up and call her blessed, and a woman who fears the LORD shall be praised (Proverbs 31:28, 30).[5]

Long-time Christian working mom Janae Gibson contends her family has thrived as she has honored and served her Savior, her husband, and her children while following the Lord's call on her life.[6]

When I read Proverbs 31, I become encouraged, inspired, and authentically excited about what the Lord has created me to do as a woman. Some read the Proverbs 31 woman as a stay-at-home mom and do-all-things domestic and *Pinteresty*. For some, that is the Proverbs 31 woman, which is wonderful because that is what the Lord has called them to be.

OK, let's get real here. This may ruffle some feathers or get some Christian mama glares, but I enjoy using my God-given gifts outside the home to make a profit. Boom—I said it! I like knowing I'm contributing to the family in this way. . . . Don't we want these women in leadership roles to be Christian influencers and radiate servant leadership? Not every woman is created to work outside their home or has the opportunity. Not every mom is called to homeschool. Not every woman will have children or a husband. However, we are ALL called to serve our Lord and adhere to *our* calling.[7]

Summary

Theologian Donald G. Bloesch writes, "The model of woman in tribal patriarchalism is the brood mare; in hedonistic naturalism, she is the bunny or plaything; in feminist ideology, she is the self-sufficient career woman; in romanticism, she is the fairy princess or maiden in distress waiting to be rescued; in biblical faith, she is the partner in ministry."[8] In what sense is the

---

5. John MacArthur, *The Fulfilled Family: God's Design for Your Home* (Nashville: Thomas Nelson, 2005), 224–26.
6. Janae Gibson in Janet Denison, "Five Steps to Becoming a Successful Christian Working Mom" in "Working Outside the Home or Inside the Home: Two Mom's Perspectives," *Christian Parenting*, May 29, 2018, https://www.christianparenting.org/articles/working-outside-home-inside-home-two-moms-perspectives.
7. Gibson in Denison, "Five Steps."
8. Donald Bloesch, *Is the Bible Sexist? Beyond Feminism and Patriarchalism* (Eugene, OR: Wipf & Stock, 2001), 100.

Proverbs 31 woman "the partner in ministry"? You must discern whether or not you believe Proverbs 31:10–31 prescribes specific roles that God wants all women to live by for all time. If so, you'll want to "be her" in as many ways as you can. For example, she is married. Is God prescribing marriage as his preferred state for all women? She has children. Are childless women incomplete? She's an entrepreneur, a real estate agent, and a seamstress who spins her own fabric. Are these worthy goals for all women?

The other option is that this is a portrait of a mother's dream daughter-in-law who lives in a different era and country with foreign customs but exhibits timeless wisdom and principles that any woman can adapt, regardless of her particular situation. If you believe the latter, when interpreting Proverbs 31:1–31, your focus should shift to looking for timeless wisdom principles to help you live well today.

REFLECTION QUESTIONS

1. What were your impressions the first time you read Proverbs 31?

2. What qualities of this ideal daughter-in-law in Old Testament times do you most admire?

3. How is your life different from hers? How is your life similar?

4. Do you believe Proverbs 31 sets forth prescribed gender roles? Why or why not?

5. What do you believe should be a woman's highest priorities in life?

PART 3

Questions Related to the
New Testament and Beyond

Women in the Gospels and Acts

What Can We Learn from the Fact That Women Traveled with and Supported Jesus's Ministry?

On her daily run, obstetrician Dr. Renee Lockey sensed God saying, "Work like a doctor; live like a nurse." Debt-free and seven years into a thriving practice, she determined to live on a quarter of her salary and give the rest away to worthy causes. With trepidation, she entered into this new way of life, one that she says radically changed her worldview and fills her with overflowing joy.[1] My pastor labeled Dr. Lockey a "VIP backstage generous investor."[2] We observe another group of "VIP backstage generous investors" in Luke 8:1–3:

> After this, Jesus traveled about from one town and village to another, proclaiming the good news of the kingdom of God. The Twelve were with him, and also some women who had been cured of evil spirits and diseases: Mary (called Magdalene) from whom seven demons had come out; Joanna the wife of Chuza, the manager of Herod's household; Susanna; and many others. These women were helping to support them out of their own means.

Who are the specific women mentioned? What exactly were they doing? What do hierarchs and heterarchs believe Luke 8:1–3 teaches about women and ministry today?

---

1. Renee Lockey, "Earn Like a Dr. Live Like a Nurse," Vimeo, https://vimeo.com/38071426.
2. Senior Pastor Neil Tomba, "Faith Uses Money," Sermon on James 5:1–6, Northwest Bible Church, Dallas, October 11, 2020.

Who Are the Specific Women Mentioned?

Mary Magdalene
Listed first, and possibly conveying some prominence, Mary Magdalene[3] exhibited lifelong commitment to Jesus during his ministry, at the cross, and at the empty tomb, when she declared to the Twelve that he had risen (Matt. 27:56; Mark 16:1–4; Luke 24:1–12). Before Jesus exorcised seven demons out of her, she was likely a social misfit, unable to function as a sane and healthy person, but because of Jesus her life dramatically changed. Her likely hometown, Magdala, is located on the Sea of Galilee and believed to be the tourist attraction known today as Migdal, where the first-century fishing industry thrived. "The industry and wealth of the town explain why Mary Magdalene conceivably had resources to support Jesus and the Twelve (Luke 8:23)."[4]

Against cultural norms, Jesus dealt directly with women like Mary who traveled with him, some leaving behind husbands and families to join his itinerant entourage. George and Dora Winston assert that he didn't consult these husbands or fathers but seemed to accept the women's own judgment, just as he did with the Twelve male disciples.[5]

Joanna
Joanna was married to Chuza, the manager[6] of the household of Herod Antipas, the first-century Jewish ruler of Galilee and Perea, placed there to do Rome's bidding. Herod was best known for ordering the execution of John the Baptist and taking part in Jesus's illegal trial. Joanna no doubt enjoyed the status of someone in the higher echelon of Jewish social, political, and economic life. Yet we find her abandoning those privileges and walking with the Twelve and Jesus on his preaching tour through Galilee and then on to Jerusalem.

Mary Magdalene and Joanna shared much in common as they followed Jesus from his early preaching ministry through his death, burial, and resurrection—the social misfit and the society lady modeled to all that Jesus came to reconcile people from every rung of the social ladder into one Christ-centered community.

Joanna possibly wooed some in the ruling classes to Jesus—even perhaps her high-ranking husband. Sociologist Rodney Stark writes, "British historian

---

3. For a full treatment of Mary Magdalene, see Karla Zazueta, "Mary Magdalene: Repainting Her Portrait of Misconceptions," in *Vindicating the Vixens: Revisiting Sexualized, Vilified, and Marginalized Women of the Bible*, ed. Sandra Glahn (Grand Rapids: Kregel, 2017), 255–72.
4. Zazueta, "Mary Magdalene," 259.
5. George and Dora Winston, *Recovering Biblical Ministry by Women: An Exegetical Response to Traditionalism and Feminism* (Fairfax, VA: Xulon, 2003), 228.
6. The NET Bible notes that this word may be political in nature and then would be translated something like "governor" or "procurator" and that in either case the gospel was reaching into the highest levels of society.

Henry Chadwick noted that 'Christianity seems to have been especially successful among women. It was often through the wives that it penetrated the upper classes of society in the first instance.'"[7] Stark explains why women were more likely to become Christians: "Christianity was unusually appealing because within the Christian subculture women enjoyed far higher status than did women in the Greco-Roman world at large."[8] And in situations where the wives converted to Christianity (which he calls primary conversions), the husbands often followed, along with the rest of the household (as secondary conversions), including servants and slaves.[9]

Susanna and "Many Others"

The third woman mentioned is Susanna and, sadly, we don't know much about her. For her to be listed by name, she was probably a woman of means. Neither do we know how many women Luke meant when he informed us that many other women traveled "with him," but we can assume it was more than a few.

What Exactly Were These Women Doing?

Luke uses two verbs to answer this question. They were *traveling* with Jesus and the Twelve (8:1), and these women were *helping to support* them out of their own means (8:3).

Men and Women Traveling Together

Jesus spent his almost-three-year earthly ministry traveling around Israel and adjacent regions. Was it common for men and women who were not family-related to travel the country together at that time? Karla Zazueta asserts that Jesus's behavior was not normative, but rather, "downright shocking and scandalous."[10]

If you had been able to join the Twelve and the women who joined them in their wandering, what do you think you would have witnessed? We know that Jesus spent a lot of time teaching and equipping the Twelve throughout their journey. As we wrote in *Mixed Ministry*, "Do you see Jesus and the twelve apostles walking along immersed in deep, important conversations while the little band of obscure women followed far behind bringing up the rear in silence, weighted down with gold to be doled out as needs arose? Would the man who welcomed Mary [of Bethany] to sit at his feet have ignored and excluded other passionate women like Mary Magdalene, Joanna, and Susanna

7. Rodney Stark, *The Rise of Christianity: How the Obscure, Marginal Jesus Movement Became the Dominant Religious Force in the Western World in a Few Centuries* (San Francisco: Harper, 1997), 99.
8. Stark, *Rise of Christianity*, 95.
9. Stark, *Rise of Christianity*, 100.
10. Zazueta, "Mary Magdalene," 262.

from learning and engaging as they sojourned together? No. Jesus intentionally included them in a culture where women were undervalued."[11] Andrew Bartlett notes that Jesus related with women in a healthy manner, "without a family connection, a chaperone or an introduction (John 4:27). He valued women as disciples."[12] Jesus created a new kind of family who joined together in harmony and moral purity, a family of sacred siblings.

Men Dependent on Women's Financial Support
    "The women who continually followed Jesus are the only recorded source of income for Jesus's itinerant ministry, providing for him 'out of their means' (Luke 8:1–3)," write Elyse Fitzpatrick and Eric Shumacher.[13] Although travelers expected the hospitality of townsfolk to provide some food and necessities, Jesus's procession of the Twelve, a company of women, and others who might follow from time to time required additional resources, and these women stepped up as providers.
    In the first century, wealthy women became patrons of gifted people like artists, students, and clergy, serving as protectors, sponsors, or benefactors. Joanna, Mary Magdalene, Susanna, and other women disciples with means stepped into this role, in effect bankrolling Jesus's ministry. Patrons used their influence to protect and assist their "clients." In the typical patron/client relationship, the client would serve the patron in response to the patron's greatly needed support. However, instead of Jesus Christ being beholden to them, these women patrons served him wholeheartedly, modeling the new radical role reversal that Jesus taught in Luke 22:25–27.[14]

What Are the Views of Hierarchs and Heterarchs?
    Heterarch Richard Bauckham insists that this text argues against the strict gender roles asserted by some hierarchs. He asserts that we cannot assume that the women who traveled with Jesus were there just to cook meals and wash and mend clothes. They may have done so, but Luke never tells us that was their purpose. Bauckham contends that neither Jesus nor any of those accompanying him on their journey engaged in work for pay, but instead generally relied on the generosity of these women of wealth.[15] Zazueta states,

11. Sue Edwards, Kelley Mathews, and Henry J. Rogers, *Mixed Ministry: Working Together as Brothers and Sisters in an Oversexed Society* (Grand Rapids: Kregel, 2008), 45.
12. Andrew Bartlett, *Men and Women in Christ: Fresh Light from the Biblical Texts* (London: InterVarsity, 2019), 309.
13. Elyse Fitzpatrick and Eric Shumacher, *Worthy: Celebrating the Value of Women* (Grand Rapids: Baker, 2020), 160.
14. Angela Ravin-Anderson, "They Had Followed Him from Galilee: The Female Disciples," *Priscilla Papers* 28, no. 2 (2014): 6–7.
15. Richard Bauckham, *Gospel Women: Studies of the Named Women in the Gospels* (Grand Rapids: Eerdmans, 2002), 112–16.

> Our Lord's practice of receiving the financial support of
> women suggests that doing so does not undermine man-
> hood. And conversely, apparently a woman's femininity is
> not violated if she financially supports a man or men. Jesus
> was not concerned with defending his manhood. His only
> concern was spreading the news about the kingdom of God.[16]

Some heterarchs stretch this text evangelastically to contend without textual
evidence that Jesus sent both the men and the women out to preach.[17] For
example, Aída Besançon Spencer writes, "The female disciples, like the males,
had spent time with Jesus and were sent out to preach God's reign. They were
with Jesus, learning from his teachings to seek God's reign, selling their pos-
sessions and giving all to the Lord's ministry, as they were taught by Jesus (Lk
12:31–34; 18:22)."[18]

Hierarch Wayne Grudem admits, "Many women accompanied Jesus and
learned from Him during His earthly ministry,"[19] but refutes that their traveling together and the women bankrolling the ministry means Jesus did not
distinguish between how men and women could lead and serve. He points
out that Jesus only called men to serve as his apostles, and when they needed
to replace Judas, Peter insisted that they chose from among the men who
had been with them (Acts 1:21).[20] Grudem writes, "Yes, Jesus undermined
the wrongful and abusive aspects of the patriarchal culture at that time, but
he did not overturn a God-given pattern of male leadership in the household
and male leadership among God's people.[21]

Another hierarch, Michael Wilkins, suggests that, besides providing financial support and because these women had experienced powerful life
change in their relationship with Jesus, "perhaps that the cultural setting it
may have been easier for these women to speak personally with the large
throngs of women who also were in attendance at many of the public appearances of Jesus (cf. Matt. 14:21; 15:38)."[22] Wilkins continues,

---

16. Zazueta, "Mary Magdalene," 265.
17. I (Sue) have used this word for many years to communicate stretching the meaning of
the text to fit one's view, although I believe I first heard it from a seminary friend, JoAnn
Hummel.
18. Aída Besançon Spencer, "Jesus' Treatment of Women in the Gospels," in *Discovering
Biblical Equality*, 3rd ed., ed. Ronald W. Pierce and Cynthia Long Westfall (Downers
Grove, IL: InterVarsity, 2021), 103.
19. Grudem, *EFBT*, 292.
20. Grudem, *EFBT*, 292.
21. Grudem, *EFBT*, 161.
22. Michael Wilkins, "Women in the Teaching and Example of Jesus," in *Women and Men
in Ministry: A Complementary Perspective*, eds. Robert L. Saucy and Judith K. TenElshof
(Chicago: Moody, 2001), 107.

The ministry team of the Twelve and the women fore-shadows the community of faith that would comprise the church, where women and men join together as witnesses to the reality of the Christian life and as brothers and sisters in Christ who share equally in the life of the Spirit. Jesus broke down barriers—economic, racial, religious, gender—by calling people into a spiritual family based on equality of discipleship. There are different roles within the family, but each person has equal value as a family member.[23]

Summary

With most hierarchs and heterarchs, George and Dora Winston conclude:

The Gospels contain at least forty different texts describing contacts between Jesus and women, clearly indicating that Jesus was introducing something new. He broke with convention in His relationships with women, treating them as individuals, associates, equals on the human plane, and simply "friends." They, just as much as His male disciples, were not considered as slaves who did not know what their master was doing (John 15:15) but as His "friends" whom he took into his confidence (v. 15b). . . . He respected women, took them seriously, believed in them, and associated freely with them in healthy, relaxed comradeship.[24]

REFLECTION QUESTIONS

1. What surprised you about the economic support women provided during Jesus's earthly ministry?

2. What especially impressed you about the specific women mentioned in Luke 8:1–3?

3. How did Jesus overturn some of the social customs of the day on behalf of women?

4. What do you admire most about these women?

5. How do you feel about women providing financial support for men?

---

23. Wilkins, "Women in the Teaching and Example of Jesus," 108–9.
24. Winston and Winston, *Recovering Biblical Ministry by Women*, 228.

What Is the Significance of Jesus Choosing Only Men as the Twelve Apostles?

During his earthly ministry, Jesus attracted many followers, both male and female. Some were drawn by his miracles only to drift away when he challenged their behaviors. Others, often known as "the seventy-two," were long-time disciples who likely traveled with him as their situations allowed. Jesus sent this group out to evangelize and perform miracles in his name (Luke 10:1–24). Yet they did not enjoy the unique privileges of the smaller group known as the apostles.[1]

We find the names of the Twelve in Matthew 10:1–4; Mark 3:13–19; Luke 6:13–16; and Acts 1:13. They devoted themselves completely to Jesus during his three years of earthly ministry. They left their homes and livelihoods to follow their rabbi, learning from and serving him in various ways. Why twelve? Why only men? We'll explore the significance of Jesus's close-knit yet diverse group of disciples, and how scholars interpret women's place and position in the church in light of the reality that Jesus chose only males for his inner group of followers.

Hierarchs

Hierarchs consider Jesus's choosing of only men as his twelve apostles crucial, but not primary, to their argument for male-only leadership in the church.[2] While women did follow Jesus, they acknowledge, Jesus had a

---

1. See Question 19 for discussion on other followers also called "apostles," but in a different sense from the Twelve.
2. John Piper, "A Vision of Biblical Complementarity: Manhood and Womanhood Defined according to the Bible," in *RBMW*, 32.

reason for not inviting them into his closest circle. John Piper contends, "But no woman in Christ's ministry was called, commissioned, or named as an apostle, or even performed in the role of an apostle. These roles and functions Christ reserved for men."[3]

James Borland lists five immediate functions of the Twelve:

1. The apostles were to be with Christ, undoubtedly to learn extensively and to be trained firsthand (Mark 3:14–15).
2. The apostles were the obvious official leaders in the early church (see Acts 2:14; 5:12, 18, 40, 42; 6:2–4; 9:29; 15:2; Gal. 1:17).
3. Special rulership was committed to the apostles. Christ promised that the apostles would sit on twelve thrones ruling over the twelve tribes of Israel (Matt. 19:28; Luke 22:30).
4. Christ promised the apostles that they would receive special revelation from God (John 16:13–15) and a special teaching ministry of the Holy Spirit (John 14:26).
5. As a testimony of the fact that male leadership in the church has been permanently established by Christ, the names of the twelve apostles are forever inscribed on the very foundations of heaven itself.[4]

Borland follows this list by saying, "None of the above roles was performed by the women who followed Christ or ministered to Him."[5] Heterarchs disagree, in part, which we will cover in the next section.

Some heterarchs counter-argue that all the apostles were also Jewish, so why aren't church leaders also limited to Jews? Borland responds, "Considering the Jewishness of Christ's mission to redeem Israel (Luke 24:21), it is not surprising to find all Jews on the initial list of apostles. It was not cultural pressure but God's plan to bring salvation through the Jews that led to twelve Jewish apostles."[6]

Hierarch Michael Wilkins points to Matthias's choice as Judas's replacement among the Twelve.

> Out of the qualifications later stipulated in the early church for replacing Judas Iscariot in the twelve apostles (Acts 1:21), the women in the ministry team qualified on at least one count, having been "with" Jesus and the Twelve . . . But the wording in the qualifications stresses that the person chosen

---

3. Piper, "Vision of Biblical Complementarity," 32.
4. James A. Borland, "Women in the Life and Teachings of Jesus," in *RBMW*, 121.
5. Borland, "Women in the Life and Teachings of Jesus," 121.
6. Borland, "Women in the Life and Teachings of Jesus," 122.

was to be a "man," using the term for the male gender (*aner*), not the more generic term (*anthropos*).[7]

He continues:

> If Jesus had wanted to go contrary to social custom by including women as apostles, He surely would not have hesitated. . . . We can see clearly that women and men are treated as equal persons who are called to equal status as Jesus' disciples. But we can also see that when Jesus did not call women to apostleship, this is an indication that there are different roles for women and men that will maximize their creation in the image of God as male and female. . . . The hint here is that there are certain positions of leadership that are appointed for men, but that in no way minimizes the status of women as persons or hinders them from participating as equal members of Jesus' ministry team.[8]

In summary, hierarchs consider the all-male membership of the original Twelve as a direct indication of Jesus's plan for leadership in his church. Only men enjoyed such proximity to Jesus, early leadership of the church, and an exalted future in the eternal kingdom ruling alongside him, all of which point to Jesus's design for male authority over his church.

Heterarchs

While acknowledging the special relationship between Jesus and the Twelve, heterarchs generally do not find great significance in the fact that they were all men as it relates to future church leadership. Spencer understands the choice to be symbolic of the twelve tribes of Israel—since Jesus's primary ministry was to the Jews, his "choice of the Twelve indicates the importance of the new covenant's being founded on the old covenant."[9] Hence the image in Revelation 21:12–14 of the new Jerusalem with foundations bearing the apostles' names and the gates bearing the tribes' names.

Jesus was also working within the first-century Jewish culture, which prioritized women's contribution to the welfare of the home. Yet he "does not

---

7. Michael Wilkins, "Women in the Teaching and Example of Jesus," in *Women and Men in Ministry: A Complementary Perspective*, eds. Robert L. Saucy and Judith K. TenElshof (Chicago: Moody, 2001), 105.
8. Wilkins, "Women in the Teaching and Example of Jesus," 106.
9. Aida Besançon Spencer, "Jesus' Treatment of Women in the Gospels," in *Discovering Biblical Equality*, 3rd ed., eds. Ronald Pierce and Cynthia Long Westfall (Downers Grove, IL: InterVarsity Press, 2021), 101.

treat women primarily as homemakers," Spencer notes.[10] He praises those who "hear the word of God and obey it" (Luke 11:28) and supports Mary of Bethany's desire to sit at his feet in the traditional pose of a student (Luke 10:38–42).

Dorothy Lee identifies Peter as the leader of Jesus's inner group of men, the Twelve, and pins Mary Magdalene as the leader of the inner group of women.[11] What women? Those mentioned in Luke 8:1–3.

These two inner groups traveled with Jesus during his earthly ministry, learning from him as they served him and those who came to him for help. Lucy Peppiatt suggests that women actively participated in his ministry in three roles: disciples, patrons, and witnesses.[12] Heterarchs argue that all three categories point to women as leaders within Jesus's circle before his ascension and, therefore, support the premise of women's leadership in the church.

Women Patrons

Patrons financed someone they wished to sponsor or support. This support put these women in a socially superior status to those they patronized. But Jesus did not object to his seemingly lower social status and welcomed the financial support of these women, who apparently were either independently wealthy or had their husband's approval (Joanna, for instance). Mary and Susanna, if single, would have likely been widowed or would have inheritance from their fathers. Whatever situation allowed them such independence, it was relatively rare in first-century Israel. But Jesus welcomed them.

Women Disciples

Women were also described as Jesus's disciples. They traveled with him and the Twelve throughout Judea and Galilee. They learned from him just like the men. Heterarchs argue that during Jesus's lifetime, the male disciples were not in authority over the female disciples. Jesus was the authority over them all. All women were encouraged to believe in and follow Jesus. His preaching reflected his open invitation. In Matthew 12:46–50 Jesus referred to his disciples as "mother, brother, sister," indicating that his call included women, then and now.

More specifically, in the story of Mary and Martha of Bethany (Luke 10:38–42), Mary was commended for sitting at Jesus's feet along with the men while Martha prepared food in the kitchen. Her story holds several layers of evidence showing Jesus's approval of female disciples.

---

10. Spencer, "Jesus' Treatment of Women in the Gospels," 97.

11. Dorothy A. Lee, *The Ministry of Women in the New Testament: Reclaiming the Biblical Vision for Church Leadership* (Grand Rapids: Baker Academic, 2021), 47.

12. Lucy Peppiatt, *Rediscovering Scripture's Vision for Women: Fresh Perspectives on Disputed Texts* (Downers Grove, IL: IVP Academic, 2019), 31.

1. Ben Witherington points out that at that time, women could attend synagogue, learn, and be educated if husbands were rabbis, but "for a rabbi to come into a woman's house and teach her specifically is unheard of."[13]

2. In *Icons of Christ*, William Witt accuses hierarch Wayne Grudem of "deliberately de-radicalizing the implications of the story." Grudem argues that people commonly sat at the feet (in front) of those teaching, that Jesus was simply commending Mary for listening, and that everyone learned from rabbis, so giving Mary a special claim as a disciple would be going too far. But the term "sitting at the feet of" is a technical formula denoting discipleship.[14] To downplay it is to ignore the obvious in favor of one's own agenda.

3. Witt, again, points to Jesus's frequent subversiveness and acts of symbolism. For instance, Jesus did not intend to overthrow Rome, yet he still rode into Jerusalem on a donkey, a symbol "clearly understood as a threat to the political order and a Messianic claim." When he cleansed the temple, he didn't dismantle the corruption but symbolically judged it. So also, Mary of Bethany sitting at his feet was "a symbolic action that was subversive of the understanding of the permissible roles for women at that time."[15]

In addition to Mary of Bethany, heterarchs use Mary Magdalene as a second example.[16] Some scholars theorize that her nickname (Magdalene) may not refer to the town of Magdala, because no town of that name can be found in the literature of that time period. If she was not named for her town, the other option is that Magdala, a derivative of *Migdal*, meaning "tower," was Jesus's nickname for Mary. Some suggest that she joined the company of men like Simon who became known as Peter, the Rock (Mark 3:16), and Joseph who became known as Barnabas, the Encourager (Acts 4:36). This nickname, "tower of strength," would underscore her role as a leader in Jesus's circle. She would not be peripheral but central to the group that traveled with and learned from Jesus.[17]

Women Witnesses

Heterarchs look to Martha of Bethany's clear witness to Jesus's identity as the Messiah. While Peter confesses Jesus as the Christ in Mark 8:29, Martha

---

13. Ben Witherington, *Women in the Earliest Churches* (New York: Cambridge University Press, 1988), 46.
14. William Witt, *Icons of Christ: A Biblical and Systematic Theology for Women's Ordination* (Waco, TX: Baylor University Press, 2020), 90–91.
15. Witt, *Icons of Christ*, 91.
16. Matt. 27:56; 28:1; Mark 15:40, 47; 16:1; Luke 24:10; John 19:25; 20:1, 18.
17. Lee, *Ministry of Women in the New Testament*, 49.

makes this same confession of faith in John's gospel. As her brother lay dead in his grave, with Jesus apparently four days too late to help, she confronts him in her grief. Jesus tells Martha, "I am the resurrection and the life. The one who believes in me, even if he dies, will live. Everyone who lives and believes in me will never die. Do you believe this?" "Yes, Lord," she said, "I believe you are the Messiah, the Son of God, who comes into the world" (John 11:25–27 CSB).

Heterarchs draw attention to the prominence of women in significant moments of Jesus's life. Dorothy Sayers wrote, "Perhaps it is no wonder that the women were first at the Cradle and last at the Cross. They had never known a man like this Man—there never has been such another."[18] Her eloquent essay reminds modern readers that Jesus's mother, Mary, witnessed the beginning of his life. And she, along with her sister and two female disciples, Mary Magdalene and the wife of Cleopas, and the apostle John, gathered around the cross to stand witness to Jesus's final hours.

And it is Mary Magdalene, argues Karla Zazueta, as the first witness to the resurrected Christ, who has been called "the apostle to the apostles"—the "one sent" to tell the "sent ones" (which is what "apostle" means), "I have seen the Lord!" "Where would we be without Mary Magdalene's testimony? What is the importance of her eyewitness account? The early church fathers, and Thomas Aquinas after them, called Mary Magdalene an 'apostle of the apostles,' and Pope John Paul II reinstated this title in 1988."[19] Heterarchs argue that Jesus again subverted the cultural norms to gift the good news first to a woman, whose testimony would not be welcome in any official judicial capacity.[20]

Jesus's Promise to the Twelve

Heterarch Andrew Bartlett suggests that just as the twelve sons of Jacob founded the nation of Israel, so the twelve apostles "signaled the founding of a new community of God's people, growing out of the Israelite community which was descended from the twelve patriarchs."[21]

Jesus told the Twelve, in Matthew 19:28, that in the new world, "you who have followed me will also sit on twelve thrones, judging the twelve tribes of Israel." But, continues Bartlett, Jesus's statement says nothing about the nature

---

18. Dorothy L. Sayers, *Are Women Human? Astute and Witty Essays on the Role of Women in Society* (Grand Rapids: Eerdmans, 2005), 68. The essay is a print version of Sayers's address to a Women's Society in 1938.
19. Karla Zazueta, "Mary Magdalene: Repainting Her Portrait of Misconceptions," in *Vindicating the Vixens: Revisiting Sexualized, Vilified, and Marginalized Women of the Bible*, ed. Sandra Glahn (Grand Rapids: Kregel Academic, 2017), 269–70.
20. Zazueta, "Mary Magdalene," 269–70.
21. Andrew Bartlett, *Men and Women in Christ: Fresh Light from the Biblical Texts* (London: InterVarsity, 2019), 289.

of leadership in future local congregations.[22] Just as the number of apostles expanded beyond twelve in the early church, so also the Jews-only leadership expanded to include Gentiles as well. In the same way, women also led church life in various ways, even though the original Twelve were only men. Perhaps church leaders were continuing the ministries begun with Jesus's female patrons and disciples.

Summary
Scholars on both sides of the issue caution against reading too much into the maleness of the apostles. Even Piper and Grudem do not argue that "merely because Jesus chose twelve men to be His authoritative apostles, Jesus must have favored an eldership of only men in the church."[23] Hierarchs do believe male-only apostleship to be *one of several* factors pointing to all-male church leadership. Heterarchs, however, point to Jesus's countercultural, welcoming interaction with his female disciples as evidence of his affirmation of their full humanity and equality with men in all areas.

REFLECTION QUESTIONS

1. What are your thoughts about Jesus choosing only Jewish men as the Twelve who were his innermost circle of followers during his earthly ministry?

2. Read Matthew 19:28–30 and discuss Jesus's promises to all his disciples through the ages.

3. Do you tend to agree more with hierarchs or heterarchs concerning the chapter's main question? Why?

4. How much weight do you give to the fact that Jesus chose only men to be his first leaders?

5. What was Jesus modeling by having both an inner circle of men and an inner circle of women travel with him during his earthly ministry?

---

22. Bartlett, *Men and Women in Christ*, 290.
23. John Piper and Wayne Grudem, "An Overview of Central Concerns: Questions and Answers," in *RBMW*, 62.

What Is the Significance That a Woman First Witnessed Jesus's Resurrection?

All four Gospels record that Mary Magdalene was the first person to proclaim the risen Christ on that glorious resurrection morning (Matt. 28:1–10; Mark 16:1–8; Luke 24:1–12). John records that she wept and hugged Jesus. He instructed her to let him go and instead to "find his 'brothers' and" tell them that he was alive (John 20:15–17). As a result, theologian Thomas Aquinas (1225–1274) referred to Mary Magdalene as an "apostle of the apostles" because he said that she announced Jesus's resurrection to the other apostles and to the world.[1] Pope John Paul II affirmed this title in 1988.[2]

What does the term "apostle" mean, and why is giving this title to a woman a bone of contention between hierarchs and heterarchs? The word "apostle" comes from the Greek verb *apostellō* meaning "to send off." Thus, the noun refers to one who is sent, an emissary, messenger, envoy, or ambassador.[3]

Hierarchs often limit the term "apostle" to men who were eyewitnesses of Jesus's ministry on earth, such as the Twelve, and those called to be the top leaders of the first churches. This second description explains why Paul could call himself an apostle, as he often introduced himself at the beginning of his epistles.[4] Many hierarchs cringe at the idea of calling any woman an apostle. Heterarchs use the term more broadly, reveling in the idea that Mary Magdalene was an apostle. They argue that, like Mary Magdalene, apostles were people of either sex sent by God as his messengers to announce the

1. Inés San Martín, "New Feast Touts Mary Magdalene as 'Paradigm' for Women," *Crux*, June 10, 2016, https://cruxnow.com/global-church/2016/06/10/new-feast-touts-mary-magdalene -paradigm-women.
2. Pope John Paul II, *Mulieris Dignitatem* (Rome: Libreria Editrice Vaticana, 1988), 5.16.
3. M. G. Easton, *Illustrated Bible Dictionary and Treasury of Biblical History, Biography, Geography, Doctrine, and Literature* (New York: Harper & Brothers, 1893), 48.
4. See Rom. 1:1; 1 Cor. 1:1; 2 Cor. 1:1; Gal. 1:1; Eph. 1:1; Col. 1:1; 1 Tim. 1:1; Titus 1:1.

good news of the gospel. For instance, in Romans 16:7, they understand Paul to refer to his coworkers Andronicus and Junia as apostles. They had been believers longer than Paul and were imprisoned with him. The privilege of apostleship carried with it responsibility and authority.

Genre Considerations

The verses about Mary Magdalene declaring, "He is risen" are narrative literature, where we must lift out what we believe the author wanted to communicate first to the original audience and then to us. Again, our lenses can easily skew our perspectives. If Paul had come right out and told us, "Mary Magdalene was an apostle and this means she and all women are unlimited in their authority and responsibility to preach and lead," our question on which view is correct would be answered. But these explicit kinds of statements are missing from Scripture.

Below are some varied ideas that we hope will help you in your search for God's truth regarding the question, What is the significance of a woman being the first witness to Jesus's resurrection?

Heterarchs

Kat Armstrong contrasts Eve and Mary Magdalene in her book *No More Holding Back*. She suggests that where Eve failed, Mary Magdalene obeyed, and shows women that they no longer need to hold back because they are not limited in their service to God. She writes: "Nothing will rival her [Mary Magdalene's] message. Jesus is the news. But we might unleash a generation of women if we teach them that secondary to the message of 'Jesus is risen' is this: a woman was the first preacher to literally *bring it*."[5] Karla Zazueta notes that this Mary was "the first to the grave, the first to see the risen Lord, the first to testify the news of his resurrection, and the only woman to consistently appear in all the lists of women disciples."[6]

N. T. Wright cites Mary Magdalene to support his argument for equality. After the disciples forsake Jesus, he says, she remains at the cross and is one of the women at his tomb. "It is the women . . . who are the first to see the risen Jesus, and are the first to be entrusted with the news that he has been raised from the dead. This is of incalculable significance. Mary Magdalene and the others are the apostles to the apostles."[7] Wright connects Mary Magdalene with Junia, whom

5. Kat Armstrong, *No More Holding Back: Emboldening Women to Move Past Barriers, See Their Worth, and Serve God Everywhere* (Nashville: W Publishing, 2019), 14–15.
6. Karla Zazueta, "Mary Magdalene: Repainting Her Portrait of Misconceptions," in *Vindicating the Vixens: Revisiting Sexualized, Vilified, and Marginalized Women of the Bible*, ed. Sandra Glahn (Grand Rapids: Kregel Academic, 2017), 272.
7. N. T. Wright, "Women's Service in the Church: The Biblical Basis," N. T. Wright Online, September 4, 2004, https://ntwrightpage.com/2016/07/12/womens-service-in-the-church-the-biblical-basis.

we meet in Romans 16:7: "We should not be surprised that Paul calls a woman named Junia an apostle in Romans 16:7. If an apostle is a witness to the resurrection, there were women who deserved that title before any of the men."[8]

Aída Besançon Spencer argues that the fact that Jesus chose women to be the first witnesses to the resurrection and the first to tell others carries with it special meaning:

> His male disciples were confounded by his consistency and even questioned the reliability of the witnesses he chose (Luke 24:10–11, 22–24). Jesus in contrast wanted women to learn and to testify before others about God's actions on earth. He wanted these women whom he had taught to go on to take authoritative leadership positions themselves. That is why they were chosen to be the first witnesses to the resurrection.[9]

Hierarchs

Wayne Grudem disputes Spencer's argument, insisting that giving testimony as an eyewitness is not equated with being a church leader: "Women did not do this in the New Testament. We should not make the text say more than it says. . . . A few days after the resurrection Peter specified that 'one of the *men*' should replace Judas among the eleven disciples (Acts 1:21, with the male-specific term *aner*)."[10]

Michael Wilkins builds on Grudem's idea that since only men were considered to replace Judas as an apostle, Mary Magdalene and the other women were not sent out as the key apostles and leaders in the early church and should not be today:

> This is an indication that there are different roles for women and men that will maximize their creation in the image of God as male and female. . . . The hint here is that there are certain positions of leadership that are appointed for men, but that in no way minimizes the status of women as persons or hinders them from participating as equal members of Jesus' ministry team.[11]

James Borland lays out the various duties of the apostles and leaders in the early church and concludes, "None of the above roles was performed by the

---

8. Wright, "Women's Service in the Church."

9. Aída Besançon Spencer, *Beyond the Curse: Women Called to Ministry* (Peabody, MA: Hendrickson, 1986), 62.

10. Grudem, *EFBT*, 165.

11. Michael Wilkins, "Women in the Teaching and Example of Jesus," in *Women and Men in Ministry: A Complementary Perspective*, eds. Robert L. Saucy and Judith K. TenElshof (Chicago: Moody, 2001), 106.

women who followed Christ or ministered to Him. Though highly valued and given a new dignity by Christ, their roles were different from those of the men Christ selected for His top leadership positions."[12]

Heterarchs counter many of these ideas by arguing that Christ did not select women for these top leadership roles in the first century because of the scandal that would have undoubtedly erupted if he had. Initially, he did not come to right all social wrongs but to bring personal redemption to all willing people through his sacrifice on the cross. When he returns to earth in his second coming, he will bring justice and righteousness to the earth in the form of a new kingdom. In the meantime, and especially since those social taboos no longer exist in many places, no believer should be limited in the use of their spiritual gifts.

Summary

Hierarchs insist that only men were and can be "apostles." Again, the hierarch's core argument relates to fixed "roles" for men and women, and the foundation for that view goes back to Genesis 2 and 3.[13] In contrast, heterarchs use the term "apostle" more broadly, appreciating the idea that Mary Magdalene was an apostle. They argue that Jesus's intentional choice of a woman as the first witness to the resurrection makes her an "apostle," or witness, to the apostles, and opens the door for equal opportunities to serve him. Weigh the ideas carefully as you form your beliefs on what the Bible teaches concerning these weighty questions.

REFLECTION QUESTIONS

1. How do you feel about the reality that the resurrected Jesus first appeared to a woman?

2. Why do you think Peter and the other disciples did not believe her at first?

3. What does the word "apostle" mean?

4. What do you think of Thomas Aquinas, Pope John Paul II, and Kat Armstrong calling Mary Magdalene an "apostle to the apostles"?

5. What is your evaluation of hierarchs' and heterarchs' interpretations?

---

12. James A. Borland, "Women in the Life and Teachings of Jesus," in *RBMW*, 121.
13. See Questions 5–10 if you need help discerning the varied perspectives on those two fundamental chapters.

What Does Jesus's Interaction with the Woman at the Well Teach Us?

On a recent Sunday morning, my husband and I (Sue) enjoyed a pastor's excellent sermon from the book of James. He dissected the text with deep insight. He inspired us with his winsome challenge. He moved seamlessly from biblical point to biblical point, bringing each section to life with vivid illustrations. Then he came to the author's two biblical illustrations: Abraham and Rahab. He expounded on Abraham with fervor and clarity. But when he came to Rahab, he hesitated and said something like, "I couldn't figure out why James added Rahab as a second example. I don't really see what she brings to the passage, except maybe to show that God can use even the lowest of the low." And he continued with his message.

I wanted to respond, "But she was in Jesus's genealogy in Matthew 1:5: 'Salmon the father of Boaz, whose mother was Rahab.' She began as a pagan madam who expressed faith in the God of the Israelites. Her words and actions saved her life, her family's lives, and those of the Israelite spies, resulting in a hall of faith legacy (Heb. 11:31). She died as a significant player in the heritage of our Lord. Her name is there for a reason. I thought 2 Timothy 3:16 applied to all passages: 'All Scripture is God-breathed and is useful for teaching.'"

I suspect this gifted young preacher, recently graduated from a reputable seminary, may have searched his commentaries on this woman and found little or nothing of real value to include in his sermon. Sadly, we find much traditional scholarship on women of the Bible lacking the breadth and depth that other texts receive. The Samaritan woman is another good example.

A Misunderstood Biblical Stereotype

What do you remember about the woman at the well? Is she really a "bad girl" exemplifying that Jesus forgives the lowest of the low? Or is there more?

John spends forty-two verses on Jesus's encounter with her, more space than some of the twelve apostles receive in all of Scripture. Yet for centuries she's endured a cursory treatment at best. What deeper insights can we glean to help us understand her as a role model for all, a passionate evangelist, and the reason Jesus "had to go through Samaria" (John 4:4)?

An Early Church Father's Surprising Praise

Archbishop of Constantinople John Chrysostom (AD 349–407), also known as "Golden Mouth,"[1] gave the woman at the well more than a cursory treatment but praised her for acting like a man.

> The woman straightway believed, showing herself much wiser than Nicodemus, and not only wiser, but more manly. For when he heard ten thousand such things [he] neither invited any others to this hearing, nor himself spake forth openly; but she exhibited the actions of an Apostle, preaching the Gospel to all, and calling them to Jesus, and drawing a whole city forth to Him. Nicodemus when he had heard said, "How can these things be?" And when Christ set before him a clear illustration, that of "the wind," he did not even so receive the Word. But the woman not so; at first she doubted, but afterwards receiving the Word not by any regular demonstration, but in the form of an assertion, she straightway hastened to embrace it. For when Christ said, "It shall be in him a well of water springing up into everlasting Life," immediately the woman saith, *"Give me this water, that I thirst not, neither come hither to draw"* (John 4:15).[2]

Chrysostom praises the Samaritan woman's wisdom and bold courage to preach the good news to all she knew. In doing so, he illustrates the complexity and diversity of ideas and opinions about these issues through the centuries. But, alas, he's the exception—if we can ignore his assertion that "manly" is better than "womanly."

Hierarchs

In their classic work *Recovering Biblical Manhood and Womanhood*, the various authors devote about three pages to the Samaritan woman.

1. "John Chrysostom: Early Church's Greatest Preacher," *Christian History*, August 2008, https://www.christianitytoday.com/history/people/pastorsandpreachers/john-chrysostom.html.
2. John Chrysostom, *Homilies on the Gospel of John*, quoted in "Saint John Chrysostom on the Samaritan Woman," OrthodoxWord, https://orthodoxword.wordpress.com/2010/05/02/saint-john-chrysostom-on-the-samaritan-woman/amp.

They use this account to argue that women are created in the image of God just as men are, that Jesus recognized their intrinsic value as persons, that everyone is responsible for their own sin, and that Jesus condemned the sin of lust.[3] Michael Wilkins also uses her to show that, "as Jesus offered salvation and healing to the people, women were equally worthy of His full-orbed ministry."[4]

Typically, the woman at the well is presented as the quintessential wicked woman, vile and depraved because Jesus reveals her history with men in John 4:18.[5] She has had five husbands and she is not married to the man she is with now. Without an understanding of the historical and cultural norms of her day, it's easy to judge her by today's standards. We mistakenly assume she enjoyed all the opportunities and possibilities available to women in most civilized nations now.

We believe in most cases hierarchs don't skip over the biblical women passages intentionally or out of malice. Many simply don't find them interesting or valuable enough to warrant the work, just like the young preacher who couldn't find the need to include Rahab as an illustration in his sermon—even though the Holy Spirit, through James, did.

A deep dive into the background and ancient customs regarding the status of women, including marriage, divorce, and societal mores, often shines new light into the accounts of biblical women like Rahab and the Samaritan woman, providing inspiring lessons for women today to pursue holiness, integrity, and purpose.

Heterarchs

In recent decades, research into historical primary source material related to women in Greece, the Roman Empire, and Israel has exploded, providing valuable insight into social norms of the day that often alter our current-day assumptions. The Samaritan woman is a prime example of a beneficiary of that new insight, and heterarchs are responsible for the majority of the work.

3. James A. Borland, "Women in the Life and Teachings of Jesus," in *RBMW*, 114–15.
4. Michael Wilkins, "Women in the Teaching and Example of Jesus," in *Women and Men in Ministry: A Complementary Perspective*, eds. Robert L. Saucy and Judith K. TenElshof (Chicago: Moody, 2001), 96.
5. Tertullian, *On Modesty* 11.1; John Calvin, *The Gospel according to St. John 1–10*, trans. T. H. L. Parker (Grand Rapids: Eerdmans, 1978), 90; Robert Jamieson, A. R. Fausset, and David Brown, *Commentary Critical and Explanatory on the Whole Bible* (1871; Oak Harbor, WA: Logos, 1997); William Barclay, *The Gospel of John*, vol. 1, New Daily Study Bible (commentary on John 4: "She was suddenly compelled to face herself and the looseness and immorality and total inadequacy of her life"); Dwight Lyman Moody, "Salvation for Sinners," in *"The Gospel Awakening": Comprising the Sermons and Addresses, Prayer-Meeting Talks and Bible Readings of the Great Revival Meetings Conducted by Moody and Sankey*, 20th ed., ed. L. T. Remlap (Chicago: Fairbanks & Palmer, 1885), 530–31.

They asked, "Could there be other explanations for her marital past? What additional evidence do we see in the account that might guide us?" Here are a few possibilities based on research by Lynn Cohick, author of *Women in the World of the Earliest Christians: Illuminating Ancient Ways of Life*.[6]

Could She Have Been Widowed?

Life expectancy in biblical times was dramatically shorter than today. Also, girls were usually married through arranged marriages at thirteen or fourteen, sometimes to older men, making widowhood common in the first century. And because women needed a male relative or husband to protect them, many widows remarried. Women could easily have been widowed more than once. Jewish historian Josephus records that by age twenty-two, the Herodian princess Berenice had been widowed twice and given birth to two children.[7]

Could She Have Been Divorced?

If the Samaritan woman was unable to conceive, more than one discontented husband might have divorced her. Generally, only husbands had the right to divorce. According to Cohick, "Women did not have direct legal recourse to the courts. They had to go through their guardian or a male representative."[8] If one or more husbands divorced her, she would have been left abandoned in a harsh culture for women without male protection.

Could She Have Been in a Forced Relationship as a Concubine?

In the Greco-Roman world, women concubines were common, preferable to a life on the streets. She might have currently been in a relationship with a Roman citizen who could not legally marry her because she might have been below him in social rank.

She might have been waiting on a dowry before a contract of marriage could be enacted. A second-century AD marriage document between Salome Komaise and Jesus son of Menahem implies that this couple lived together before marrying without specific reasons as to why they were now entering into a marriage contract.[9] Examining first-century legal records and contracts brings to light varying possibilities and situations foreign to us today.

---

6. Lynn H. Cohick, *Women in the World of the Earliest Christians: Illuminating Ancient Ways of Life* (Grand Rapids: Baker Academic, 2009), 122–28.
7. Josephus, *Antiquities of the Jews* 19.277.
8. Cohick, *Women in the World*, 124.
9. Tal Ilan, "Premarital Cohabitation in Ancient Judea: The Evidence of the Babatha Archive and the Mishnah (Ketubbot 1.4)," *Harvard Theological Review* 86 (1993): 247–64; reprinted in her book, *Integrating Women into Second Temple History* (Peabody, MA: Hendrickson, 2001), 235–51.

Could She Have Been a Second Wife?

Historical evidence shows that polygamous relationships existed in the first century. For example, in the Babatha archives we learn that Babatha became the second wife of a man named Judas who was already married to a woman named Mariam.[10] Josephus also admitted this practice existed, citing Herod Archelaus and Herod Antipas as illustrations.[11] It's possible that the Samaritan woman's new companion was already married to someone else, and she may have accepted this arrangement in order to eat. As we consider the customs of the day, we can deduce a number of scenarios that explain why she had five husbands and her current companion was not legally her husband. Whatever it was, Jesus knew about it, responded with compassion, and traveled out of the way, through Samaria, to find her.

Additional Evidence from the Text

Additional evidence comes right out of the narrative. The townfolks' response to her testimony in John 4:28–30 may shed some light: "Then the woman left her water jar, went off into to the town and said to the people, 'Come, see a man who told me everything I ever did. Surely he can't be the Messiah, can he?' So they left the town and began coming to him" (NET).

They believed her immediately! John records that no one doubted the validity of her evidence, even in a culture that did not allow women to give testimony in a trial. If she had been the town "bad girl," would the townspeople have listened, much less dropped what they were doing and set out to find Jesus?

John even makes a point of telling us in 4:39, "Now many Samaritans from that town believed in him because of the report of the woman who testified" (NET). She was the first to share her faith to the town, like an evangelist—an unlikely role for a degenerate woman.

Also, unlike the woman caught in adultery (John 8:1–11), Jesus never rebukes her or advises her to "go now and leave your life of sin" (v. 11). Instead, Jesus uses this situation to teach his disciples that the harvest is ripe, and it's a harvest that includes Samaritans and women, people the disciples devalued.

> Don't you say, "There are four more months and then comes the harvest?" I tell you, look up and see that the fields are already white for harvest! The one who reaps receives pay and gathers fruit for eternal life, so that the one who sows and the

---

10. Naphtali Lewis, Yigael Yadin, and Jonas C. Greenfield, eds., *The Documents from the Bar Kokhba Period in the Cave of Letters*, Judean Desert Studies 2 (Jerusalem: Israel Exploration Society, 1989), 80.
11. Josephus, *Antiquities of the Jews* 17:350.

one who reaps can rejoice together. For in this instance the saying is true, "One sows and another reaps." I sent you to reap what you did not work for; others have labored, and you have entered into their labor. (John 4:35–38 NET)

Jesus tells the disciples that they will reap what others have sown, and that they can rejoice together over what God has done through those who sow. Could Jesus have been referring to the woman at the well, the woman right before them, as the one who sowed?

Summary

What does Jesus's interaction with the woman at the well teach us about his view of women in ministry? First, Jesus went out of his way to pass through Samaria to minister to this woman and to reveal himself to her as the Messiah, "I, the one speaking to you, am he" (John 4:26 NET), as well as to a town of people despised by the Jews. Obviously, this woman and this town mattered greatly to Jesus. In addition, he used this woman's testimony to win souls and begin to spread the truth that their Messiah had come to the entire nation of Samaria. She serves as a role model today for women who believe they are called to be evangelists.

Second, we can't know whether this woman's many marriages resulted from sinful choices on her part or from desperate circumstances that should arouse our compassion, or a combination of both. We can observe that Jesus approached her with more compassion than judgment and did not disqualify her or ignore her because of her past. And John included forty-two verses in his gospel focused on her story. All Scripture is inspired, and therefore it is a worthy pursuit to study her faith and faith-filled actions with the same scholarship that we afford other biblical characters, rather than many hierarchs' practice of jumping to the assumption that she's just another immoral woman and ignoring the rest of her story.

Women need heroines just like men need heroes. If we have always viewed the woman at the well as just another shameful temptress or sinful woman, perhaps it's time to look again.

REFLECTION QUESTIONS

1. What assumptions have you heard others make about the Samaritan woman?

2. What assumptions have you made?

3. How might knowing the social issues of the time make a difference in how people interpret this account?

4. What new lessons did you learn from this chapter about the Samaritan woman's encounter with Jesus and her response to him?

5. What other women in the Bible would you like to learn more about in light of new discoveries related to the social customs of the day?

What Is the Significance of the Spirit's Work on Pentecost for Men and Women?

Hierarchs and heterarchs alike celebrate the coming of the Holy Spirit at Pentecost, when the third person of the Godhead anointed and indwelt the 120 believers gathered in Jerusalem. Shortly before Jesus ascended into heaven, the apostles gathered around him and asked, "Lord, are you at this time going to restore the kingdom to Israel?" (Acts 1:6). Jesus responded, "It is not for you to know the times or dates the Father has set by his own authority. But you will receive power when the Holy Spirit comes on you; and you will be my witnesses in Jerusalem, and in all Judea and Samaria, and to the ends of the earth" (Acts 1:7–8). All scholars apply Jesus's marvelous revelation not only to the apostles who originally heard it but to all future believers, both men and women.

J. I. Packer describes the monumental impact of the Holy Spirit's ministry in the lives of Christian men and women from Pentecost forward:

> The Christian's life in all its aspects—intellectual and ethical, devotional and relational, upsurging in worship and outgoing in witness—is supernatural; only the Spirit can initiate and sustain it. So apart from him, not only will there be no lively believers and no lively congregations, there will be no believers and no congregations at all. But in fact the church continues to live and grow, for the Spirit's ministry has not failed, nor ever will, with the passage of time.[1]

Both heterarchs and hierarchs affirm that women, just like men, are empowered to achieve significant acts for God's glory through the Spirit.

---

1. J. I. Packer, *Keep in Step with the Spirit: Finding Fullness in Our Walk with God* (Grand Rapids: Revell, 1984), 9.

To prepare for this original, wondrous empowering, men and women prayed together for days, waiting for the Holy Spirit to come. Acts 1:12–2:4 tells the story of their assembly and the miraculous result of the Spirit's coming. As the disciples returned to Jerusalem after Jesus's ascension, "they all joined together constantly in prayer, along with the women and Mary the mother of Jesus, and with his brothers. In those days Peter stood up among the believers (a group numbering about a hundred and twenty)" (Acts 1:14–15).

Many more men and women had joined the Twelve and the women who originally followed Jesus. After the ascension they all regrouped in Jerusalem. Luke, the author of Acts, then described how they chose a replacement for Judas, settling on Matthias to round out the twelve men (1:26). Immediately following that, we read:

> When the day of Pentecost came, they were all together in one place. Suddenly a sound like the blowing of a violent wind came from heaven and it filled the whole house where they were sitting. They saw what seemed to be tongues of fire that separated and came to rest on each of them. All of them were filled with the Holy Spirit and began to speak in other tongues as the Spirit enabled them. (Acts 2:1–4)

Were women present at Pentecost? Did the Spirit anoint them along with the men? The text clearly reveals that they were, and he did. We observe the results when God-fearing Jewish men and women who were visiting the temple from all over the known world began to speak and understand one another, proclaiming, "We hear them declaring the wonders of God in our own tongues!" (Acts 2:11). Amazingly and miraculously, people could speak and understand languages they did not know. By this event, God seems to be declaring that the Jews were no longer going to be his primary representatives on earth, but his gospel was going out into all nations and to all peoples, and both men and women would be part of this worldwide mission.

Immediately following this event, uneducated Peter, a former fisherman, stood up and exhibited the Holy Spirit's enabling power when he preached to the confused masses in the city, quoting from the prophet Joel:

> This is what was spoken by the prophet Joel:
> "In the last days, God says,
> I will pour out my Spirit on all people.
> Your sons and daughters will prophesy,
> your young men will see visions,
> your old men will dream dreams.
> Even on my servants, both men and women,

> I will pour out my Spirit in those days,
> and they will prophesy." (Acts 2:16–18)

By these words, Peter affirmed that God would use women as well as men to carry out his new agenda on the earth, and his speech bore incredible fruit—three thousand came to faith in Jesus that day (Acts 2:41).

Immediately following Pentecost and Peter's speech, Luke describes the Christian house churches that erupted in Jerusalem, where these new believers began to grow in their faith. Some hierarchs point out that in these first churches, the apostles were the primary teachers and, since they were males, men should be the primary teachers in the church today (Acts 2:42).[2] Heterarchs George and Dora Winston counter by writing,

> The apostles' doctrine was uniquely authoritative because it was apostolic, not because it was teaching or even male teaching. Nobody today, male or female, is teaching in the identical sense as the twelve original apostles. From the moment inspired Scripture was written down, the locus of authority shifted from the teacher to the teaching as enscripturated. There is still authoritative apostolic doctrine in the Scriptures. There is no authoritative apostolic succession in the church. Every attempt to ascribe teaching authority (magisterium) today to the person of the human teacher (in addition to that of the Bible he is teaching) is a threat to the principle of *Sola Scriptura*.[3]

These first Christians demonstrated a beautiful unity that attracted others to join them daily (Acts 2:47). Packer writes, "In Acts 2–5 we read of a church with, it seems, no buildings of its own, with loose and sometimes improvised leadership, but with each member apparently pulling his or her own weight in the work and witness that went on, and the impact on Jerusalem was great."[4]

In our research, we find little disagreement on the implications of Pentecost regarding women and men. All agree that men and women alike are indwelt and empowered, given spiritual gifts, and encouraged to yield to the Spirit's leading in every good work. Every believer since then experiences

---

2. Hierarchs Robert Saucy and Clinton Arnold write, "Living together in a complementary relationship, the ultimate responsibility for community leadership rested with men" ("Woman and Man in Apostolic Teaching," in *Women and Men in Ministry: A Complementary Perspective*, eds. Robert L. Saucy and Judith K. TenElshof [Chicago: Moody, 2001], 113).

3. George and Dora Winston, *Recovering Biblical Ministry by Women: An Exegetical Response to Traditionalism and Feminism* (Fairfax, VA: Xulon, 2003), 364.

4. Packer, *Keep in Step with the Spirit*, 254.

the same empowerment and opportunity to use specific gifts for the good of the church and the world. "There are different kinds of gifts, but the same Spirit distributes them. There are different kinds of service, but the same Lord. There are different kinds of working, but in all of them and in everyone it is the same God at work. Now to each one the manifestation of the Spirit is given for the common good" (1 Cor. 12:4–7).

All agree that spiritual gifts are given by God's will, not according to gender, race, ethnicity, or any other category. He empowers people as he wills, to further his purposes. Does this mean that scholars agree that women can be gifted in leadership and teaching? Yes, scholars across the board agree that such gifts are given by the Spirit's determination, not by gender. So where do the differences lie? Notably, only in the circumstances under which women can use certain gifts.

Heterarchs

Gifts determine service, heterarchs believe. If a person is gifted to teach, he or she should pursue teaching opportunities in order to build up the body of Christ. If a believer is gifted as a shepherd, he or she should pursue opportunities to shepherd fellow believers. In the early church, when Paul's letters were written, these occasions would have happened within families and among small house churches.

Heterarchs see no division in official leadership positions versus volunteer or women-only settings in which women can use their gifts of teaching, shepherding, leadership, or any other. For example, if they can teach, then the church leadership should encourage and facilitate their efforts to do so. If they are gifted to evangelize, they should work to win people to faith. If God calls them to serve as a missionary, they should follow God's leading.

Hierarchs

Most hierarchs teach that women with teaching and leadership gifts must limit their exercise of those gifts to women and children. Some are comfortable with women teaching in a mixed setting of both men and women, as long as it's not in the large assembly of the entire congregation; others are not.

In *Recovering Biblical Manhood and Womanhood,* the following question arises: Do you deny women the right to use the gifts God has given them? Does not God's giving a spiritual gift imply that he endorses its use for the edification of the church? Their answer:

> Having a spiritual gift is not a warrant to use it however we please. John White is right when he writes, "Some people believe it to be impossible that the power of the Holy Spirit could have unholy consequences in an individual's life. But it can." Spiritual gifts are not only given by the Holy Spirit, they

are also regulated by the Holy Scriptures. This is clear from 1 Corinthians, where people with the gift of tongues were told not to use it in public when there was no gift of interpretation, and prophets were told to stop prophesying when someone else had a revelation (14:28–30). We do not deny to women the right to use the gifts God has given them. If they have gifts of teaching or administration or evangelism, God does want those gifts used, and He will honor the commitment to use them within the guidelines given in Scripture.[5]

Summary

At Pentecost, both men and women were anointed by the Holy Spirit and gifted with spiritual gifts meant to honor God and serve others. Today, church leaders across the theological spectrum agree that women can be imbued by the Spirit with gifts typically used in leadership positions. Though some disagree about exactly where they should be allowed to use those gifts, all encourage women to serve in their God-given strengths.

REFLECTION QUESTIONS

1. Why is Pentecost so important in the history of the church?

2. How can a Christian identify his or her spiritual gifts?

3. What spiritual gifts do you sense God has given you?

4. How do you believe God wants you to use these spiritual gifts?

5. Where do you think men and women are free to use their spiritual gifts?

---

5. John Piper and Wayne Grudem, "An Overview of Central Concerns: Questions and Answers," in *RBMW*, 77.

What Is the Significance of Priscilla Correcting Apollos's Theology?

A Jewish couple, Aquila and Priscilla, made tents for a living. They met Paul, also a tentmaker, in Corinth, and the three went into business together (Acts 18:1–4). Later, following the guidance of the Holy Spirit, the three moved their business to Ephesus. Knowing Paul, it's reasonable to assume the three talked theology while busy at work, and that Priscilla was an astute pupil. We know from Paul's writings that the couple was prominent in ministry in Ephesus and that a church met in their home. While Paul was away, the couple continued to minister and seemed to take an important role combating incorrect teaching in a particular situation recorded by Luke. Acts 18:24–28 reads:

> Now a Jew named Apollos, a native of Alexandria, arrived in Ephesus. He was an eloquent speaker, well-versed in the scriptures [Old Testament]. He had been instructed in the way of the Lord, and with great enthusiasm he spoke and taught accurately the facts about Jesus, although he knew only the baptism of John [probably lacked knowledge of the Holy Spirit and possibly other important doctrines]. He began to speak out fearlessly in the synagogue, but when Priscilla and Aquila heard him, they took him aside and explained the way of God to him more accurately. When Apollos wanted to cross over to Achaia, the brothers [and sisters] encouraged him and wrote to the disciples to welcome him. When he arrived, he assisted greatly those who had believed by grace, for he refuted the Jews vigorously in public debate, demonstrating from the scriptures that the Christ was Jesus. (NET, additions ours)

Luke knew about this situation and decided to include it in his writings so that we may "know the certainty of the things" we have been taught (Luke 1:1–4). What can we learn about women teaching men theology from this account? Not surprisingly, hierarchs and heterarchs agree on some conclusions and disagree on others.

The Order of Their Names

Normally, when a husband and wife are mentioned in the first century, the husband's name comes first. Priscilla's name is mentioned with her husband, Aquila, six times in the New Testament. In the first instance when Paul met them in Corinth, Luke lists Aquila's name first (Acts 18:1–3), as does Paul in his early connection with the couple (1 Cor. 16:19). But in the following four instances, Priscilla's name is listed first (Acts 18:18, 26; Rom. 16:3; 2 Tim. 4:19). Twice, Paul calls her "Prisca," possibly a sisterly nickname. Robert Saucy, a hierarch, writes that Priscilla's name is mentioned first "perhaps because she was more prominent and influential in the church."[1] Hierarch Wayne Grudem insists that it's not possible to be certain about the significance of the order of their names but suggests that maybe it was because she held a superior social status.[2]

Priscilla as a "Coworker"

Fourteen men were described as "coworkers" in the New Testament, including Paul's close associates Timothy, Titus, Luke, and Epaphroditus. In addition, three women were listed: Priscilla, Euodia, and Syntyche. Heterarch Philip Payne insists that the term "fellow worker" connotes "one who labors with Paul as commissioned by God in the shared work of mission preaching."[3] Hierarch Saucy admits that women like Priscilla would "surely have been looked up to by the average members of the church as functional leaders in church ministry"[4] but denies that this meant women served in the senior position of elder or overseer, as this leadership role was open only to men.[5]

Was Priscilla's Teaching "Public" or "Private"?

One of the key disputes between scholars is what constitutes "public" ministry from "private" ministry in the first century. The issue is complicated

1. Robert L. Saucy, "The Ministry of Women in the Early Church," in *Women and Men in Ministry: A Complementary Perspective*, eds. Robert L. Saucy and Judith K. TenElshof (Chicago: Moody, 2001), 163.
2. Wayne Grudem, *EFBT*, 180.
3. Philip Payne quotes W. H. Ollrog, *Paulus und seine Mitarbeiter*, WMANT 50 (Neukirchen: Neukirchener, 1979), 63–72, esp. 67; cf. James D. G. Dunn, *Romans 9–16*, WBC 38B (Grand Rapids: Zondervan, 1988), 892.
4. Saucy, "Ministry of Women in the Early Church," 172.
5. Saucy, "Ministry of Women in the Early Church," 172–73.

because, unlike today, Christians generally did not worship in public buildings, but in private homes. We can learn much about the first gatherings in Jerusalem from Acts 2:42–47:

> They devoted themselves to the apostles' teaching and to fellowship, to the breaking of bread and to prayer. Everyone was filled with awe at the many wonders and signs performed by the apostles. All the believers were together and had everything in common. They sold property and possessions to give to anyone who had need. Every day they continued to meet together in the temple courts. They broke bread in their homes and ate together with glad and sincere hearts, praising God and enjoying the favor of all people. And the Lord added to their number daily those who were being saved.

Even a quick list of the differences between the first-century believer's experience and the typical church worship experience today shows that their church picture was drastically unlike ours.

- The first church met in one of the outer temple courts "every day" instead of their own "church" building once a week for a "service." Once first-century believers left Israel to escape persecution, they settled throughout the Roman Empire. Then they gathered in homes that were different from ours. Archeology reveals much of the "private" home was open-aired with courtyards and spaces where passersby could see and hear everything going on. The woman who wiped Jesus's feet with her hair wasn't invited to the "private" party but found access to the patio where they were eating (Luke 7:36–50). Did Christians meet inside, outside, or both? Were there multiple house churches as their numbers grew? Did they continue to meet "every day"? When did an actual "church service" begin on a certain day, and what did it look like? When did actual paid clergy come on the scene?
- Their fellowship was often around meals in homes where we know from Paul's letter to Corinth that they took Communion as part of the meals they shared. Here we observe a mixture of what we consider "public" and "private." How structured was this mealtime together? Was it a "service" where formal teaching occurred or more like informal discussions where everyone, including women, participated and contributed?
- What about the structure of the worship? Did the leaders teach only at "meeting times" or, like Jesus had modeled, was teaching going on all the time in various ways? We really don't know. Did they sing and pray together at a certain time in a service like we often do now, or

was this spontaneous according to needs? Without watches or clocks, concepts of time were radically different in these early cultures.

It's easy but probably unwise for any of us to assume that worship in the early church looked like it does today. To discern truth, we would be wise to look carefully into biblical contexts without attempting to pour what we see into a modern mold, or to attempt to fit the picture into our preconceived perspectives, wherever we land on these various issues. That said, let's look at the varied interpretations of verse 26 and then examine several scholars' diverse views.

Varied Interpretations of Acts 18:26

In Greek, Acts 18:26 actually says, "And this man [Apollos] began to speak boldly in the synagogue. And hearing him *Priscilla and Aquila took him* and more accurately to him explained the way of God" (emphasis added). In the original language, Luke doesn't say where they took him, but different translators impute their interpretations into the verse. Examples include the following:[6]

- King James Version: "And he began to speak boldly in the synagogue: whom when Aquila and Priscilla had heard, *they took him unto them*, and expounded unto him the way of God more perfectly."
- American Standard Version: "And he began to speak boldly in the synagogue. But when Priscilla and Aquila heard him, *they took him unto them*, and expounded unto him the way of God more accurately."
- Common English Bible: "He began speaking with confidence in the synagogue. When Priscilla and Aquila heard him, *they received him into their circle of friends* and explained to him God's way more accurately."
- Complete Jewish Bible: "He began to speak out boldly in the synagogue; but when Priscilla and Aquila heard him, *they took him aside* and explained to him the Way of God in fuller detail."
- New International Version: "He began to speak boldly in the synagogue. When Priscilla and Aquila heard him, *they invited him to their home* and explained to him the way of God more adequately."

Obviously, different interpreters have added their own opinions about where and how Priscilla and Aquila corrected Apollos.

Heterarchs

Andrew Bartlett considers Priscilla a strong teacher:

---

6. Emphasis added to the following Scripture citations.

With her husband, Priscilla corrected Apollos, a prominent male preacher, and taught him the way of God more accurately, as narrated by Paul's companion, Luke (Acts 18:26). . . . Luke considered Priscilla's correction of Apollos sufficiently important to include it in his short history. Teaching Apollos was no minor task. He was a forceful public exponent of the gospel, with an expansive ministry (Acts 18:24–28). When he moved on to Corinth, his ministry there was more influential with some believers even than Paul's (1 Cor. 1:12).[7]

Stanley Grenz and Denise Muir Kjesbo add,

Contrary to complementarian [hierarch] opinion, the text of Acts will not allow us to transform this narrative into anything other than a clear indication of authoritative teaching by a woman in the church. The text gives no warrant to importing a distinction between private teaching in a home and authoritative teaching in the church. To pass by this incident as "*unofficial* guidance" as distinct from "*official* teaching leadership" is to draw too fine a line between authoritative and so-called non-authoritative teaching among the people of God.[8]

Hierarchs

Grudem counters by arguing that although "Scripture encourages men and women to talk with each other about the Bible and Christian doctrine in private discussions, to say that there is no distinction between private and public teaching is to ignore the . . . context."[9] He insists that the phrase "they took him" indicates that "they waited to speak to him until they could take him aside, out of public view,"[10] and that this example "does not give warrant for women to teach the Bible in the assembled church."[11] Thomas Schreiner agrees: "This Scripture does not indicate 'that women filled the pastoral office or functioned as regular teachers of the congregation. All believers are to instruct one another. . . . But such mutual encouragement and instruction is

---

7. Andrew Bartlett, *Men and Women in Christ: Fresh Light from the Biblical Texts* (London: InterVarsity, 2019), 207.

8. Stanley J. Grenz and Denise Muir Kjesbo, *Women in the Church: A Biblical Theology of Women in Ministry* (Downers Grove, IL: InterVarsity, 1995), 82–83.

9. Grudem, *EFBT*, 178.

10. Grudem, *EFBT*, 178.

11. Grudem, *EFBT*, 179.

not the same thing as a woman being appointed to the pastoral office or functioning as the regular teacher of a gathering of men and women."[12]

Summary

From what Luke actually says about Priscilla's role in teaching Apollos, we don't believe it's possible to conclude with certainty where they "took him" or, for that matter, since "they" is plural, who took him. Did Priscilla and Aquila take him to their home where other believers who had heard Apollos joined them? Were they alone in their home or with "their circle of friends," as some interpreters have surmised? Or did Priscilla and Aquila just take him aside outside the synagogue after he spoke there? The only thing we can know for sure is that Apollos listened, learned from their competent theological instruction, and went on to become a great orator of the gospel (Acts 18:28). We contend that if Priscilla weren't such a controversial character, all sides would be more honest in their assessments.

REFLECTION QUESTIONS

1. Where do you think Priscilla and Aquila learned deep truths about God?

2. What are your thoughts concerning why Paul listed Priscilla's name before her husband's four times?

3. What are the differences between the early church services and typical services today?

4. Taking into account the original language, what can we know about whether Priscilla and Aquila took Apollos to a public or private space to instruct him?

5. How do you feel about women teaching theology?

---

12. Thomas R. Schreiner, "Women in Ministry: Response," in *Two Views on Women in Ministry*, eds. Stanley N. Gundry and James R. Beck (Grand Rapids: Zondervan, 2001), 191.

Women in the Epistles

What Is the Significance of the Women Commended by Paul in Romans 16?

I used to think Romans 16 was the most boring chapter in the letter,"[1] admits heterarch scholar N. T. Wright. Hierarch William R. Newell agrees, beginning his commentary on the chapter by asserting that it's "neglected by many to their own loss."[2] Why? Because the chapter contains a list of unfamiliar names, and we tend to skip over it. But like the pearl of great price in Jesus's parable (Matt. 13:45–46), we discover gems of insight into Paul's relational heart for friends, and especially women co-laborers for Christ. Newell continues: "It is by far the most extensive, intimate and particular of all the words of loving greeting in Paul's marvelous letters. No one can afford to miss this wonderful outpouring of the heart of our apostle toward the saints whom he so loved—which means all the real Church of God!"[3] Obviously, Paul valued, celebrated, considered himself a brother and son in the faith too, and worked beside many women for the cause they shared.

Women Listed in Romans 16

Ten women are listed in Paul's greeting to the church in Rome. Their names are Phoebe, Priscilla, Mary, Junia, Tryphena, Tryphosa, Persis, Julia, and two that we know by their relationship to others, Rufus's mother and Neureus's sister. This list makes us wonder how many other women ministered beside their brothers in other first-century churches.

---

1. N. T. Wright, "Women's Service in the Church: The Biblical Basis," N. T. Wright Online, September 4, 2004, https://ntwrightpage.com/2016/07/12/womens-service-in-the-church-the-biblical-basis.
2. William R. Newell, *Romans Verse by Verse* (1938; Grand Rapids: Baker, 1987), 548.
3. Newell, *Romans Verse by Verse*, 554.

We know little about many of the women Paul greeted. Mary (v. 6) is such a common name; we only know that news of her energy and hard work for the churches in Rome had reached Paul's ears, and she was probably a personal friend as well. Tom Constable writes that Tryphena (v. 12) means "dainty" and Tryphosa means "delicate." He thinks they may have been sisters since both names derive from the verb *truphao*, meaning to live delicately or luxuriously,[4] although they were commended for their diligent service, as was Persis (v. 12).

Paul lauded Rufus's "mother" (v. 13) and declared she had also been a "mother to me." It's doubtful she was actually Paul's mother but obviously, at some time in the past, she had acted like a mother to him, earning his deep affection. Paul's commendation alerts us to the important part older women can play in the lives of younger Christian men who need their wisdom and guidance. Paul wasn't above placing value on these kinds of relationships. "Let Christian mothers find here a great field for that wonderful heart of instinctive loving care given by God to mothers,—that they extend their maternal care beyond their own family circle, to all Christians, and especially to all laborers for Christ. The Lord will remember it at His coming!"[5]

Verse 14 may refer to a group of men and women from the same house church that he calls "brothers and sisters," in his typical manner of using family language for his dear friends.

Verse 15 contains another list of names including Julia and Nereus's sister. William Barclay speculates that Nereus may have been the slave of the consul of Rome, the highest political office in the city. His name was Flavius Clemens, and he was executed for being a Christian by the emperor Domitian. Flavius's wife of royal blood, Domatilla, was banished to the island of Pontia for her Christian faith. Could it have been Nereus who led Flavius and Domatilla to the Lord, and their faith was so strong that Flavius was later martyred for the cause of Christ? If so, it's likely the other people named in verse 15 may have been involved or at least were aware of this incident.[6] Constable concludes:

> Paul's acknowledgement of his co-workers (vv. 3, 9; cf. v. 7) shows that he was not a "lone ranger" minister. He had strong personal connections with several of the people whom he named. The significant number of women (nine) mentioned in these verses argues against the view of some that Paul was a woman-hater. Obviously women played important roles in the ministry of the early church, and Paul appreciated them.[7]

---

4. Tom Constable, "Dr. Constables' Notes on Romans," 300, Sonic Light, Plano Bible Chapel, 2021, https://www.planobiblechapel.org/tcon/notes/html/nt/romans/romans.htm.
5. Newell, *Romans Verse by Verse*, 554.
6. William Barclay, *The Letter to the Romans*, Daily Study Bible Series (Philadelphia: Westminster, 1957), 237.
7. Constable, "Notes on Romans," 301.

In our research, we found that both hierarchs and heterarchs share the opinion that many women were active, esteemed participants in the early church. Notes in the margin of my (Sue) Bible identify these Romans 16 women as "hidden heroes that were all in" and "you celebrate what you value."[8] However, heterarchs and hierarchs differ on the meaning of the ministry roles of Phoebe, Priscilla, and particularly Junia.[9]

Was Junia an Apostle?

First, we will focus on Junia, in verse 7.[10]

> Greet Andronicus and *Junia*, my fellow Jews who have been in prison with me. They are *outstanding among the apostles*, and they were in Christ before I was. (NIV)

> Greet Andronicus and *Junia*, my compatriots and my fellow prisoners. They are *well known to the apostles*, and they were in Christ before me. (NET)

> Greet Andronicus and *Junias*, my kinsmen and my fellow prisoners, who are *outstanding among the apostles*, who also were in Christ before me. (NASB 1995)

These different interpretations highlight three controversies around verse 7.

The First Controversy: Was Junia(s) a Man or a Woman?

For most of church history, almost all Bibles identified the second person in verse 7 with the feminine name "Junia." Examples include Wycliffe Bible (1382), Tyndale (1525), Geneva New Testament (1557), King James Version (1611), and Webster (1833).[11] The first time the name was assumed to be masculine was in the early fourteenth century, but this concept became more popular when Martin Luther adopted the masculine name "Junias" when he translated the Bible for the common people from Latin into German. However, "Junias" is not found elsewhere in secular literature or inscriptions and artifacts at that time and would have to be a shortened form of the name "Junianus." Most now admit that's a stretch, especially since the name "Junia"

---

8. From a sermon preached by hierarch Neil Tomba at Northwest Bible Church in Dallas, Fall 2020.
9. We discuss the controversy around Phoebe in Question 33 and Priscilla in Question 18.
10. Emphasis added to the following Scripture citations.
11. Dennis J. Preato, "Junia, a Female Apostle: An Examination of the Historical Record," *Priscilla Papers* 33, no. 2 (2019): 8, www.cbeinternational.org/sites/default/files/PP332-3-Preato.pdf. For a thorough treatment of the historical background on this issue, read the entire article.

was a common Roman name for a woman. As a result, most scholars now agree that Paul was referring to a woman.[12]

The Second Controversy: What Kind of Apostle Was She?
Robert Saucy, a hierarch, admits that Paul called Junia an "apostle" but believes that the term is used in four different ways in the New Testament:

1. for the original Twelve;
2. for those who were eyewitnesses to Jesus's ministry and commissioned by him;
3. for those sent out by a church to perform a particular task; and
4. for a missionary.

He believes that Andronicus and Junia were probably a husband-wife missionary team who were outstanding among other missionaries at that time.[13] John Stott agrees with this overall premise, writing, "It is impossible to suppose that an otherwise unknown couple have taken their place alongside the apostles Peter, Paul, John, and James."[14]

However, heterarch Amy Peeler makes an interesting case from Paul's description of Andronicus and Junia in verse 7. She contends that they may have qualified as a kind of apostle: they were Jews, they suffered as prisoners possibly with Paul, and they were among the earliest Jewish converts to the faith. She argues that since Paul experienced his dynamic encounter with Jesus on the Damascus Road in AD 33 or 34, and verse 7 says Andronicus and Junia became believers before Paul, they were probably among the early Christians he was still hunting down and imprisoning. They could have been present at the cross and seen the resurrected Christ. If so, at the time Paul wrote Romans, they had been boldly sharing the gospel for some twenty years, the reason they had been incarcerated for their faith.[15]

Richard Bauckham agrees and also suggests that Junia may be the Latinized version of the name Yohannah, whom we know as Joanna in English. Joanna was one of the women who traveled with Jesus and the Twelve, supporting them out of their own wealth (Luke 8:1–3). She was also one of the women with Mary

---

12. Preato, "Junia, a Female Apostle," 8–15.
13. Robert L. Saucy, "The Ministry of Women in the Early Church," in *Women and Men in Ministry: A Complementary Perspective*, eds. Robert L. Saucy and Judith K. TenElshof (Chicago: Moody, 2001), 177–78.
14. John Stott, *Romans: God's Good News for the World* (Downers Grove, IL: InterVarsity, 1994), 396.
15. Amy Peeler, "Junia/Joanna: Herald of the Good News," in *Vindicating the Vixens: Revisiting Sexualized, Vilified, and Marginalized Women of the Bible*, ed. Sandra Glahn (Grand Rapids: Kregel, 2017), 273–85.

Magdalene who first saw the resurrected Jesus (Luke 24:1–12).[16] Peeler states, "It was a common practice for Jewish people to adopt Greek or Latin names that sounded similar to their given Hebrew names. . . . This would allow Greek or Roman neighbors more ease in pronouncing their names."[17] Peeler concludes that Junia had the same qualifications as others, besides the Twelve, who had also been designated as apostles: she was a Jewish eyewitness to Jesus's ministry, an early believer, and she had been imprisoned for her faith. She argues that Paul may have been commending her with the title *apostle* on that basis.[18]

Heterarch Eldon Epp summarizes the interpretive journey of Andronicus and Junia this way:

> The male "Junias" and the female "Junia" each has his or her alternating "dance partners"—first one, then the other: first and for centuries, Junia with "prominent apostle"; then Junias with "prominent apostle." Then for a time Junia disappears from the scene, hoping upon her return to team up once again with "prominent apostle," only to encounter "known to the apostles" cutting in during this latest "dance."[19]

The Third Controversy: Was Junia Outstanding Among the Apostles or to the Apostles?

Hierarchs

In 2001 Michael Burer and Daniel Wallace published a paper arguing that the more likely meaning of verse 7 is "'well known to the apostles" instead of "notable among the apostles.'"[20] Their work relies on technical linguistic understanding of Greek, involving the adjective and the prepositional phrase as a unit. Burer, in a follow-up article, asserts that the phrase in question "is more naturally taken with an exclusive force rather than an inclusive one."[21]

> By exclusive we meant that the person described by the adjective was not considered part of the group referred to by the prepositional phrase; this is the interpretation we advanced

16. Richard Bauckham, *Gospel Women: Studies of the Named Women in the Gospels* (Grand Rapids: Eerdmans, 2002), 172–80.
17. Peeler, "Junia/Joanna," 279.
18. Peeler, "Junia/Joanna," 280.
19. Eldon Jay Epp, *Junia: The First Woman Apostle* (Minneapolis: Fortress, 2005), 72.
20. Michael H. Burer and Daniel B. Wallace, "Was Junia Really an Apostle? A Re-examination of Rom 16.7," *New Testament Studies* 47 (2001): 90.
21. Michael H. Burer, "*Episēmoi en tois Apostolois* in Rom 16:7 as 'Well Known to the Apostles': Further Defense and New Evidence," *Journal of the Evangelical Theological Society* 58, no. 4 (2015): 732.

for Rom 16:7. By inclusive we meant that the person described by the adjective was part of the group referred to by the prepositional phrase; this is the more traditional interpretation of "notable among the apostles."[22]

Their argument is outside the bounds of this book, but their articles are readily available on the internet to read. While Burer and Wallace advocate for their view as *possible* (and even likely) within the semantic range of the words in verse 7, Wayne Grudem insists theirs is the only correct view. He admits that Junia is a woman's name but writes that it makes no difference since she wasn't an apostle; she was simply known to the apostles.[23]

Heterarchs

Andrew Bartlett contends that hierarchs ask Christians to believe ideas based on evidence that, viewed without bias, appear completely unlikely. He cites three reasons below:

- We would have to believe that for 1,500 years commentators familiar with Greek failed to see the true meaning of what Paul wrote, even as a possibility; instead, they misunderstood him as definitely commending Junia's apostleship.
- This happened even though those commentators included native Greek speakers in the early centuries after Paul.
- This happened even though those commentators were strongly opposed to women holding any position of leadership, so they had a strong motive to notice a different interpretation if the text so allowed.[24]

Heterarchs' strongest evidence that Paul commended Junia because she was *outstanding among the apostles*, possibly along with her husband Andronicus, stems from a sermon preached by church father John Chrysostom in the fourth century AD. A leading intellectual, native Greek speaker, and archbishop of Constantinople, his writings and messages earned him the names "Golden Mouth" and "Doctor of the Church." Today some six hundred sermons and two hundred of his letters survive.[25] Here are the words taken directly from his ancient sermon on Romans 16, verse 7:

---

22. Burer and Wallace, "Was Junia Really an Apostle?," 732.
23. Wayne Grudem, *EFBT*, 224–25.
24. Andrew Bartlett, *Men and Women in Christ: Fresh Light from the Biblical Texts* (London: InterVarsity, 2019), 305.
25. "John Chrysostom: Early Church's Greatest Preacher," *Christian History*, August 2008, https://www.christianitytoday.com/history/people/pastorsandpreachers/john-chrysostom.html.

Then another praise besides. *"Who are of note among the Apostles."* And indeed to be apostles at all is a great thing. But to be even among these of note, just consider what a great encomium [tribute] this is! But they were of note owing to their works, to their achievements. Oh! How great is the devotion (φιλοσοφία) of this woman, that she should be even counted worthy of the appellation [name or title] of apostle! But even here he [Paul] does not stop, but adds another encomium [tribute] besides, and says, *"Who were also in Christ before me."* For this too is a very great praise, that they sprang forth and came before others.[26]

Heterarchs argue that Chrysostom's misogynistic views on women make his comments even more remarkable.[27]

Summary

Paul's mention of so many women friends and coworkers in Romans 16 affirms that he worked with, respected, and valued women. Junia is probably the most debated person in his list, and scholars have disagreed as to whether this person was a woman or a man, and still disagree on how Paul referred to her. As you can see, respected theologians come down on different sides of the arguments, generally according to their preconceived perspectives on women in ministerial leadership. We agree with Amy Peeler who states, "Junia alone cannot bear the weight of the 'women's question' in the church,"[28] and that even if we had irrefutable evidence that Paul viewed her as a bona fide apostle, she still would not be considered in the ranks of the Twelve, and we still would have all the other related passages to wrestle with that shine light on our final conclusions and resulting actions. Nevertheless, we commend Peeler when she writes:

No matter where one is located on the spectrum of the debate . . . [Junia's] existence serves as a needed reminder of the points that unite us: Everyone should hear the gospel, everyone should be willing to suffer for Christ, and everyone should respect those who are worthy of honor, without concern for gender. . . . Whether one perceives Junia to be an apostle or not, reflecting on her witness should make

---

26. John Chrysostom, *Homilies on Romans* 31, New Advent, https://www.newadvent.org/fathers/210231.htm. Definitions added by the authors.
27. Bartlett, *Men and Women in Christ*, 301.
28. Peeler, "Junia/Joanna," 274.

Christians neither ignore her nor fight over her, but desire to emulate her life.[29]

REFLECTION QUESTIONS

1. Why do you think many people initially find Romans 16 boring?

2. What did you think was most interesting about this chapter?

3. What did you learn about how much Paul valued relationships?

4. Why do you think some people see Paul as a "woman hater"?

5. How might Romans 16 change that perception?

---

29. Peeler, "Junia/Joanna," 274–75.

Can Women Teach or Prophesy?

At first glance, the question before us can be answered very simply by looking at the biblical text. Deborah was a prophet (Judges 4–5), and Priscilla taught Apollos (Acts 18:26)—both with the approval of their faith communities. So why is there controversy? Some passages that seem to contradict others have confused scholars and Bible readers. Are there cultural issues at play? Are women limited in where, when, and how they can teach or prophesy? We'll explore both activities and introduce various perspectives that attempt to reconcile opposing conclusions.

Teaching

By teach, we mean to impart God's truth to another person, whether it originated from God himself or from his holy writings. The biblical text gives ample evidence that women were empowered and allowed to offer God's truth—to men as well as to other women: Abigail (1 Samuel 25), Mary (Luke 2), or the woman of Proverbs 31.

Of course, God appointed Deborah (Judges 4–5) as judge and prophet over Israel. Priscilla taught God's word authoritatively alongside her husband (Acts 18:24–28; Romans 16). The gift of teaching is given to both male and female believers as the Holy Spirit wills, to be used in encouraging, correcting, and instructing others.

Paul encouraged women to teach in church. First Corinthians 14:26 states, "Whenever you come together, each one"—which includes men and women—"has a . . . teaching [*didachē*]" (CSB). Likewise, Colossians 3:16 encourages all believers (cf. v. 11) to "teach and admonish one another with all wisdom."[1]

---

1. Philip Payne, "Examining the Twelve Pillars of Male Hierarchy" (audio recording), Christians for Biblical Equality International, July 31, 2012, https://www.cbeinternational .org/resource/audio/examining-twelve-pillars-male-heirarchy.

However, in 1 Timothy 2:8–15, Paul seems to tell Timothy that he does not allow a woman to teach a man—hence the controversial discussion on what limitations God may have given women regarding teaching his Word, which we'll cover in another chapter.[2] We will devote the rest of this chapter to the topic of prophecy.

Prophesying

A prophet is God's spokesperson, one through whom God speaks to his people. Sometimes his word related to a future event, which we call foretelling, but prophecy also refers to any direct revelation from God. So a prophet teaches, though not all teachers prophesy.

The Old Testament features prominent female prophets such as Deborah (Judges 4–5), who was also a judge, and Huldah, the first prophet to authenticate a text as the Word of God (2 Kings 22:14–20).[3]

The New Testament also speaks of women prophesying during Jesus's time and in the early church. Shortly after his birth, Anna the prophetess spoke about him in the temple "to all who were looking forward to the redemption of Jerusalem" (Luke 2:38). On the day of Pentecost, the apostle Peter declared that the coming of the Holy Spirit was the beginning of the "last days" spoken of by the prophet Joel: "I will pour out my Spirit on all people. Your sons and daughters will prophesy, your young men will see visions, your old men will dream dreams. Even on my servants, both men and women, I will pour out my Spirit in those days, and they will prophesy" (Acts 2:17–18, quoting Joel 2:28–29).

During the apostle Paul's journeys, he met up with Philip the evangelist, who "had four unmarried daughters who prophesied" (Acts 21:9). When Paul wrote to the church in Corinth, he gave instructions on the appropriate apparel of "every man who prays or prophesies" and "every woman who prays or prophesies" (1 Cor. 11:4–5). His language indicates that he expected women to prophesy as a normal part of worship. Just as some would pray, so others would prophesy.

What About 1 Corinthians 14?

While heterarchs point to evidence that God did choose to speak through women in a variety of situations, all scholars (both hierarchs and heterarchs) note 1 Corinthians 14, where Paul appears to flat-out deny women permission to speak in church. The relevant section reads:

> As in all the churches of the saints, the women should be si-
> lent in the churches, for they are not permitted to speak, but
> are to submit themselves, as the law also says. If they want to

---

2. We cover the 1 Timothy passage in great detail in Questions 23, 24, and 25.
3. See Question 11 for more on women prophets.

> learn something, let them ask their own husbands at home, since it is disgraceful for a woman to speak in the church. Or did the word of God originate from you, or did it come to you only? (1 Cor. 14:33–36 CSB)

Most contemporary scholars acknowledge the potential for confusion in Paul's words here. Paul wrote about issues he assumed his readers would understand. The rest of us are separated by time and culture and left attempting to grasp the end of a conversation whose beginning we have not heard. Every interpretation includes some degree of speculation, but not all are equally speculative. Neither can we separate the arguments easily between heterarch and hierarch, as various scholars across the spectrum hold similar and different views about this passage.

Hierarchs work under the assumption that male headship is God's created design, while heterarchs view Scripture through the lens of parity in the male/female partnership. Below, we sketch a variety of options that have been suggested to understand this passage.

- **Theory 1:** Verses 34–35 are interpolations, text added by later scribes—possibly in the wrong place. Respected heterarchs who study early manuscripts have noted irregularities among ancient texts that open up the possibility that Paul either (1) did not write these verses or (2) originally wrote them in a different location.[4] If true, we do not need to interpret these two verses in their current context, and no limitation on women's speech in church is needed.

  Response: The verses appear in all New Testament manuscripts. If they were added, the change would have had to happen at an extremely early date. Also, the language in the verses echoes common words from verses surrounding it, which makes it all fit together rather well. While some questions remain, most scholars affirm the verses are original to the text.

- **Theory 2:** Paul was quoting a Corinthian saying in order to refute it.[5] In verse 36, he exclaimed, "What! Did the word of God originate with you, or are you the only ones it has reached?" The context shows, starting in verses 11–12, that Paul had been establishing the

---

4. Philip Payne argues a thorough case for verses 34–35 as a non-Pauline interpolation. See Philip B. Payne, *Man and Woman, One in Christ: An Exegetical and Theological Study of Paul's Letters* (Grand Rapids: Zondervan, 2009), 227–65.
5. Lucy Peppiatt, *Women and Worship at Corinth: Paul's Rhetorical Arguments in 1 Corinthians* (Eugene, OR: Wipf & Stock, 2015), 130.

primacy of prophecy as a desired spiritual gift, even over teaching and tongues, and encouraging all—including women—to aspire to prophecy because it built up the church rather than the speaker. Why then would he restrict women from using their gift *in the church gathering*, where it was of most use?

Response: The original texts of the Bible did not have punctuation, so we cannot see any written hints that verses 34–35 were quoted from outside sources. Most scholars hesitate to "put words in Paul's mouth," but this theory is less objectionable than the idea that the verses were never written by him at all (theory 1). The lack of punctuation, on the other hand, also leaves theory 2 open as a legitimate option.

- **Theory 3:** Since the word for "woman" in Greek is also the word for "wife," Paul could have been speaking of wives only. So, if wives were interrupting their husband's prophecies with questions, Paul could have been restoring order by having them be quiet. Immediately preceding these verses, Paul had explained how to properly practice their gift of prophecy and then said, "God is not a God of disorder but of peace—as in all the congregations of the Lord's people" (v. 33). Even more specifically, some heterarchs see Paul directing wives to stop judging their husbands' prophecies *in public* because it might break civil law ("as the law says," v. 34b). The Jewish law made no reference to women being silent in worship, but Corinthian laws required submission from wives. Paul would have wanted order in the house churches so that the civil authorities would have no cause to object.[6]

  Response: These options take into account local customs and laws, fit within the larger context of 1 Corinthians 11 and 14, and are consistent with the grammar (i.e., it is more likely that he meant wives in this context because husbands are referenced as well).

- **Theory 4:** Because prophecies were considered authoritative speech, and women were not permitted any church-wide teaching authority, Paul required them to stay quiet during the judging of prophecies.[7] Yet the scholars who prefer this view also invert the importance of

---

6. Sandra Glahn, "1 Corinthians 14: Are Women Really Supposed to Be Silent in Church?," *Engage* (blog), Bible.org, May 8, 2018, https://blogs.bible.org/1-corinthians-14-are-women -really-supposed-to-be-silent-in-church.

7. D. A. Carson, "Silent in the Churches: On the Role of Women in 1 Corinthians 14:33b–36," in *RBMW*, 52–53. See heterarch Craig Keener's response to Carson in *DBE*, 146–58.

teaching and prophecy: they maintain that prophecy in the church did not hold the same authority as that of the Old Testament prophets, therefore teaching was more important. And women were prohibited from teaching. If a wife were to judge her husband's prophecy, his headship would be threatened and their relationship "out of order."

Response: Hierarchs favor this view due to their belief that male headship underpins all male/female relationships and acceptable behavior in the church. The text, however, does not specify judging but rather mere speaking, so this conclusion is speculative. Neither does the passage refer to headship, a concept that is inferred from letters Paul wrote to other churches. Their claim that prophecy in the church was less authoritative than Old Testament prophets is also contradictory to Paul's emphasis on prophecy over other gifts like tongues, interpretation, and giving instruction (1 Cor. 14:1, 26–31).

Summary

Paul's admonition to the Corinthian church has confused Bible readers for centuries. Save for some church fathers who believed women were subhuman and intellectually inferior, few scholars believe the statement "women should remain silent in the churches. They are not allowed to speak" means absolute silence. As a result, many scholars attempt to clarify, temper, and explain how, or even if, verses 34–35 could be interpreted and harmonized with the rest of the Bible.

Does God gift men and women alike as he wills? Yes, including teaching and prophecy. Concerning prophecy, Paul is very clear earlier in chapter 14 that he's speaking to the entire Corinthian church. He clarified how best to practice spiritual gifts within a church service so that order was maintained and the church body was built up in Christ.

The explanations included here give each reader permission to explore Paul's intent. We close with Sandra Glahn's encouragement:

> Understanding Paul as saying women cannot open their mouths at any time in church actually contradicts his repeated desire that all prophesy and his earlier assumption that women would prophesy. Hopefully, by seeing that there are a number of options for how we understand "let the women keep silent," we will lose our misogynistic interpretations and recover the spirit of the apostle's instructions.[8]

---

8. Glahn, "1 Corinthians 14."

REFLECTION QUESTIONS

1. What are some of the challenges women with teaching gifts face in the church?

2. Do you think it's possible that God has given you a teaching gift? If so, how might you use it to minister to others?

3. What is the difference between teaching and prophesying?

4. Of the different theories explaining the mysterious verses, 1 Corinthians 14:33b–36, which makes the most sense to you and why?

5. How would you advise a woman with a gift of teaching and a desire to serve the Lord to move forward?

What Does Paul Mean When He Uses the Metaphor *Head*?

It's natural for any of us, including scholars harboring preset convictions, to interpret metaphors to support an overall agenda. As seekers of truth, we must avoid this pitfall and attempt to set aside our biases for an honest look. This chapter's goal is to examine what various scholars believe biblical authors meant when they used the Greek metaphor for "head" (*kephalē*). Then you'll need to decide for yourself what you think, and how these conclusions impact your overall views on women in ministry, the home, and the community.

As we begin our quest, we must define the term *metaphor*: it is a word or phrase that describes something in a way that isn't literally true but helps explain it by comparing it to something else. For example, if you call someone "the black sheep of the family," you are using a metaphor. Do you really have sheep in your family? Of course not, but every native English speaker knows what you mean.

Metaphors in the Bible can be tricky because we live in a different culture than the original audience. Sometimes a metaphor might be perfectly clear to people in biblical times, but it doesn't make much sense to us today. When the topic is controversial, scholars can impart their own biased meaning onto the metaphor and end up disagreeing. That's the case with the biblical metaphor "head": "There is always a danger that metaphors move from being useful descriptive tools to becoming markers of loyalty to an entire school of thought. If we are not careful, we serve metaphors instead of having them serve us."[1] Interpreting biblical metaphors is messy. We must either put in the hard work to sort out the meaning ourselves or rely on scholars we trust to do so and assess their work to see what rings true in light of the whole of God's Word. This

---

1. Jonathan Downie, "The Problem with Metaphors," *Still Thinking* (blog), January 26, 2019, https://jonathandownie.wordpress.com/2019/01/26/the-problem-with-metaphors.

is especially needed if an important doctrine depends on the interpretation of that particular metaphor—like the metaphor *head* that we're looking at in this chapter.

How to Interpret Biblical Metaphors Correctly

1. *Look for clues in the context.* Do any of the related verses in the passage shed light on the author's likely intended meaning? Great literature, like the Scriptures, often communicates as a unit of thought, and other parts of the passage may provide valuable evidence concerning the author's overall meaning.
2. *See how this metaphor was used in other biblical passages.* But even there, you must make judgment calls, since—again—it's a metaphor, a comparison, and seldom as clear as direct language. And a metaphor may mean one thing in one passage and something different in another.
3. *Find out all you can about what that metaphor meant to the people who lived at that time.* Look at ancient religious and secular artifacts like letters, tombstones, and manuscripts to see if it's possible to discern how the metaphor was used back then. Sometimes these artifacts are available and sometimes they aren't, although new ones are being discovered all the time.

The English Meaning of "Head"

"Head" has multiple meanings in the English language. Before the twelfth century, this word simply meant a physical head that sits on top of a body.[2] But since then, a plethora of meanings have become part of the English language. These are just a few of the many English meanings according to the *Merriam-Webster* dictionary:

- the source of a stream (the head of the Nile)
- one side of a coin (heads or tails)
- the mind (two heads are better than one)
- a toilet (the head on a ship)
- someone in charge of a department (head of the chemistry department)
- the foam on an effervescing liquid (the head of a beer)
- to hit or propel with one's head (head a soccer ball)

---

2. *Merriam-Webster*, s.v. "head," accessed April 8, 2022, https://unabridged.merriam-webster.com/unabridged/head.

Our task is to set aside any English assumptions and determine what this metaphor probably would have meant in biblical times.

Three Views on the Meaning of *Head* in Ephesians 5:21–33

One of the most debated texts relates to what Paul meant when he used the metaphor *head* is Ephesians 5:21–33.[3] The text says:

> Submit to one another out of reverence for Christ.
>
> Wives, submit yourselves to your own husbands as you do to the Lord. For the husband is the head [*kephalē*] of the wife as Christ is the head [*kephalē*] of the church, his body, of which he is the Savior. Now as the church submits to Christ, so also wives should submit to their husbands in everything.
>
> Husbands, love your wives, just as Christ loved the church and gave himself up for her to make her holy, cleansing her by the washing with water through the word, and to present her to himself as a radiant church, without stain or wrinkle or any other blemish, but holy and blameless. In this same way, husbands ought to love their wives as their own bodies. He who loves his wife loves himself. After all, no one ever hated their own body, but they feed and care for their body, just as Christ does the church—for we are members of his body. "For this reason a man will leave his father and mother and be united to his wife, and the two will become one flesh." This is a profound mystery—but I am talking about Christ and the church. However, each one of you also must love his wife as he loves himself, and the wife must respect her husband. (Eph. 5:21–33)

Scholars believe *head* here means either (1) authority, (2) source, or (3) part of a one-flesh union.

Authority

Throughout John Piper and Wayne Grudem's book *Recovering Biblical Manhood and Womanhood,* the various authors argue that when Scripture uses the word *kephalē* as a metaphor related to the relationships of husbands and wives, it always means that the husband has authority over his own wife.[4]

---

3. The other most debated passage is 1 Corinthians 11:3. See Question 22 for insight on 1 Corinthians 11:3.
4. See Grudem's explanation in *RBMW*, Appendix 1, "The Meaning of *Kephalē* ('Head'): A Response to Recent Studies," 499–567. Here, Grudem responds to studies that refute his conclusion.

In Grudem's later book *Evangelical Feminism and Biblical Truth*, he suggests more than fifty examples in ancient literature where *kephalē* means authority or ruler. He includes examples from Old Testament verses containing the Hebrew word for head (*rosh*) and New Testament verses containing the Greek word for head (*kephalē*), and he quotes from ancient writers. Many of the examples relate to military and political works or passages. He argues that these examples prove that when Paul used the word *kephalē* he meant an authoritative leader.[5]

Robert Saucy describes the kind of leadership he believes the Bible teaches because the husband is the authoritative *head*.

> The husband will "lead" his family rather than boss his partner; the husband will be in tune with his wife's needs and strive to meet them; the husband will value what his wife can give him that he needs and does not have without her. . . . The husband will cast a vision and direction for the family oriented around God's Kingdom purposes—in other words, he will have a strategic plan for how his household will serve the Lord in the church and community.[6]

Most hierarchs espouse this view today.

Source

Heterarch Philip Payne believes that instead of *authoritative leader*, Paul meant for the metaphor *head* to communicate *source*. One reason is because Paul calls Jesus the *Savior* and not the *leader* in his relationship with the church; thus Paul is saying that the husband is more the savior than the authority in relationship to his wife.[7] "Paul explains that 'head' means 'savior' here, for Christ is the source of life, love, and nourishment for the church as husbands should be for their wives. 'Source' is better established as a meaning for 'head' in Hellenistic Greek than 'leader' or 'authority.'"[8]

Payne backs up this concept with passages like Colossians 1:15–20, where Paul describes Jesus as "the head of the body, the church" (v. 18). This passage emphasizes that the church is sourced in Christ because he is the Christian's

---

5. Grudem, *EFBT*, Appendix 3, "Over Fifty Examples of *Kephalē* ('Head') Meaning 'Authority Over/Ruler' in Ancient Literature," 544–51.
6. Robert Saucy, "The Ministry of Women in the Early Church," in *Women and Men in Ministry: A Complementary Perspective*, eds. Robert L. Saucy and Judith K. TenElshof (Chicago: Moody, 2001), 137.
7. Philip B. Payne, *Man and Woman, One in Christ: An Exegetical and Theological Study of Paul's Letters* (Grand Rapids: Zondervan, 2009), 283–90. For a fuller explanation of this view, see chap. 15, "Ephesians 5:21–33 and Colossians 3:18–19: Husband-Wife Relationships," 271–90.
8. Payne, *Man and Woman*, 290.

creator and reconciler, and by his blood he is the source of their redemption. In the same way, the husband provides love, protection, nourishment, and tender care for his wife. He is her savior in the sense that he saves her from physical harm and all kinds of difficulties. Payne writes that in the first century, "Wives depended on their husbands as the source of food, clothing, shelter, the physical source of her children, and her emotional source of love."[9] Thus, the emphasis is not on his authority over her but on his cherishing and providing for her. He contends, "When a husband is the 'head' of his wife in this sense, his wife has good reason to submit to him . . . [as] a joyous response."[10]

Payne provides fifteen key reasons why *kephalē* should be translated as "source" and not "authority," to refute Grudem's appendix of examples that he insists show that this metaphor must be interpreted as authority.[11] William Witt agrees with Payne that the metaphor *head* is best translated as "source" or "origin" and adds another consideration in response to Grudem.

> For Paul, "head" (*kephalē*) and "origin" (*arche*) seem largely equivalent. . . . Crucial for the discussion in Ephesians, however, is not how the metaphor might or might not have been used in military or political settings—which are not the context here—but how it was used in reference to the family, and how it is used in reference to Christ.[12]

He also aligns with Payne by saying that the context of Ephesians 5:21–33 does not allow for the notion of a top-down giving of orders, but of mutual love and care, nourishment and protection, and like Christ who gave himself sacrificially for the church, the husband gives himself sacrificially for his wife.[13]

Many heterarchs have argued that when Paul used the metaphor *head* in Ephesians 5:21–33, he was communicating that the husband serves as the source of many blessings in the life of his wife and that the context does not support the English meaning of *head* as boss or authority. They base this principle on Ephesians 5:21, "Submit to one another out of reverence for Christ," and the mandates in the text that wives submit to their husbands and husbands sacrifice for their wives, constructing a mutual environment of giving, sharing, and working together.

---

9. Payne, *Man and Woman,* 288.
10. Payne, *Man and Woman,* 289.
11. Payne, *Man and Woman,* 118–37; Grudem, "Appendix 1," *EFBT*, 425–68.
12. William Witt, *Icons of Christ: A Biblical and Systematic Theology for Women's Ordination* (Waco, TX: Baylor University Press, 2020), 113.
13. For Witt's full argument, see *Icons of Christ,* 112–43.

Andrew Bartlett argues that Grudem and Payne are correct that *kephalē* was used to mean both authority and source in ancient times[14] but counters that "metaphorical meaning is not determined by usage elsewhere but by context."[15]

One-Flesh Union

Sarah Sumner offers an alternative view. She argues that wives are commanded to submit to their husbands, and nowhere in Scripture are husbands commanded to specifically submit to their wives.[16] But neither does the Bible say anywhere that husbands are to lead their wives. The words "lead," "leader," or even "servant leader" or "spiritual leader" are absent from any biblical text on marriage.[17] While wives are to submit to their husbands, husbands are to sacrifice for their wives, making marriage more of a complementary lifting one another up for mutual edification rather than one exercising authority over another.[18] She also contends that the word "headship" is absent in the Bible and nowhere can we find the common saying that "the husband is the head of the home,"[19] as if he is the boss of everything that goes on there. Instead, she insists that the husband as the head of the wife evokes an entirely different concept.

She bases this idea on her interpretation of the metaphor *head* as neither authority nor source. Her argument goes something like this: Marriage is a one-flesh union. The metaphor Paul uses here is the picture of this physical union: The husband is the head, the upper part of this organic physical body. "Head" simply means "head." And the wife is the body, the part under the head of this organic physical body. She comes under him to lift him up, and then he does the same for her. Together they compose one body. This union is deeply mysterious and the biblical picture of one flesh.[20]

Sumner argues that the context of Ephesians 5:21–33 supports this interpretation of the one-flesh metaphor *head*:

- In 5:23 Paul says, "the husband is the head of the wife as Christ is the head of the church, his body, of which he is the Savior." So Paul clearly

14. Andrew Bartlett, *Men and Women in Christ: Fresh Light from the Biblical Texts* (London: InterVarsity, 2019), 117–20.
15. Bartlett, *Men and Women in Christ*, 120.
16. In 1 Corinthians 7:3–5, Paul does remind his readers of a husband's and wife's mutual authority over the other's body.
17. Sarah Sumner, *Men and Women in the Church: Building Consensus on Christian Leadership* (Downers Grove, IL: InterVarsity, 2003), 160. See also Ronald W. Pierce and Elizabeth A. Kay, "Mutuality in Marriage and Singleness: 1 Corinthians 7:1–40," *DBE*, 108–25.
18. Sumner, *Men and Women in the Church*, 169–71.
19. But Paul admonishes the women to "manage their homes" (1 Tim. 5:14) from the Greek οἰκοδεσποτέω, which means to rule over the house.
20. Sumner, *Men and Women in the Church*, 161–71.

makes the comparison—the husband is the head of the wife, his body, as Christ is the head of "his body," the church. As a result, we commonly call the church the "body of Christ." And Paul emphasizes that as the *head*, Christ is the *Savior* of the body. As such, he submitted himself to save the body.

- In 5:28 Paul instructs the husband to love his wife the way he loves his own body. He is to treat and care for the needs of his wife as he cares for himself. In other words, she is him; they are one.
- In 5:31 Paul quotes Genesis 2:24 in describing the beauty and mystery of marriage, "For this reason a man will leave his father and mother and be united to his wife, and the two will become one flesh."[21]
- Paul goes on to describe this unity of husband and wife as a "profound mystery" in verse 32. Sumner asks, "What is mysterious about a leader being coupled with his helper? Not very much. Nor is it particularly inspiring. But it is altogether breathtaking to see the biblical picture of body and head joined mysteriously as one."[22]

She argues that Jesus's response to the Pharisees when they questioned him on divorce (Matthew 19:1–6) supports this interpretation of the metaphor *head*.

> "Haven't you read," he replied, "that at the beginning the Creator 'made them male and female,' and said, 'For this reason a man will leave his father and mother and be united to his wife, and the two will become one flesh'? So they are no longer two, but one flesh. Therefore what God has joined together, let no one separate." (vv. 4–6)

Sumner then compares divorce to a bloody decapitation, one of the reasons God is so vehemently opposed to it.[23]

Lucy Peppiatt gives this analogy an application: "If the husband is the 'head' in an analogous sense to Christ as the head, he is the one who lays down his life in order to raise his wife up. He behaves to her as Christ behaves to her as the one who confers love, loyalty, dignity, status, honour, and power; he is the lifter of her head."[24]

---

21. Sumner lays out her view on pp. 161–62. For the full argument see chapter 13, "The Husband *Is* the Head," 154–72.
22. Sumner, *Men and Women in the Church*, 167.
23. Sumner, *Men and Women in the Church*, 164–67.
24. Lucy Peppiatt, "Talking Heads 1: The Cornerstone," *Theological Miscellany*, WTC Theology, Feb. 10, 2016, https://wtctheology.org.uk/theomisc/talking-heads-cornerstone.

Summary

Clearly, we need to determine our interpretation of *head* in the New Testament to help us know God's desires concerning how men and women best relate to one another in marriage, in the church, and in the community. We've just scratched the surface concerning scholars' research on this topic, but we hope this overview provides some insight into the varied approaches. We've attempted to give you reliable sources to follow up as you make your determination. It's just one more piece of the puzzle, so keep learning, thinking, and trusting God to guide you into his truth.

REFLECTION QUESTIONS

1. What is a metaphor?

2. Why can interpreting biblical metaphors be tricky?

3. What did you think when you learned that the phrase "the husband is the head of the home" isn't in the Bible?

4. Of the three explanations of "head" in Ephesians 5:21–33, which rings most true for you? Why?

5. If you are married, what difference would adopting one of these views of "head" make in your marriage?

Must Women Cover Their Heads in Church?

For many decades, women paraded into Easter Sunday church services displaying their newest bonnet or hat. In fact, in the United States, women wore hats regularly during worship and social occasions, and even today, in the American South at least, observers can still witness men pulling off their caps during public prayer. Primarily a cultural phenomenon, the wearing and removing of head coverings during worship has echoes (and perhaps roots) in Scripture.

The body of believers in Corinth struggled with a number of besetting sins, including immorality (1 Cor. 3) and frivolous lawsuits (1 Cor. 6). In 1 Corinthians 11:3–12, the apostle Paul addressed those praying and prophesying in the church with yet another correction. This one involved their appearance.

When I (Sue) taught the Bible in Rwanda, Africa, some of my female students wore brightly colored headdresses to match their outfits in response to this text, while others did not. And when time came for questions, the first question concerned which group of women was right. How would you have answered?

Let's walk our way through this controversial, confusing, and difficult passage verse by verse. Entire books have been written on it and theories abound, continuing to spark disagreements between Bible experts as well as everyday people who desire to obey the Bible but don't really know what this passage requires them to do.

Why Does Paul Begin by Talking About "Heads"?

"But I want you to realize that the head of every man is Christ, and the head of every woman is man, and the head of Christ is God" (1 Cor. 11:3). Paul starts off his argument making a point about their "heads." He establishes a principle that they need to know in order to understand his directives that follow. What does he mean by the metaphor *head*? Scholars disagree. In Question 21, we look in detail at varied views, but here's a recap.

Hierarchs

Hierarchs believe "head" (*kephalē*) communicates the idea of "authority," so they interpret the metaphors in verse 3 this way:

> Christ holds authority over men.
> Men hold authority over women.
> God holds authority over Christ.[1]

Verse 3 is a pivotal passage for hierarchs, who see the text as saying Christ is the authority over the church, men are authorities over women, and God, the Father, has authority over Christ, the Son, who responds with submission.[2] Thus, the stage is set to see Paul's mandates that follow in light of men's authority over women and how that authority will be fleshed out in their appearances.

Heterarchs

Most heterarchs don't believe the term "head" in verse 3 denotes "authority." They point out that if Paul wanted to emphasize a ranking of authority, he would have listed the heads there in a hierarchical way, God first, then Christ, and then man—but he did not. Instead of what one might expect if hierarchy were in view, the order is Christ, Man, God.

> Hierarchical order: God, Christ, Man
> Paul's order: Christ, Man, God

As a result, they argue that verse 3 must mean something else as a foundation for what follows.

Gilbert Bilezikian writes that Paul's order doesn't reflect a hierarchy but instead a chronological historical order. He contends that first-in-sequence Christ

---

1. See, e.g., Jack Cottrell, *Feminism and the Bible: An Introduction to Feminism* (Joplin, MO: College Press, 1992), 14; Mark C. Black, "1 Cor. 11:2–16—A Re-Investigation," in *Essays on Women in Earliest Christianity*, vol. 1, ed. Carroll D. Osburn (Eugene, OR: Wipf & Stock, 2007), 191; Thomas R. Schreiner, "Head Coverings, Prophecies, and the Trinity: 1 Corinthians 11:2–16," *RBMW*, 127.
2. Some charge that insisting that the Father is the authority over Christ is not biblical and similar to a heresy from Arius, a theologian in the fourth century who relegated the second person of the Trinity, the Son, to a lesser position within the Godhead. To avoid charges that such a view of Christ leans too close to Arianism, some proponents of the view that "head" here means "authority" clarify that Christ's submission to the Father was limited to Jesus's earthly mission. In Question 39, "How Does One's View of the Trinity Shape Relationships between Men and Women?" we discuss this debate (known as the "Subordination Debate") and the various related views.

was the source of Adam in the sense that he created Adam (Col. 1:15–16). Next, Adam's body became the source of woman when she was created out of him. And finally, God, as the Holy Spirit in Mary's womb, became the source of Jesus at his earthly birth. Thus, this opening section of Paul's arguments refers to the unity, interdependence, and connection of the pairs rather than one of them being the boss or authority over the other. This pairing relates to Paul's later reference to man and woman's interdependence in 1 Cor. 11:11–12.[3]

Philip Payne and Andrew Bartlett also interpret "head" as "source," reading the metaphors chronologically as follows:[4]

> Christ is the source of humankind's creation.
> Man is the source of woman, who was created out of his body.
> God is the source of Jesus because of the incarnation in which he sent Jesus to redeem humankind.[5]

Thus, they also understand these relationships to be highlighting what they believe is the interconnectedness and closeness communicated by the pairings. In this view, Paul is emphasizing the interdependence and mutuality between men and women and between God the Father and God the Son. So instead of Paul emphasizing Jesus's authority over people, he's emphasizing that Christ is their source of life, unconditional love, and salvation, based on passages like Colossians 1:15–20: "The Son is the image of the invisible God, the firstborn over all creation. For in him all things were created. . . . He is before all things, and in him all things hold together. . . . For God was pleased to have all his fullness dwell in him, and through him to reconcile to himself all things." This view sets up the reader for an entirely different meaning related to what follows.

Appearances Concerning Corinthian Men's and Women's Heads

> Every man who prays or prophesies with his head *covered* dishonors his head. But every woman who prays or prophesies with her head *uncovered* dishonors her head—it is the same as having her head shaved. For if a woman does not cover her head, she might as well have her hair cut off; but if it is a disgrace for a woman to have her hair cut off or her head shaved, then she should cover her head. (1 Cor. 11:4–6, emphasis added)

3. Gilbert Bilezikian, *Beyond Sex Roles: What the Bible Says about a Woman's Place in Church and Family* (Grand Rapids: Baker, 1985), 138.
4. Philip B. Payne writes an entire chapter on verses 2 and 3 that lays out his view in detail ("1 Corinthians 11:2–3: Head/Source Relationships," in *MWOC*, 113–39).
5. Andrew Bartlett, *Men and Women in Christ: Fresh Light from the Biblical Texts* (London: InterVarsity, 2019), 144.

Before we attempt to discern what Paul wants Corinthian men and women to do related to their "heads," let's observe three important points we can glean from these two verses.

- Both men and women are praying and prophesying in the public gathering. Paul seems to affirm that both voices contribute something worthwhile, and this practice is fine.
- There is a distinction between what women and men are to do; thus, Paul affirms the brilliant and beautiful reality that God created men and women differently and the way they look needs to reflect that.
- Historically, a woman's shaved head was a natural sign of disgrace. For example, after World War II, British and French women who consorted with Nazi soldiers had their heads shaved to shame them and draw attention to their disloyalty.

What's Hair Got to Do with It?

On the surface, the way English translations read would lead us to the conclusion that Paul is saying that women should wear some kind of head covering, maybe a veil or shawl over their heads, or for my African sisters, brightly colored headdresses. This fits with our pictures of Israeli women on our Christmas cards or Muslim women's veils or burkas. But Corinth is not in Israel or the Middle East. It's an important first-century city in the Gentile Roman Empire. And the word "head covering" is not in the text. Instead, Greek verbiage in verse 4 actually says, "having down from the head." Consequently, this phrase could mean a cloth head covering, or it could just as easily be the way men and women were wearing their hair and what that communicated in that culture. To discern Paul's meaning, we need to know if it was typical for Greek and Roman women to wear veils, burkas, or any kind of headdresses, as well as what men's hairstyles communicated to others. What were the first-century Corinthian social conventions related to heads and hairstyles?

Greek and Roman Women's Hairstyles

Apparently, some female Corinthian women were doing something shameful—breaking social conventions related to their heads—and Paul is correcting them. What then would communicate godly beauty at that time? "The extensive evidence from portraiture, frescos, sculpture, and vase paintings in Greek and Roman cities of Paul's day almost universally depicts respectable women with their hair done up."[6] Most artifacts of Paul's day don't show women wearing veils or any covering over their hair. Instead, they wore their

---

6. One can find illustrations of first-century Greek and Roman women in Rolf Hurschmann, "Hairstyle," in *New Pauly Encyclopedia of the Ancient World*, eds. Hubert Cancik and Helmuth Schneider (Leiden: Brill, 2005), 5:1099–1103.

hair in all sorts of elaborate and even ostentatious massive beehives and ornate patterns, requiring lengthy grooming sessions. It's likely that some Christian women were imitating these extreme fashions, as some women do today—so much so that Paul asked women in Ephesus to "dress modestly, with decency and propriety, adorning themselves, not with elaborate hairstyles" (1 Tim. 2:9). But this doesn't mean that Paul was instructing women to wear their hair down, loose and wild, or to cover up their head with a cloth. Richard Hays explains: "For women to have loose hair in public, however, was conventionally seen as shameful, a sign associated either with prostitutes or—perhaps worse from Paul's point of view—with women caught up in the ecstatic worship practices of the cults associated with Dionysius, Cybele, and Isis."[7]

If women were not to wear their hair loose or imitate the ostentatious styles of done-up hair that worldly women in Corinth were wearing, what was Paul asking godly women to do? Bruce Winter writes, "Statue types displayed the simple hairstyles which epitomized the modest wife and were worn by members of the imperial family. These statues were replicated throughout the Empire and represented 'fashion icons' to be copied by modest married women."[8]

We believe that Paul is suggesting that a Christian woman in Corinth wear her hair neatly over her head, typically twisted and tied up with some sort of fastener, so as not to call undo attention to herself as she prayed and prophesied, but to focus attention on Christ. Later, we will talk about a related principle we can draw out of the text and apply today in any culture.

Heterarchs Bartlett and Payne agree that in 1 Corinthians 11:2–16 Paul isn't instructing women to cover their heads to express they are under the authority of their husbands. Rather, Paul is concerned about something else that men's and women's hairstyles could communicate when they were praying and prophesying. Bartlett writes:

> Paul's concern is not about hair itself, but about the dishonourable message given by the Corinthians' hairstyles. Their conduct should honour God's purposes for men and women as taught in Genesis. . . . Relevantly, those purposes involve faithful, monogamous, heterosexual marriage. Paul also emphasizes redemption in Christ: though differentiated by their sexuality in creation, in redemption men and women are united in the Lord. . . . Prayer and prophecy should be

7. Richard B. Hays, *First Corinthians: Interpretation: A Bible Commentary for Teaching and Preaching* (Louisville: Westminster John Knox, 2011), 185–86.
8. Bruce W. Winter, *Roman Wives, Roman Widows: The Appearance of New Women and the Pauline Communities* (Grand Rapids: Eerdmans, 2003), 104.

undertaken . . . in a way that honours God, the source both
of creation and of redemption.[9]

Sandra Glahn suggests, "Most likely the wives in Corinth were 'letting down
their hair,' a practice probably associated with spiritual freedom in Dionysus
worship. But doing so was the equivalent to taking off their wedding rings,
which shamed their husbands and suggested they were 'available.'"[10]

Social Conventions Related to Men's Hairstyles

H. Herter documents the moral indignation over effeminate hairstyles
by men with over a hundred references to effeminate hair from classical antiquity, the greatest number coming from around Paul's time.[11] Men adver-
tised their desire for homosexual liaisons by their effeminate hair,[12] coming
"down from the head," and dressing like women, just as they sometimes do
today. We observe long, effeminate hair on first- and second-century statues
of Dionysus—a member of the Greek pantheon. And Dionysus was apparently celebrated in Corinth.[13]

A quick look at busts, coins, and artifacts of first-century honorable men
in the Roman Empire reveals that most wore their hair short-cropped, sometimes with forked locks or ringlets around the forehead. Paul is concerned
about what is "proper" for godly men in Corinthian culture too.

What's the Point?

It's simple. God created men and women distinct from one another and
their appearance and actions need to picture propriety, dignity, honor, respect,
biblical morality, and modesty; however, those qualities are communicated in
the culture where they live. Both men and women represent Jesus to outsiders.
When our appearance and behavior draw people to Jesus, God delights. In this
instance, if a veil or headdress is meaningless to people who don't know Jesus,
don't wear them. That's what I told my African students, and they cheered.

---

9. Bartlett, *Men and Women in Christ*, 158.
10. Sandra Glahn, "Who Were the Women with Shaved Heads (1 Cor. 11:5)?," *Engage* (blog),
    Bible.org, Sept. 30, 2014, https://blogs.bible.org/who-were-the-women-with-shaved-heads
    -1-cor-115.
11. H. Herter, "Effeminatus," *Reallexikon fuer Antike und Christentum*, 4:620–50. See also
    James B. Hurley, "Man and Woman in 1 Corinthians: Some Exegetical Studies in Pauline
    Theology and Ethics" (PhD diss., University of Cambridge, 1973), 54.
12. David F. Greenberg, *The Construction of Homosexuality* (Chicago: University of Chicago
    Press, 1988), 154.
13. Pausanias, in the second century AD, wrote, "On the market-place [of Corinth], where most
    of the sanctuaries are, stand . . . wooden images of Dionysus, which are covered with gold
    with the exception of their faces; these are ornamented with red paint" (*Description of Greece*,
    vol. 2, *Corinth*, trans. W. H. S. Jones [Cambridge, MA: Harvard University Press, 1918],
    2.2.6–7, https://sourcebooks.fordham.edu/ancient/pausanias-bk2.asp).

What's Glory Got to Do with It?

"A man ought not to cover his head, since he is the image and glory of God; but woman is the glory of man. For man did not come from woman, but woman from man" (1 Cor. 11:7–8). Traditionally, scholars thought Paul was saying that, compared with woman, man is a more direct reflection of God and man has a more direct relationship with God. Such status resulted in seeing men as superior to women and thus holding more authority in contrast to the inferior and subordinate status of woman. Eighteenth-century preacher John Gill summarizes this line of thinking: "Man was first originally and immediately the image and glory of God, the woman only secondarily and mediately through man. The man is more perfectly and conspicuously the image and glory of God, on account of his more extensive dominion and authority."[14] A desire to distance themselves from this "traditional" view of women is part of why hierarchs coined the label "complementarian." Those who self-describe with this label embrace man's authority in relation to woman while rejecting the superiority/inferiority foundation that once undergirded it.

Verse 7 says that "woman is the glory of man." What do current scholars think Paul meant by this phrase? What does it mean that women are men's "glory"? Hierarchs and heterarchs disagree.

Hierarchs

Hierarch Thomas Schreiner grounds his view of this text in male authority. He states, "Since woman came from man, she was meant to be his glory, i.e., she should honor him."[15] Because men are in authority over women (v. 3), women should wear a head covering to honor them. "Paul's point is that one should always honor and respect the source[16] from which one came. And woman honors man by wearing a head covering, thereby showing that man is the head, i.e., the authority."[17]

John Coe describes men as the "radiant and weighty self-expression of God, the chief agent to exalt Him, so woman is created out of man, and, as such, is his glory, the radiant and weighty expression of man."[18] He goes on to claim that verse 7 "flies in the face of the contemporary view that woman's

---

14. John Gill, *Exposition of the Entire Bible* [1746–1763], Internet Sacred Texts Archive, https://www.sacred-texts.com/bib/cmt/gill/index.htm.

15. Schreiner, "Head Coverings, Prophecies, and the Trinity," 133.

16. Note how Schreiner simultaneously embraces both metaphors, ascribing to *kephalē* the meaning of both source and authority. His explanation of 1 Corinthians 11 remains the dominant hierarchical argument.

17. Schreiner, "Head Coverings, Prophecies, and the Trinity," 133.

18. John Coe, "Being Faithful to Christ in One's Gender: Theological Reflections on Masculinity and Femininity," *Women and Men in Ministry: A Complementary Perspective*, eds. Robert L Saucy and Judith K. TenElshof (Chicago: Moody, 2001), 216.

flourishing is not necessarily tied to the man's or vice versa."[19] He asserts that growth in Christ for both men and women is connected to them functioning in their proper roles in the church, home, and in society.[20]

Andreas and Margaret Köstenberger write, "Paul again echoes Genesis 2, contending that the woman's purpose is essentially oriented toward the man. Rather than arguing that authority and submission are completely interchangeable, Paul affirms the difference and distinctiveness of male and female in the creation order and the divine purpose for the man and the woman."[21]

Schreiner agrees that "woman was created to assist and help man is clear from the Pauline commentary in verses 7–9."[22]

Heterarchs

Philip Payne sees the meaning of "woman is the glory of man" in a much different light, more related to Paul's previous comments about condemning homosexuality and affirming gender distinctiveness and biblical morality by one's appearance and actions. He believes that Paul is saying that "woman, not another man, is the glory of man" in that woman is the proper sexual partner for man.[23] He writes,

> The glory of someone is the person in whom he glories, as the man glories over the woman in Genesis 2:23. Woman is depicted as the crowning glory of creation made specifically to be man's partner. Most men would agree that of all creation, woman is the most beautiful. The history of art typically exalts woman as the fairest of God's creation. . . . When husbands treat their wives as their glory, marriage is beautiful.[24]

He insists that looking at the text from this perspective in no way implies or suggests that woman is any less in the image of God or the glory of God, but that men and women reflect God's glory together.[25]

Concerning verses 8 and 9 ("For man did not come from woman, but woman from man; neither was man created for woman, but woman for man"), Payne asserts, "Man was the source from which God made woman. Woman is the glory of man, for she came from him. It is because she corresponds to

19. Coe, "Faithful to Christ in One's Gender," 216.
20. Coe, "Faithful to Christ in One's Gender," 216.
21. Andreas J. Köstenberger and Margaret E. Köstenberger, *God's Design for Man and Woman: A Biblical–Theological Survey* (Wheaton, IL: Crossway, 2014), 176.
22. Thomas R. Schreiner, "Women in Ministry: Response," in *Two Views on Women in Ministry*, eds. James R. Beck and Craig L. Blomberg (Grand Rapids: Zondervan, 2005), 227.
23. Philip B. Payne, *MWOC*, 179.
24. Payne, *Man and Woman, One in Christ*, 179.
25. Payne, *Man and Woman, One in Christ*, 180.

him, having come from him, that she can complement him as his mate. God's central purpose in creating woman from man was to create an intimate and procreative partner for man (Gen 1:27–28, 2:20)."[26]

Bartlett also sees this passage as including a warning to the Corinthians as relating to sexual mores. If men were growing their hair long, he reasons, they were looking effeminate—not honoring their status as God's image-bearers charged with procreation and filling the earth (Gen. 1:27–28). Women should put their hair up to avoid any hint of promiscuity, evidently a cultural practice in Corinth, thereby allowing their husbands to "glory"—delight—in them.[27]

Whose Authority?

> It is for this reason that a woman ought to have *authority over her own head*, because of the angels. (1 Cor. 11:10 NIV, emphasis added)

> That is why a wife ought to have *a symbol of* authority on her head, because of the angels. (1 Cor. 11:10 ESV, emphasis added)

Notice the opposite meanings between these two interpretations.[28] One says women should exercise their own authority, and the other says someone else should have authority over them. In the original Greek, the phrase "a symbol of" does not exist. Yet several English translations add it to the verse. Why?

Hierarchs who see authority structures throughout this passage assume Paul is speaking of the authority of man over woman, so in order to make Paul's sentence make sense, translators had to add the phrase "a symbol of." The head covering becomes the symbol of male authority.[29]

Heterarchs refer to the original Greek and ask why translators add a phrase that reverses the meaning of the original? For a woman to have authority on her own head could mean Paul is telling her to exercise authority over her own hair—to pin it up![30] He could be directing her to use discretion and remember that her appearance reflects Christ.

---

26. Payne, *Man and Woman, One in Christ*, 181–82.
27. Bartlett, *Men and Women in Christ*, 146.
28. Note also that the old King James Version reads, "For this cause ought the woman to have power on her head," whereas the New King James Version reads, "For this reason the woman ought to have *a symbol of* authority on *her* head."
29. Schreiner, "Head Coverings, Prophecies, and the Trinity," 135.
30. Bartlett, *Men and Women in Christ*, 149.

What About the Angels?

Next, Paul gives a reason why some of the Corinthians need to amend their appearance and actions—"because of the angels." What in the world is he talking about? Scholars espouse several ideas as possibilities, but we don't know for sure:

- Perhaps Paul was referring to angels, spiritual witnesses, who delight when worshippers honor God and one another by their appearances and actions. If so, watching the Corinthians' poor worship habits may have grieved them.
- The word *angelos* means "messenger," and while most often the Bible refers to spiritual servants of God, sometimes the word refers to human beings sent as messengers. Winter offers the suggestion that perhaps local officials were visiting church services to verify that Christian gatherings conformed to civil law. Given Paul's concern that the church avoids offending those in the believers' surrounding culture, perhaps he wrote to instruct them on more appropriate appearance during public worship, since such messengers would be present.[31]

Interconnectedness and Mutuality

"Nevertheless, in the Lord woman is not independent of man, nor is man independent of woman. For as woman came from man, so also man is born of woman. But everything comes from God" (1 Cor. 11:11–12). Paul finishes this part of his instructions with a beautiful passage that highlights the joy and delight that should be evident when Christian brothers and sisters respect, honor, and depend on one another. Note that he emphasizes that this attitude and behavior is expected when men and women are "in the Lord." He expects Christians to act humbly and to view our lives, relationships, and "everything" as coming from the Lord.

Neither sex, he admonishes, should be too quick to claim dominance. Woman is sourced in man in creation, but Paul highlights that in giving birth, woman is man's source. This may be an intentional statement to counterbalance any misunderstanding of his earlier teaching, which some men might use to mistreat or undervalue women. Both sexes are necessary and valuable—"and all things come from God."

Summary

First Corinthians is an important and pivotal text to help us understand how God wants men and women to treat one another and function together both in ministry and in the home. Some see Paul affirming their view that for Christians to thrive and represent God well in the world, they must live

---

31. Winter, *Roman Wives, Roman Widows*, 89.

according to God's creation order in Genesis and desired male authority. Others believe this text doesn't uphold those beliefs but instead affirms the beauty of gender differences, proper sexual identity, and mutuality, as well as how appearance and actions should communicate these values and differences.

Whatever you determine Paul is communicating in this important passage, we hope that we will all echo Michelle Lee-Barnewall's sentiments when she writes,

> The corporate identity of the church, not individual rights or personal power and position, provides a more fitting perspective for understanding gender. The goal of the church as Christ's body and bride is to be wholly dedicated to him and through the Spirit to live in holiness and in loving and sacrificial relationships with one another. The orientation is not simply toward the benefits or rights of women and men in the new age. Rather believers are called to become a community that pursues holiness, submission, and devotion to God through the Spirit in imitation of Christ.[32]

REFLECTION QUESTIONS

1. What experiences have you encountered with this so-called command that women should wear hats or veils in church?

2. What were the meanings of hairstyles for men and women in the Roman Empire at the time Paul wrote this letter?

3. What difference would these first-century hairstyles make in what Paul's directions would mean for the original audiences?

4. What do you think Paul would want for Christians attempting to follow his directions today?

5. What confusion has the various interpretations of this passage caused through the ages?

---

32. Michelle Lee-Barnewall, *Neither Complementarian nor Egalitarian: A Kingdom Corrective to the Evangelical Gender Debate* (Grand Rapids: Baker Academic, 2016), 177.

How Do Christians Reach Different Conclusions on 1 Timothy 2:11–15?

Heterarchs tend to appeal to the cultural and historical situation in Ephesus, where Timothy was, for their interpretation of this controversial text. Hierarchs dispute heterarchs' analysis and how it applies to the meaning of 1 Timothy 2:11–15. What do we mean by appealing to the cultural and historical context?

In his letters, Paul addresses a variety of situations specific to each church. In Question 4, we discussed when a biblical issue is "cultural" and when the meaning should be taken at face value, just as it's written on the page, without taking the situation into consideration. We talked about our mandate to figure out what the original author meant for the original audience.

To do that in Paul's first letter to Timothy, heterarchs argue that it's critical to understand the historical and cultural context to understand the author's original intent. Hierarchs also affirm that the historical and cultural context is important, but heterarchs charge that in the instance of this critical text, they fail to do so.

If the concept of considering the cultural context is new to you, we suggest you mark your place, turn back, and digest Question 4. Then you'll be better prepared to understand the different views on 1 Timothy 2:11–15, possibly the most controversial of the arguments between heterarchs and hierarchs.

The Problem

Paul wrote this personal letter to his protégé Timothy, who was serving as his emissary in Ephesus, to help him address a number of problems there. The passage pertaining to women teaching, 2:11–15, includes many confusing or potentially contradictory ideas. Many heterarchs believe that without knowing what was going on at the time in Ephesus, we cannot truly understand why Paul wrote the way he did. They insist that this knowledge will help us reconcile what Paul meant with other biblical passages.

The Charge Concerning Some Hierarchs' Interpretive Approach

Heterarchs charge that in the case of 1 Timothy 2:11–15, some hierarch scholars and pastors use a more literalist approach to Paul's words, without considering enough what was going on in Ephesus at the time. They claim that, for this reason, when Paul writes in 2:12, "I do not permit a woman to teach or to assume authority over a man; she must be quiet," hierarchs insist that Paul was stating a universal principle for all time. Some hierarchs counter the heterarchs' charge by saying that an attempt to interpret Paul's words in light of cultural considerations would lead down a "slippery slope" to other errors and misinterpretations.

For example, to interpret differently than hierarchs do would open the door to excusing other prohibitions in the Bible, like homosexuality, and that those who reject the male authority they see taught in 1 Timothy 2:12 do not hold a high view of Scripture. Albert Mohler writes, "Simply put, the only way to affirm women serving in the pastoral role is to reject the authority and sufficiency of biblical texts such as . . . 1 Timothy 2."[1] Thomas Schreiner admits that "the complementarian position seems unloving and discriminatory to many, and the general atmosphere of our society encourages people to liberate themselves from traditional views."[2] But he insists that "the truth or falsity of both views must be established by an intensive exegesis of the biblical text."[3] He claims that heterarchs "rightly insist that the life setting of the letter must inform our interpretation and application of specific passages" but pushes back against many of the heterarchs' ideas related to culture, insisting that heterarchs use fragmentary cultural evidence to make a case that cannot stand up to rigorous analysis and hierarchs' rebuttals.[4]

The Heterarch View

First, many heterarchs conclude that cultural and historical context always helps readers understand a biblical passage. They insist that this method of studying the text is not "liberal" or a convenient way to get around the literal words on the page. By examining history and culture, they argue, readers learn about events, practices, people, beliefs, and places relevant to what's

---

1. Albert Mohler, "Women Pastors, Women Preachers, and the Looming Test of the Southern Baptist Convention," AlbertMohler.com, May 10, 2021, https://albertmohler.com/2021/05/10/women-pastors-women-preachers-and-the-looming-test-of-the-southern-baptist-convention.
2. Thomas R. Schreiner, "An Interpretation of 1 Timothy 2:9–15: A Dialogue with Scholarship," in *Women in the Church: An Interpretation and Application of 1 Timothy 2:9–15*, 3rd ed., eds. Andreas J. Köstenberger and Thomas R. Schreiner (Wheaton, IL: Crossway, 2016), 164–65.
3. Schreiner, "Interpretation of 1 Timothy 2:9–15," 165.
4. Schreiner, "Interpretation of 1 Timothy 2:9–15," 168. See the full chapter for a thorough treatment of Schreiner's argument, 163–225.

going on at the time. Although often this information isn't provided within the text per se, contextual clues shed light on the biblical writer's words and meaning.

In addition, if an author appears to be contradicting himself or other parts of Scripture, it's reasonable to look beyond a surface-level interpretation. Heterarchs insist that for many reasons, which we'll investigate in the following two chapters, 1 Timothy 2:11–15 fits this criterion. Thus, history and culture can play a part in examining the text as we seek to understand it more accurately.

For example, in 1 Timothy 2:15, Paul says, "Woman will be saved through childbearing." In order to understand this strange statement accurately, say heterarchs, we must look beyond the superficial, "plain" meaning to see what else may have been influencing Paul's choice of words. This is not "pulling the culture card" but instead doing due diligence with the text. Heterarchs charge that hierarchs, who acknowledge the importance of cultural and historical context in other texts, refuse to consider this when it comes to this particular passage.

What Issues Require an Examination of Culture?

Heterarchs insist that examining what was happening in the first century when Timothy was pastoring in Ephesus enables us to bring relevant clues into our evaluation of Paul's letter. Doing so testifies to a scholar's respect for Scripture and the desire to seek accurate interpretation in this text just like any other. Hierarchs agree that understanding culture is necessary, but they simply come to different conclusions in light of the historical and cultural context.[5]

Below are several arguments that heterarchs use to explain why it's reasonable to consider these cultural clues in order to draw out Paul's meaning. The points cited below will be covered in detail in the following two chapters, where you can decide for yourself which perspective best reflects what you think Paul meant.

We Already Appeal to Backgrounds to Interpret 1 Timothy 2

In verse 8, Paul writes, "Therefore, I want the men everywhere to pray, lifting up holy hands without anger or disputing." He exhorts Ephesian men to raise their hands when praying, but we have never heard anyone teach that men literally must do so today even though he says "everywhere." That seems to be an issue specific to Ephesus. Thus, a consistent approach requires us also to consider the cultural background to understand verses 11–15 concerning what Paul instructs women to do in Ephesus.

---

5. For an in-depth chapter on first-century Ephesian culture, see S. M. Baugh, "A Foreign World: Ephesus in the First Century," in *Women in the Church*, 25–64.

Scripture Itself Gives the Background

Acts 19 gives us the context for what was happening in Ephesus. In this chapter, we discover how Paul founded the church there. We also learn about some of the pagan practices involved in the worship of the goddess "Artemis of the Ephesians" (Acts 19:28). We understand her influence on the city, not only from history or archaeology, but also from Paul's experience in Ephesus as recorded by Luke in Acts. Artemis had such a hold on the city that a riot broke out, begun by merchants profiting from Artemis worship. People in Ephesus celebrated a yearly festival in her honor that brought tourists from all over the Roman Empire.

Angry over Paul's interference with their profits, the merchants drove Paul out of the city. Heterarchs argue that current research tells us more than ever about the Artemis cult, adding validity to the suggestion that the pagan worship of Artemis may have played a part in the accurate interpretation of several confusing Scripture passages. This research will be explained further in the following chapters.

Acknowledging Culture Is at Play Resolves Numerous Contradictions

Heterarchs use 1 Timothy 5 as an example to show how understanding the cultural setting can shed light on understanding a scriptural passage. In that text, Paul says he wants younger widows to marry and have children (v. 14). That differs drastically from the advice he gave people in Corinth (1 Corinthians 7:8–9). Readers have three options as to why he gives opposite advice: (1) Paul contradicts himself; (2) Paul changes his views on marriage; (3) Paul is addressing a cultural situation in Ephesus that differs from the one in Corinth with its rampant immorality. Hierarchs provide other explanations, which we will get to.

An Example Heterarchs Use

First Timothy 1:3 is another example of where culture might play an important role in interpretation, according to some heterarchs. They contend that Paul's first letter to Timothy influences the gender discussion because it contains the passage hierarchs use most to argue that women must not teach men in the Sunday service or church in general.[6] Let's examine it.

> As I urged you upon my departure for Macedonia, remain on at Ephesus so that you may instruct certain *men* not to teach strange doctrines. (NASB 1995)

> As I urged you when I was leaving for Macedonia, stay on in Ephesus to instruct certain *people* not to spread false teachings. (NET)

---

6. See Questions 24 and 25 for further discussion of 1 Timothy 2:11–15.

The first says "men," and the second says "people." Does it matter? Heterarchs say "yes," because they use 1 Timothy 1:3 to argue that hierarchs have misapplied the critical text, 1 Timothy 2:11–15.

Heterarchs insist that one reason the application of 1 Timothy 2:11–15 is limited to Ephesus and not for all time is because women, not just men, were teaching "strange doctrines." (In fact, Paul's reference in 1 Timothy 1:3 to leaving Timothy behind when he went to Macedonia refers to the account of his encounter with the Artemis cult in Acts 19–20, especially 20:1–6.) Heterarchs argue that the reality of Paul referencing both men and women is borne out by a number of passages in the letter, but that that truth is lost when the opening of the letter incorrectly makes it sound like only men were teaching. Sandra Glahn writes:

> English-speaking evangelicals are three to four times more likely than the population at large to use male wording when the original author had "people" in mind. And 1 Timothy 1:3 is an example of an instance in which it hurts us to do so. While we know the word "men" can really mean "people," we still tend to read the word "men" in 1 Timothy 1:3 as "males." And that leaves us thinking that males were the ones doing all the teaching, including falsehood, in Ephesus. Yet the word rendered "men" in 1 Timothy 1:3 is indeed the neuter pronoun *tisin*. *Tisin* carries no suggestion of male or female (as the NET Bible's rendering, "people," correctly suggests). So Timothy was to teach certain *people* not to teach strange doctrines.[7]

Where does culture enter into the picture? asks Glahn. Hierarchs believe that men do the teaching, so they naturally assume that Paul means men, and that translation supports their preconception, in spite of the fact, says Glahn, that the Greek pronoun is gender neutral, and really should be translated as "people." But the reader without knowledge of the Greek doesn't know that. Glahn continues, "Bible versions that choose the generic 'men' in 1 Timothy 1:3 skew readers' perception of Ephesian teaching: they will assume only men do it, when later portions of the letter talk about women engaged in false teaching as well."[8]

Other examples from 1 Timothy that heterarchs argue relate to both men and women teaching false doctrine include the following:

---

7. Sandra Glahn, "Does Paul Really Think Women are Gossips and Busybodies?," *Engage* (blog), Bible.org, April 29, 2015, https://blogs.bible.org/does-paul-really-think-women-are -gossips-and-busybodies.

8. Glahn, "Does Paul Really Think . . . ?"

As I urged you when I went to Macedonia, stay there in Ephesus so that you may command certain people not to teach false doctrines any longer or to devote themselves to myths and endless genealogies. Such things promote controversial speculations rather than advancing God's work— which is by faith. The goal of this command is love, which comes from a pure heart and a good conscience and a sincere faith. Some have departed from these and have turned to meaningless talk. They want to be teachers of the law, but they do not know what they are talking about or what they so confidently affirm. We know that the law is good if one uses it properly. (1:3–8)

In the same way, the women are to be worthy of respect, not malicious talkers but temperate and trustworthy in everything. (3:11)

The Spirit clearly says that in later times some will abandon the faith and follow deceiving spirits and things taught by demons. Such teachings come through hypocritical liars, whose consciences have been seared as with a hot iron. They forbid people to marry and order them to abstain from certain foods, which God created to be received with thanksgiving by those who believe and know the truth. . . . If you point these things out to the brothers and sisters, you will be a good minister of Christ Jesus, nourished on the truths of the faith and of the good teaching that you have followed. Have nothing to do with godless myths and old wives' tales; rather, train yourself to be godly. (4:1–3, 6–7)

As for younger widows, do not put them on such a list. For when their sensual desires overcome their dedication to Christ, they want to marry. Thus they bring judgment on themselves, because they have broken their first pledge. Besides they get into the habit of being idle and going about from house to house. And not only do they become idlers, but also busybodies who talk nonsense, saying things they ought not to. (5:11–13)

If anyone teaches otherwise and does not agree to the sound instruction of our Lord Jesus Christ and to godly teaching, they are conceited and understand nothing. They have an unhealthy interest in controversies and quarrels about words that result in envy, strife, malicious talk, evil suspicions, and constant friction between people of corrupt mind, who have been robbed of the truth and who think that godliness is a means to financial gain. (6:3–5)

Timothy, guard what has been entrusted to your care. Turn away from godless chatter and the opposing ideas of what is falsely called knowledge, which some have professed and in so doing have departed from the faith. (6:20–21)

Heterarch Linda Belleville contends that the entire text must be read in light of Paul's concern for the false teaching going on, and that this concern consumes about thirty-five percent of Paul's writing in his letter to Timothy.[9] She suggests that women were at "the center of this storm," and it was more serious than "nosiness or gossiping," evident from Paul's evaluation that "some have in fact already turned away to follow Satan" (1 Tim. 5:15).[10] She continues, "This would explain why women are the particular focus of Paul's prohibition in 1 Timothy 2:12–15. . . . Paul is not giving routine instruction. He is responding to a situation that has gotten out of hand."[11]

Heterarchs argue that undoubtedly many Ephesian women came to faith out of the pagan Artemis cult. History and archeology affirm that women were extremely involved and were also key leaders in the kinds of occult practices that Luke wrote about in Acts 19. Paul's writings to Timothy affirm that many Ephesian women liked to express themselves to others and could easily have believed that they should be the ones teaching in the house churches. Many may have tried to do that.

Heterarchs suggest the possibility that women who had been former Artemis worshippers and even leaders in that pagan cult attempted to step into leadership and teaching roles before they were mature and had learned sound doctrine. In that case, Paul's limitations for women might not be universal, for all women for all time, but instead just for those particular women in Ephesus.

Hierarchs disagree. The Köstenbergers say that the political climate in Ephesus was decidedly Roman and not feminist, overseen by the Roman emperor, Augustus.[12] They acknowledge, "The religious climate was dominated by the Artemis cult, centered in the Artemisium, the largest building in the Greek world (four times larger than the Athenian Parthenon). Nevertheless,

9. Linda L. Belleville, *Women Leaders and the Church: Three Crucial Questions* (Grand Rapids: Baker, 2000), 165.
10. Belleville, *Women Leaders and the Church*, 166–67.
11. Belleville, *Women Leaders and the Church*, 167
12. Andreas J. Köstenberger and Margaret E. Köstenberger, *God's Design for Man and Woman: A Biblical-Theological Survey* (Wheaton, IL: Crossway, 2014), 197.

the cult hierarchy of Artemis Ephesia was controlled by the male political establishment."[13] S. M. Baugh agrees. He writes,

> A thorough presentation of all the institutions of Ephesus is not possible here, but in general, one must conclude from the abundant extant evidence (including an estimated six thousand recovered inscriptions) that Ephesus resembled other Hellenic city-states of the time with a fundamentally patriarchal social and political structure. . . . Some individual women rose to prominence in Ephesus, particularly in the second and third centuries. . . . But in the first century, based on our substantial evidence base, no woman at all filled municipal magistracies . . . , though a few did fill particular high-status priesthoods in the city and province. So the city is still best described as somewhat typically patriarchal.[14]

Will Including Cultural Context Solve Some Interpretive Problems?

According to heterarchs, many of the interpretive problems are solved when we limit Paul's admonition that women must not teach men to the text's particular setting and particular time in history. In addition, limiting Paul's command to the Ephesian Christian women helps us synthesize this controversial passage with other parts of the Bible. Glahn provides several examples:

1. We can reconcile contradictory advice given to Corinth versus Ephesus (1 Cor. 7:8; 1 Tim. 5:14).
2. We can reconcile 1 Timothy 2:11–15 with the whole canon that has women in numerous settings filled with the Spirit and proclaiming the Word publicly with men present.
3. We can eliminate the question of how old a male must be when he must stop learning from women (1 Tim. 2:12).
4. We can see that all humans who are given spiritual gifts can use them for the good of the body and are not limited to the nuclear family (1 Cor. 12:21–31).
5. We solve the issue of how it could be possible that women are restricted from teaching because of Eve (the logic being she is worse for being deceived) but men are not restricted because of Adam, who knowingly sinned, with full comprehension that he was doing wrong. Rather, we can read the creation story as both the man and the woman being fully responsible. This also resolves the apparent contradiction between 1 Timothy, where Eve is seen as more responsible,

---

13. Köstenberger and Köstenberger, *God's Design for Man and Woman*, 198.
14. Baugh, "Ephesus in the First Century," 32.

and Romans 5, where the man appears more responsible. We can't
have it both ways.[15]

Hierarchs provide different answers to these difficult interpretive problems,
and they come to different conclusions on the basis of their extensive research
and arguments. The following two chapters will address the varied views on
1 Timothy 2:11–15 in detail and give you an opportunity to understand how
it is possible that well-meaning, godly, Bible-believing Christians reach such
vastly different conclusions concerning this pivotal text.

REFLECTION QUESTIONS

1. What do you think regarding women teaching men?

2. Where did your ideas come from?

3. Can you think of biblical passages that we apply differently today because
   they mean something different in our culture?

4. What do you think are some reasons why it might be better if women don't
   teach men?

5. What do you think are some reasons why it might be helpful if women do
   teach men?

---

15. Glahn, "Does Paul Really Think . . . ?"

What Are the Different Views of 1 Timothy 2:11–12?

No one talking about women in the church can get around 1 Timothy 2:11–12. When my (Sue's) students raise their hands to ask a question concerning women in ministry, often it's about understanding this text. Hierarchs feel compelled to comply with the "plain reading" of Scripture. Heterarchs insist that, in contrast, we should dig beyond surface appearances. As we might suspect, the two groups come to different conclusions, although they both admit that the passage includes some of the most confounding phrases in Scripture.

Hierarchs, "soft" and "hard" complementarians, point to this passage as their primary reasoning for women's limited activity in church leadership. Different translations use different wording:

> A woman should learn in quietness and full submission. I do not permit a woman to teach
>
> - or to assume authority (NIV)
> - or to have authority (CSB, NRSV, RSV, NKJV)
> - or to exercise authority (ESV, NET)
> - nor to usurp authority (KJV)[1]
>
> over a man; she must be quiet. For Adam was formed first, then Eve. And Adam was not the one deceived; it was the woman who was deceived and became a sinner. But women

---

1. The meaning of the verb αὐθεντεῖν, a hapax legomenon (a term used only one time in the Bible), is a critical piece on which translators disagree. Its significance will be addressed in the coming sections.

> will be saved through childbearing—if they continue in faith,
> love and holiness with propriety. (1 Tim. 2:11–15 NIV)

William Witt, a heterarch, calls it "the only passage in the entire Bible that on a literal reading might seem to exclude women from teaching or having authority over men."[2] Heterarchs agree that it is a critical passage to understand, while noting that almost every word in the verse is in some way controversial. We cannot cover the entire passage in one chapter but have split it up into three chapters. The last chapter covered interpretive issues related to this text, and this chapter and the next will discuss the text itself.

In this chapter, we will approach 2:11–12 by addressing a number of major questions, defining terms and grammatical issues, and eventually comparing how hierarchs and heterarchs use this passage to explain their stances.

What Is the Meaning and Significance of *Authentein*?

The word Paul uses for authority in 1 Timothy 2:12 is *authentein*. This term is found only here in the whole Bible. Heterarch scholars point out that Paul could have easily used the other more common term for authority (i.e., *exousia*). This term communicates the idea of giving permission, the right, the liberty, or the power to do something, and appears over and over throughout the New Testament. Heterarchs ask why Paul would choose the utterly unique and rare term *authentein* if he meant the same sort of authority that *exousia* would have communicated. Belleville charges:

> Without a doubt, the most difficult part of 1 Timothy 2:11–15
> to unpack is *didaskein de gynaiki ouk epitrepo oude authen-*
> *tein andros*—although the average person in the pew would
> not know it. English translations stemming from the 1940s
> to the present tend to gloss over the difficulties. A hierar-
> chal, noninclusive understanding of leadership is partly to
> blame. Women are not supposed to be leaders, so the lan-
> guage of leadership where women are involved, tends to be
> manipulated.[3]

This charge makes it clear that it behooves us to dig deeper into the meaning and use of *authentein*, and that it is necessary for us to consult other literature of that era for help in understanding its specific meaning. Greek dictionaries offer these definitions of *authenteō*, the root word of *authentein*:

---

2. William Witt, *Icons of Christ: A Biblical and Systematic Theology for Women's Ordination* (Waco, TX: Baylor University Press, 2020), 155.
3. "Teaching and Usurping Authority, 1 Timothy 2:11-15," *DBE*, 3rd ed., 210. For more insight into Belleville's translation concerns, see *DBE*, 3rd. ed., 210–21.

- To control in a domineering manner[4] (negative)
- To have full power over[5] (neutral)
- Strictly, of one who acts on his own authority; hence have control over, domineer, lord it over[6] (negative)
- Give orders to[7] (neutral)
- Domineer, have authority over[8] (negative)
- (1) One who with his own hands kills another or himself. (2) One who acts on his own authority, autocratic. (3) An absolute master. (4) To govern, exercise dominion over one.[9]

As you can see, some of these denote a negative meaning—a writer might use the term to condemn a practice done that way. Others denote a more neutral meaning—a writer might use the term not to condemn but just to communicate a fact, without implying whether it's recommended or discouraged, whether it's good or bad. These definitions range from neutral to negative. Predictably, so do the preferences of scholars in their interpretation of the term.

Hierarch Douglas Moo chooses to translate *authentein* in a more neutral sense, implying that Paul uses the word to mean that he never permits a woman to "exercise authority" over a man.[10] Thus he sees no reason for Paul to use the more common word for authority, *exousia*, since the word connotes no judgment on whether or not the practice is good or bad. He also questions the origin and development of *authentein*, when shown as a negative term.[11] Understanding *authentein* as a general, neutral term for authority compels hierarchs to interpret verse 12 broadly, limiting women from all kinds of authority over men for all time.

The Köstenbergers agree, writing:

> Some argue that "to teach or have authority" shouldn't be taken to imply that Paul prohibits women from teaching in

4. Johannes P. Louw and Eugene Albert Nida, *Greek-English Lexicon of the New Testament: Based on Semantic Domains* (New York: United Bible Societies, 1996), §37.21.
5. H. G. Liddell, *A Lexicon: Abridged from Liddell and Scott's Greek-English Lexicon* (Oak Harbor, WA: Logos Research Systems, 1996).
6. Timothy Friberg, Barbara Friberg, and Neva F. Miller, *Analytical Lexicon of the New Testament* (Grand Rapids: Baker, 2000).
7. *Lexham Analytical Lexicon to the Greek New Testament* (Oak Harbor, WA: Logos Research Systems, 2008–2013).
8. Barclay M. Newman Jr., *A Concise Greek-English Dictionary of the New Testament* (Stuttgart: German Bible Society, 1993).
9. *Enhanced Strong's Lexicon* (Oak Harbor, WA: Logos Bible Software, 1995).
10. Douglas Moo, "What Does It Mean Not to Teach or Have Authority over Men? 1 Timothy 2:11–15," in *RBMW*, 186.
11. Moo, "1 Timothy 2:11–15," 186.

general but that he merely doesn't want them to teach error or heresy, giving the word commonly translated "to have authority" (*authenteō*) a negative connotation and subordinating it to the word "teach" (*didaskō*). They claim that there was a specific problem of false teaching at Ephesus that Paul didn't want women to perpetuate. Several important word studies have contributed to our better understanding of the meaning of the word *authenteō*. The word is found only here in the New Testament and is also rare in extrabiblical writings, occurring only twice in Greek literature prior to 1 Timothy 2:12. Arguably, this is an insufficient data base for adjudicating the matter on the basis of word study alone, even though some have inappropriately used this data to establish a negative connotation for the word *authenteō*.[12]

Heterarchs disagree with Moo's and the Köstenbergers' assertion that Paul's Greek contemporaries used *authentein* in a neutral sense. Cynthia Westfall's research of first-century Greek literature finds that "the verb *authenteō* refers to a range of actions [in which] the targets of these actions are harmed, forced against their will."[13] Westfall's study of *authenteō* also revealed that, in ancient Greek literature closest to Paul's time, human authority written as *authentein* depicts the writer as framing the incident as something bad, a negative event.

Lucy Peppiatt claims it's impossible to glean a clear understanding of the term *authentein* and all these confusing passages unless we consider the cultural context, especially related to Ephesian women and the likelihood that many of them had recently come out of a lifetime in the Artemis cult before they accepted Christ. This view has been strengthened in the eyes of some heterarchs because of the research of Gary H. Hoag published in 2015. He cross-referenced terms in Paul's letter to Timothy with an ancient Greek novel *Ephesiaca*, written at the same time as Paul's ministry.[14] Originally, this ancient novel was thought to have been written after Paul wrote this letter in the second or third century AD, but the novel has recently been authenticated to have been penned in the middle of the first century AD, around the time of Paul's ministry.

This novel chronicles a love story of two Ephesians, Habrocomes and Anthia, both devoted to Artemis. They met during a worship ceremony to Artemis, with Anthia leading a procession of other young women into the

12. Andreas J. Köstenberger and Margaret E. Köstenberger, *God's Design for Man and Woman: A Biblical-Theological Survey* (Wheaton, IL: Crossway, 2014), 208.

13. Cynthia Westfall, *Paul and Gender: Reclaiming the Apostle's Vision for Men and Women in Christ* (Grand Rapids: Baker Academic, 2016), 291–93.

14. Gary G. Hoag, *Wealth in Ancient Ephesus and the First Letter to Timothy: Fresh Insights from Ephesiaca by Xenophon of Ephesus* (Winona Lake, IN: Eisenbrauns), 2015.

temple. According to some heterarchs, this novel now provides us with valuable insight into the beliefs and practices, particularly of women leaders, in the cult. Hoag argues that evidence from the novel shows these Ephesian women to be assertive, competitive, vocal, and well-versed in their religion. "They recite prayers, serve piously, and fiercely compete to attain various religious roles linked to their adornment and activities."[15]

Peppiatt writes, "If women like the ones we encounter in *Ephesiaca* are joining the church, it is easily imaginable how they end up assuming authority, control, and might have taken to teaching others without seeing the need to receive instruction."[16] She agrees with Hoag that Paul was instructing these ex-Artemis worshippers to "cease propagating heresy that promoted women as the usurper of authority of man, the woman as the originator of man, and that man was the one deceived in the creation account."[17] These ideas were all sourced in the Artemis cult.[18]

To conclude this section, how one defines *authentein* informs the way one interprets Paul's caution regarding women teaching men. Hierarchs understand the term as neutral, not condemning or affirming the practice. This assessment supports their conclusion that women are never to teach men in the church. Many heterarchs claim we must consider cultural issues related to the Artemis cult, and when we do, we will see that *authentein* is a negative word, showing that Paul was correcting women from teaching in a domineering or abusive way—not prohibiting them from all teaching and authority.

Is Paul Restricting Women from One Activity or Two?

Should readers understand verse 12 as two separate actions, "I do not permit a woman to teach men *nor* to have authority over men," or as one complete action, "I do not permit a woman to teach in an authoritative manner." Why would one interpretation matter over the other? Scholars argue that both options are grammatically acceptable. If Paul was speaking of two separate actions, women would be denied permission to teach as well as the ability to be in authority over men. If it's one action combined, then Paul was only limiting presumptive women from teaching with a controlling, domineering attitude over men. Not surprisingly, hierarchs argue for the former and heterarchs the latter.

Many heterarchs argue that the grammar allows that the two infinitives in verse 12, teach and exercise authority, contribute to one concept, with the second describing how the first is being performed. Heterarch Philip Payne

---

15. Hoag, *Wealth in Ancient Ephesus*, 88.
16. Lucy Peppiatt, *Rediscovering Scripture's Vision for Women, Fresh Perspectives on Disputed Texts* (Downers Grove, IL: IVP Academic 2019), 150.
17. Hoag, *Wealth in Ephesus*, 228.
18. Peppiatt, *Rediscovering Scripture's Vision for Women*, 150.

provides multiple examples, insisting that the grammatical construction in the "undisputed letters of Paul combine two elements to express a single idea."[19] He compares these examples to the English equivalents when two expressions combine together to convey a single idea such as, "Don't eat 'n' run." This mandate prohibits leaving right after eating rather than prohibiting eating or leaving by itself, as two separate actions. Other examples include "hit 'n' run" and "nice 'n' easy," and "black 'n' white."

These expressions combine both actions to form one meaning, and Payne argues that in an abundance of instances in Paul's letters, he uses this grammatical construction to be interpreted this way. For example, in 1 Corinthians 3:2, Paul writes, "I gave you milk, not solid food, for you were not yet ready for it. Indeed, you are still not ready." These two concepts of milk and not solid food are meant to be taken together in a combined meaning.[20] Paul doesn't just mean he gave them milk and they are not yet ready for it. Nor does he mean only that he didn't give them solid food. Only the combined idea of "milk and not solid food" conveys what he's trying to say. Payne concludes, "This verse does not prohibit women such as Priscilla from teaching men, as long as their authority is properly delegated, not self-assumed. It simply prohibits women from assuming for themselves authority to teach men."[21]

Conversely, hierarch Moo believes that the grammatical construction in verse 12 communicates two separate prohibitions. He states directly, "We think 1 Timothy 2:8–15 imposes two restrictions on the ministry of women: they are not to teach Christian doctrine to men and they are not to exercise authority directly over men in the church. These restrictions are permanent, authoritative for the church in all times and places and circumstances."[22]

Thomas Schreiner agrees and uses this verse to deny women's permission not only to pastoral office but also to teach men in any capacity, such as a guest lecturer or Sunday school teacher: "When we read 1 Timothy 2:12, it doesn't directly speak to the issue of office; it addresses the matter of function, prohibiting women from teaching and exercising authority over a man."[23] In other words, women can't ever teach men in a ministry context, even if invited by male leaders or as a co-teacher, much less hold an office that puts them in a position of leading or teaching men.

Is Paul discussing one or two activities? How we determine our answer will influence our understanding of the passage as a whole. If he speaks of

---

19. Philip B. Payne, *Man and Woman, One in Christ: An Exegetical and Theological Study of Paul's Letters* (Grand Rapids: Zondervan, 2009), 338.
20. Payne, *Man and Woman*, 337–59.
21. Payne, *Man and Woman*, 338.
22. Moo, "1 Timothy 2:11–15," 180.
23. Thomas Schreiner, "Should Women Teach? Thoughts on Function, Office, and 1 Timothy 2:12," *9Marks*, Dec. 10, 2019, https://www.9marks.org/article/should-women-teach -thoughts-on-function-office-and-1-timothy-212.

two activities, Paul limits women from both teaching and authority over men, which includes both the function (teaching) and office (authority) of elder/pastor, in the eyes of hierarchs. If the two terms work together, Paul is prohibiting presumptive women from teaching men in an authoritative way or without proper invitation.

What Is the Nature of Paul's Prohibition of Women Teaching?

Verse 12 opens with a verb, *epitrepō*, which means either "I do not permit" or "I am not now permitting." The grammar of *epitrepō* is written in the first person singular ("I") and present active indicative, which conveys an ongoing state of action. Is it a universal command or a statement that Paul at that time did not permit a woman to *authentein*?

Why do we care about Greek grammar here? Because we can translate that phrase into English with slightly different wording, each giving different connotations that affect our understanding of Paul's intent. Every major translation of 1 Timothy 2:12 opens with, "I do not permit/allow a woman" or "I permit no woman." The wording leaves open the idea that Paul was speaking to a specific situation as well as the option that he was decreeing a general universal principle. One cannot know which option by the current English phrasing.

Hierarchs interpret this verse with the phrasing "I do not permit" as one of their reasons for believing Paul was setting down a universal decree. They dismiss the second grammatical option as unreasonable[24] or unknowable.[25] Heterarchs prefer the second interpretive option, "I am not permitting": "By saying, 'I am not permitting,' Paul focuses particularly on the situation in Ephesus. Such language as this, as well as the 'I want' in v. 8, lacks any sense of universal imperative for all situations."[26] Payne contends that in comparing the grammatical construction of 1 Timothy 2:12 with other letters from Paul, we find four identical situations. "In every case, it expressed [Paul]'s current desire and not a universal command."[27]

In summary, Paul's introductory phrase in verse 12 remains a point of contention among scholars. Is Paul speaking specifically to the situation at Ephesus or did he announce a general principle?

Do Women Have to Remain Quiet or Silent?

The Greek word translated "quiet" (ESV, NIV, CSB, NET) or "silent" (KJV, RSV, NRSV) is *hēsychia*. It has the connotation of silence, quietness, or settling down, as in 2 Thessalonians 3:12, "We command and exhort all such

---

24. Kevin DeYoung, *Men and Women in the Church: A Short, Biblical, Practical Introduction* (Wheaton, IL: Crossway, 2021), 80.
25. Moo, "1 Timothy 2:11–15," 185.
26. Gordon D. Fee, *1 and 2 Timothy, Titus*, Understanding the Bible Commentary Series (Grand Rapids: Baker, 2011), 71.
27. Payne, *Man and Woman*, 320.

people to work quietly." *Hēsychia* emphasized an attitude toward learning that precluded one from speaking out of turn or acting like a busybody (see 1 Tim. 5:13). Paul, like any teacher of his time period, expected a teachable spirit and respectful attitude, not absolute silence.

Hierarchs and heterarchs alike agree that "quiet" rather than "silent" is the more appropriate term in this context. In his other letters, Paul mentions women speaking in church, doing such things as praying or prophesying (cf. 1 Cor. 11:5). So complete silence in church cannot be his intent here, especially if he's laying out a universal rule for all women for all time.

Summary

First Timothy 2:11–12 is the first half of a passage fraught with meaning for church life. Verses 11–12 give instructions while 13–14, which we'll look at next, offer support for them. We will sum up the opposing views, with the understanding that the following chapter continues the conversation.

Hierarchs

Hierarchs differ from one another greatly in their application of 1 Timothy 2:11–12. Paul's instructions, say hierarchs on one end of the spectrum, apply to all women for all time in the setting of the gathered church. For many, a woman may learn of God and Scripture but not ever teach it to men. Nor can she exercise any kind of authority over men. This means she may not hold the position of elder or pastor, since they are functionally the same thing, involving authority and ability and opportunity to teach the Bible. In addition, she may not teach doctrine with men or in the presence of men in any setting, regardless of her training or giftedness. And when boys reach the designated age of manhood, she must not attempt to influence them through any sort of teaching or authoritative action.

For other hierarchs, these restrictions vary. For example, women may not teach men doctrine to the whole congregation but may teach in smaller settings like Sunday schools and small groups. Some allow women to speak from the pulpit on Sunday morning as long as they are not teaching doctrine, but they can share an experience, present a devotional, or give a testimony. Still others allow women to preach doctrine from the pulpit as part of a team if they do not serve in the office of senior pastor or elder. Nevertheless, the hierarchical interpretation of 1 Timothy 2:11–12 offers them a solid foundation for male authority in the church.

Heterarchs

Heterarchs believe the overall message of verses 11–12 is that if a woman is learning, she should do so quietly, in a settled manner, not interrupting with disruptive speech or teaching things she doesn't know in a controlling or domineering way. William Witt notes that verse 12 may parallel 1 Timothy

5:13, in which Paul refers to women who are "saying things they ought not" and "the false teachers of Titus 1:11, who 'teach things they ought not.'"[28]

Heterarchs point to Paul's unusual choice of words in verses 11–12 as reason to delve beneath the hierarch's interpretations of Paul's instruction. The context allows for several grammatical choices. What does *authentein* mean? They say that the strongest linguistic evidence points to a negative, harsh form of authority best rendered "control or dominate." If true, they assert, then Paul was probably only speaking to the Ephesian women, many highly influenced by the cultic background from which they came, as they learn the way of Jesus and sit under Timothy's teaching. Instead of teaching what they don't yet know, they should learn quietly. They should not insist on teaching in a presumptuous manner when they are ill prepared.

Heterarchs insist that their understanding of verses 11–12 leads to a theology of freedom for women in pastoral leadership. Women are allowed to use their gifts of teaching, exhortation, leadership, and more to encourage both men and women in the body of Christ. And women are eligible to be considered for ordination as well.

The next chapter will pick up in verse 13, which offers the reasons for Paul's instruction to Timothy.

REFLECTION QUESTIONS

1. If you were acquainted with 1 Timothy 2:11–12 before reading this chapter, what did you think it meant and why?

2. What are your thoughts regarding Paul's use of the word *authentein* for authority rather than *exousia*?

3. In verse 12, do you think Paul was restricting women from one activity or two, and why does this distinction matter?

4. What are your thoughts regarding verses 11–12 now that you have read the various opinions on its meaning?

5. What difference does the interpretation make for women who are called to ministry?

---

28. Witt, *Icons of Christ*, 158.

What Does Paul Mean When He Talks About Creation, Eve, and Childbearing in 1 Timothy 2:13–15?

A woman should learn in quietness and full submission. I do not permit a woman to teach or to assume authority over a man; she must be quiet. For Adam was formed first, then Eve. And Adam was not the one deceived; it was the woman who was deceived and became a sinner. But women will be saved through childbearing—if they continue in faith, love· and holiness with propriety. (1 Tim. 2:11–15)

In the previous question, we examined competing interpretations of 1 Timothy 2:11–12, where Paul gave instructions on the proper way for women to learn Scripture, and whether or not they should be allowed to teach men, either in an overbearing way according to heterarchs, or not at all or not in some situations, according to hierarchs.[1] In verses 13–15, Paul continues his instructions to Timothy. Let's begin by looking at verses 13 and 14.

What Is "For" There For?
"For Adam was formed first, then Eve. And Adam was not the one deceived; it was the woman who was deceived and became a sinner" (1 Tim. 2:13–14). Paul begins verse 13 with the word "for." The Greek word is *gar*, which usually means "because," and acts as a simple connecting word followed by reasons. However, *gar* can also introduce an example or illustration of what was said before.

---

1. We encourage you to read these two chapters as a unit since they are so closely related.

Why Did Paul Reference Eve's Birth Order and Deception?

Hierarchs

For centuries, hierarch scholars understood verse 13 to mean that women were not to teach men because they were intellectually inferior to men. Witt writes, "Women were considered less rational, more gullible, and more susceptible to temptation, and thus were restricted not only from church office, but from any position of authority over any men in any sphere whatsoever."[2] Their subordinate rank to men came about because they were defective in their personhood.

Today's hierarchs have largely abandoned inferiority as a reason for women's subordination, acknowledging that women are no more gullible or less intelligent than men. Instead, they point to 1 Timothy 2:13 and Genesis 2—creation order. Because Paul grounded his argument in creation, a universal truth, he was speaking of all women in a universal sense when he told Timothy that they could not teach men. Thomas Schreiner writes,

> In any case, Paul appeals to the created order. Those scholars who posit that false teaching or lack of education stimulated the prohibition ignore the reason the text actually gives (the created order) and insert something absent from the text (false teaching and lack of education) to explain the proscription. I do not deny that women were influenced by the false teaching (1 Tim. 5:11–15; 2 Tim. 3:6–9), and it is even possible (though far from certain) that some of the women were teaching the heresy. But Paul doesn't ground his prohibition in women teaching falsely. If both men and women were involved in the heresy (and we know that men were certainly involved), why does Paul forbid only the women from teaching men?[3]

Hierarchs contend that we should translate *gar* to mean "because." Thus, Paul seems to be reasoning that women must learn "in quietness and full submission" and they cannot teach men because they were created after them. For hierarchs, verse 13, *for Adam was formed first, then Eve*, is the linchpin of their argument for male authority. Witt explains, "The complementarian interpretation of this passage [1 Tim 2:13–14] focuses on Paul's appeal to creation order (Adam was formed first, then Eve) to argue that Paul is arguing for a

---

2. William Witt, *Icons of Christ: A Biblical and Systematic Theology for Women's Ordination* (Waco, TX: Baylor University Press, 2020), 146.
3. Thomas R. Schreiner, "An Interpretation of 1 Timothy 2:9–15: A Dialogue with Scholarship," in *Women in the Church: An Interpretation and Application of 1 Timothy 2:9–15*, 3rd ed., eds. Andreas J. Köstenberger and Thomas R. Schreiner (Wheaton, IL: Crossway, 2016), 205–6.

hierarchical relationship between men and women based in the pre-fall creation as the reason why women may not teach or have authority over men."[4]

Douglas Moo connects the dots from verse 12 to the idea of headship: "for Paul, the man's priority in the order of creation is indicative of the headship that man is to have over woman."[5] Because Adam was formed before Eve, women may not teach men. The Köstenbergers add,

> Paul's argument, then, is twofold: woman ought not to teach or exercise authority over a man because, first, Adam was created first, then Eve (the man's priority in creation); and second, the woman was deceived first, then the man (the woman's priority at the fall). Because of God's creation order (Adam-Eve) and because of the negative consequences that ensued when the first man and the first woman subverted that creation order (Eve-Adam), Paul urges that men, rather than women, teach and exercise authority in the church.[6]

The Köstenbergers give another reason why Paul referred to Eve's deception but admit this reason is harder to understand.[7] They write,

> Was Adam not also deceived? In verses 13–14, Paul is simply reading the Genesis narrative and registering some basic observations. The Serpent approached the woman and deceived the woman, not the man. Why did the Serpent approach the woman when the man was in charge and had received both the direct mandate to cultivate the garden and the direct prohibition from God concerning the Tree of the Knowledge of Good and Evil? Paul reminds his readers what happened historically when the woman acted apart from the man, leading him into disobedience, rather than the man fulfilling his role and leading the woman.[8]

Schreiner adds,

> Paul would be reminding Timothy that Eve transgressed first, and yet Adam was held responsible for the sin that was imputed

4. Witt, *Icons of Christ*, 160.
5. Douglas Moo, "What Does It Mean Not to Teach or Have Authority over Men? 1 Timothy 2:11–15," *RBMW*, 248.
6. Andreas J. Köstenberger and Margaret E. Köstenberger, *God's Design for Man and Woman: A Biblical-Theological Survey* (Wheaton, IL: Crossway, 2014), 211–12.
7. Köstenberger and Köstenberger, *God's Design for Man and Woman*, 211.
8. Köstenberger and Köstenberger, *God's Design for Man and Woman*, 211.

to the whole human race (Rom. 5:12–19). By referring to Eve sinning first, Paul subtly reminds Timothy that Adam bore primary responsibility for sin entering the world (note that in Genesis 3 God approached Adam first after the sin).[9]

Heterarchs

However, heterarchs argue that hierarchs' reasoning is flawed and that it has perplexed some scholars through the centuries. For example, John Calvin (1509–1564), theologian, pastor, and reformer in Geneva during the Protestant Reformation, candidly wrote, "Yet the reason Paul assigns, that woman was second in the order of creation, appears not to be a very strong argument in favour of her subjection; for John the Baptist was before Christ in the order of time, and yet was greatly inferior in rank."[10] Heterarchs do not accept the idea that creation order in Genesis 1 and 2 implies hierarchy or male headship, but instead they insist that these passages describe the mutual calling, oneness, and divine image-bearing of men and women.[11]

Heterarchs also refute the idea that women are primarily to blame for the fall and are more easily deceived, which they say verse 14 seems to imply on the surface but isn't supported by other biblical texts. They look to Romans 5:12–19. "For if, by the trespass of the one man [Adam], death reigned through that one man, how much more will those who receive God's abundant provision of grace and the gift of righteousness reign in life through the one man, Jesus Christ" (v. 17). They argue that although Eve was deceived, Adam knowingly sinned against God, and both are equally accountable. In addition, men have proven to be just as easily deceived through the ages as women.[12] And since Paul also wrote Romans 5 assigning blame for the fall on Adam, Paul must have meant something else in 1 Timothy 2:13–14.

Heterarchs maintain that an understanding of the local culture in the first century explains and illuminates the confusing references in these verses. They point out that *gar* in verse 13 does not only mean "because" but also is used to set up an example.[13] Therefore, Paul could be offering a local, temporary example to explain why these particular uneducated Ephesian women were especially susceptible to deception and temptation and therefore ill prepared at that time to teach. Witherington contends that "the point of the

---

9. Schreiner, "Interpretation of 1 Timothy 2:9–15," 214–15.
10. John Calvin, *Commentary Timothy, Titus, Philemon*, Christian Classics Ethereal Library, ccel.org/ccel/calvin/calcom43.iii.iv.iv.html.
11. See Questions 6 and 21 for more detailed discussion on creation order and the meaning of "head."
12. See Question 29 that addresses whether women are more easily deceived than men.
13. Witt, *Icons of Christ*, 161.

example [of Adam and Eve] is to teach women not to emulate Eve"[14] and to counter pagan myths embraced by Artemis worshippers. Heterarchs argue that we cannot truly understand why Paul brought up Eve's creation after Adam and her deception without understanding the mindset of many first-century Ephesian women. Paul encountered this mindset when he founded the Ephesian church in Acts 19. The women he referenced in 1 Timothy had been immersed in the pagan worship of the goddess Artemis and the related stories they grew up with. As former female Artemis worshippers, they were likely still influenced by their previous religion and the worldly culture of the city where they lived. And because the primary deity they worshipped in Ephesus was a woman, they had an elevated view of the status of women over men. Clifton Arnold, in his extensive research on the Artemis cult, writes, "One undisputed characteristic of the Ephesian Artemis is the unsurpassed cosmic power attributed to her."[15]

In addition, heterarchs draw attention to the mythological creation story of Artemis and her male twin Apollo. According to this story they were the children of Zeus, the king of all the other gods, and Leto, a Titan goddess. Artemis was a virgin, the mother of all life as creator, the guardian of young children, and the protector of women in labor. In contrast, Apollo was a male god with many lovers, and he's the one who brought sin into the world.[16] In the Artemis creation narrative, the woman came into the world before the man, exactly the opposite of the creation account in Genesis.

Heterarchs claim that, as relatively new Christians, Ephesian women were still under the influence of their past beliefs and were desperately in need of learning sound Christian doctrine. Even worse, some who had enjoyed the elevated status of women in the upper echelons of the pagan priesthood may have, out of ignorance, synthesized the two belief systems and were spreading their false ideas. This would account for Paul's continued rebuke of those who "want to be teachers of the law, but they do not know what they are talking about or what they so confidently affirm" (1 Tim. 1:7). Paul was correcting these women, telling them to stop promoting these myths in the house of God. In 4:7, Paul wrote, "But reject those myths fit only for the godless and gullible, and train yourself for godliness" (NET). The accompanying note by NET Bible scholars reads, "*Those myths* refer to legendary tales characteristic of the false teachers in Ephesus and Crete."[17] Sandra Glahn adds:

---

14. Ben Witherington, *Women in the Earliest Churches* (New York: Cambridge University Press, 1988), 122.

15. Clifton E. Arnold, *Power and Magic: The Concept of Power in Ephesians* (Grand Rapids: Baker, 1992), 21.

16. Mike Greenberg, "Who Was the Twin of Artemis?," Mythology Source, Sept. 23, 2020, https://mythologysource.com/who-was-the-twin-of-artemis.

17. NET Bible, New English Translation, Second Beta Edition (Dallas: Biblical Studies Press, 2003), 2180n9.

In these gentiles' [Ephesians'] creation narrative, the woman came first, and that gave her preeminence as the first twin. Competition persisted between cities that worshiped one or the other of the twins, with Artemis's followers insisting she was superior because she was born first. So in Timothy's context, the creation story from Genesis contrasts completely with the local story and would have served as a logical corrective.[18]

Having been immersed in Artemis worship, women who had converted to faith in Jesus could have exported old domineering habits into the church, insisting they be allowed to teach when they were not yet competent, and demanding they be given unqualified authority. Glahn suggests that the author of 1 Timothy may have had in mind local laws that prevented women from intervening in public arenas, which would describe a house church. A wife lording it over her husband would have reflected poorly on the church in their community.[19] Paul specifically advised these women to learn in submission and not assume prominence as they did under Artemis, but rather humble themselves and remember that the first woman had been deceived just like they were being deceived. Glahn notes:

> Seeing the reference to Eve's creation order in 1 Timothy 2:13 as an all-time prohibition against females imparting spiritual content to males has created far more textual difficulties than it has resolved. But seeing it as an apologetic against false teaching in Ephesus fits the context and allows interpreters to better synthesize the whole counsel of God.[20]

Hierarchs respond that all this is speculation and a stretch, and what they believe is a more straightforward and logical meaning. Schreiner writes, "There is no clear evidence in Paul's letter that the Artemis cult played a role. Paul does not mention the cult, nor is there any specific notion in the text that shows the influence of the cult."[21]

How Are Women Saved Through Childbearing?

"But women will be saved through childbearing—if they continue in faith, love and holiness with propriety" (1 Tim. 2:15). Verse 15 is notoriously

---

18. Sandra Glahn, "The First-Century Ephesian Artemis: Ramifications of Her Identity," *Bibliotheca Sacra* 172 (October–December 2015): 450–69.
19. Glahn, "First-Century Ephesian Artemis," 460.
20. Glahn, "First-Century Ephesian Artemis," 464.
21. Thomas R. Schreiner, "Women in Ministry: Response," in *Two Views on Women in Ministry*, 2nd ed., eds. James R. Beck and Craig L. Blomberg (Grand Rapids: Zondervan, 2005), 108.

difficult to interpret, and various suggestions have dominated through the centuries. Heterarchs and hierarchs agree on some aspects and disagree on others, so they are not easily categorized.

The Greek word for "saved" (*sōzō*) takes on a variety of different biblical meanings that the astute Bible reader must discern through the context. Usually, Christians use the word to denote what happens when a person puts their faith in Jesus Christ to receive eternal life. "For it is by grace that you have been saved, through faith—and this is not from yourselves, it is the gift of God—not by works, so that no one can boast" (Eph. 2:8–9). Obviously, women do not receive salvation by bearing children, which would be by works, but by accepting the undeserved gift of life through faith in what Christ did on the cross on their behalf. So, Paul must mean something else.

Hierarchs

Some hierarchs argue that Paul was using the term *saved* in the sense of Philippians 2:12: "continue to work out your salvation with fear and trembling." Thus, verse 15 would apply to all women. Moo comments,

> We think it is preferable to view verse 15 as designating the circumstances in which Christian women will experience (work out; cf. Philippians 2:12) their salvation—in maintaining as priorities those key roles that Paul, in keeping with Scripture elsewhere, highlights: being faithful, helpful wives, raising children to love and reverence God, managing the household.[22]

Wayne Grudem adds, "Women are not eternally lost because of Eve's sin, but they will be saved and will experience the outworking of their salvation throughout their Christian lives if they follow the roles God has given to them and continue in faith and obedience."[23]

Andreas Köstenberger concludes that Paul means *sōzō* ("saved") in the sense of "to be kept safe." He writes, "Women will be spiritually preserved (saved) if they devote themselves to their God-given role in the domestic and familial sphere."[24] He continues, "The apostle is extending God's original design for men and women to the life of the church, redirecting the aspirations of women from teaching and exercising authority over men in the church to the domestic, familial realm." He asserts that women who stray outside these realms put themselves in danger of "satanic deception" when they, like Eve,

---

22. Douglas Moo, "What Does It Mean Not to Teach or Have Authority over Men? 1 Timothy 2:11–15," in *RBMW*, 192.

23. Grudem, *EFBT*, 74

24. Andreas Köstenberger, "Saved through Childbearing?," *CMBW News* 2, no. 4 (1997) https://cbmw.org/wp-content/uploads/2013/05/2-4.pdf.

believe, "You can do better than abiding by God's design and submitting to the man."[25]

Glahn counters the Grudem-Moo-Köstenberger view: "Mothering, in this view, is the appropriate outlet for a woman's desire to minister to the body of Christ through teaching. But why would the author [Paul] limit women to teaching only those most vulnerable to false doctrine?"[26] In other words, if women are easily deceived, why would Paul instruct them to teach impressionable children?[27]

Other hierarchs and some heterarchs suggest that since the word "save" usually denotes what happens when a person puts their faith in Jesus Christ to receive eternal life, then the phrase *tēs teknogonias* should be understood as "*the* childbearing." Rather than having anything to do with Ephesian women bearing children, it's a reference to the birth of Christ, the promised Savior. In this sense, all women will be saved through Mary giving birth to Jesus when women place their faith in Christ—if they continue in faith, love, and holiness with propriety.[28]

Schreiner, however, insists this view is "quite improbable" because the term "saved" "always has the meaning of spiritual salvation in the Pastoral Epistles" and because "Mary was not saved by virtue of giving birth to Jesus, nor does Paul elsewhere say that salvation comes through the incarnation."[29] Instead, he argues that Paul is actually referring to childbearing because it "represents the fulfillment of the woman's domestic role as a mother in distinction from the man."[30] He writes,

> More likely, Paul saw the woman's function of giving birth a divinely intended and ongoing difference of function between men and women. This does not mean that all women must have children in order to be saved. Though the underlying principle is timeless, Paul is hardly attempting to be comprehensive here. . . . He selects childbearing because it is the most notable example of the divinely intended difference in roles between men and women and because many women throughout history have had children. Thus, Paul generalizes from the experience of women by using a representative example of women maintaining their proper role.[31]

---

25. Köstenberger and Köstenberger, *God's Design for Man and Woman*, 216.
26. Glahn, "First-Century Ephesian Artemis," 465.
27. For a thorough discussion on women teaching children, see Question 29.
28. Philip Payne and Andrew Bartlett are among the heterarchs adopting this view. George W. Knight, as well as church fathers Tertullian, Ignatius, Irenaeus, are among hierarchs who do.
29. Schreiner, "Interpretation of 1 Timothy 2:9–15," 217, 219.
30. Schreiner, "Interpretation of 1 Timothy 2:9–15," 221.
31. Schreiner, "Interpretation of 1 Timothy 2:9–15," 222.

Schreiner addresses the issue of salvation by works rather than by faith by arguing that good works are the result of authentic salvation and a changed life, which involves adhering to one's proper role, as well as other Christian virtues like those Paul mentions. For this reason, Paul writes that women must persevere in virtues like faith, love, and holiness.[32]

Heterarchs

Some heterarchs believe it's only possible to glean a clear understanding of this confusing text if we consider the cultural context, especially related to Ephesian women and the likelihood that many of them had recently come out of a lifetime in the Artemis cult before they accepted Christ. As discussed in the previous chapter, this view has been strengthened in the eyes of some heterarchs because of the research of Gary H. Hoag published in 2015. He cross-referenced terms in Paul's letter to Timothy with the ancient Greek novel *Ephesiaca*, written at the same time as Paul's ministry.[33] This novel chronicles a love story of two Ephesians, Habrocomes and Anthia, both devoted to Artemis, and paints a picture of the lives of women in the Artemis cult that may be helpful when we attempt to understand what Paul wrote in verse 15.

Although exact maternal and child mortality in the first-century Roman empire can only be guessed at, they were likely high. For example, rough yet conservative estimates suggest that there were twenty-five maternal deaths and three hundred infant deaths for every thousand live births.[34] Glahn writes that although some have speculated that Artemis was a nourishing mother figure, that is inconsistent with the evidence. According to the myth, Artemis was born first and saw the painful nine-day labor of her twin brother Apollo.[35] Thus, she vowed to remain a virgin. As a result, Glahn says, "Artemis had no desire to give birth herself, so she asked her father to make her immune from Aphrodite's arrows, a request that Zeus granted. Thus, Artemis, having special sympathy for women in travail from her first days, came to be associated with virginity and especially, in Ephesus, with midwifery."[36] Thus, Ephesian women looked to Artemis to protect them during childbirth.

Hoag agrees and suggests that understanding the identity of the goddess provides a clearer explanation of why Paul would write that women will be "saved through childbearing—if they continue in faith, love and holiness with propriety" (v. 15). Christian women who came out of this cult where they

---

32. Schreiner, "Interpretation of 1 Timothy 2:9–15," 222–24.

33. Gary G. Hoag, *Wealth in Ancient Ephesus and the First Letter to Timothy: Fresh Insights from Ephesiaca by Xenophon of Ephesus* (Winona Lake, IN: Eisenbrauns, 2015).

34. "Childbirth in Ancient Rome: From Traditional Folklore to Obstetrics," *Australian and New Zealand Journal of Obstetrics and Gynaecology* 47, no. 2 (2007): 82–85.

35. Sandra L. Glahn, "The Identity of Artemis in First-Century Ephesus," *Bibliotheca Sacra* 172 (July–September 2015): 319.

36. Glahn, "Identity of Artemis," 319.

believed they were protected by Artemis, the goddess of childbearing, might naturally be fearful that they were offending the goddess by leaving the cult. And they were especially in danger when giving birth. Hoag argues that Paul is attempting to soothe their fears and encourage them to trust in God by persevering in "faith, love, and holiness" rather than returning to their old beliefs that would show they were still living in fear of the goddess.[37] Peppiatt agrees: "Clearly this would provide an adequate explanation of the reference to Christian women being saved/delivered through childbirth by God if they continue to place their trust in him by living Christianly and not with a foot in either camp."[38]

Glahn contends that if "saved" here means physical deliverance, the verse might be promising that faithful women who had turned from Artemis to Christ would bear children in safety and health. Paul may be asserting Christ's superiority, making "a promise in this foundational period of the church that their God would prove greater than the pagans' god. . . . Someone turning from the false goddess of midwifery was not going to die in childbirth when turning to the true Savior."[39] Schreiner counters this heterarch's views by writing,

> Our problem with the text is in the main not exegetical but practical. What Paul says here is contrary to the thinking of the modern world. We are confronted here with a counter-cultural word from the Scriptures. This countercultural word should modify and correct both our thinking and our behavior. . . . These are not idle topics, for the happiness and strength of the church today will be in direct proportion to our obedience to the biblical text.[40]

Although heterarchs come to different conclusions concerning the meaning of the text, they agree with Schreiner's last statement.

Summary

In the end, the numerous options for interpreting 1 Timothy 2:13–15 make it difficult and probably a bit prideful for any of us to insist that we know its meaning for certain. We agree with Lynn Cohick that

> the fluidity of the term "saved," whose meaning ranges from preservation from physical harm to one's eternal salvation,

37. Hoag, *Wealth in Ephesus*, 228.
38. Lucy Peppiatt, *Rediscovering Scripture's Vision for Women: Fresh Perspectives on Disputed Texts* (Downers Grove, IL: IVP Academic, 2019), 152.
39. Glahn, "First-Century Ephesian Artemis," 469.
40. Schreiner, "Interpretation of 1 Timothy 2:9–15," 225.

allows for either an interpretation that locates the verse's impact in the here and now or one that situates it in the hereafter. The preposition can be understood as "by" or "through," though some have argued "during," which muddies the waters further. Finally, the Greek noun translated "childbirth" reflects a breadth that encompasses pregnancy, delivery, childrearing, and (metaphorically) general domestic duties. It is impossible to know with any certainty how the initial recipients of the letter understood the verse, but women of childbearing years and their families would have been concerned about the dangers inherent in pregnancy and delivery, and about the viability of the infant. Any promise that such dangers could be averted would have been welcomed.[41]

If there is any passage in Scripture that we should all approach with humility, it's this one. The fate of half the church as they live out their lives in their homes and churches rests upon wise and discerning hearts.

REFLECTION QUESTIONS

1. Why do you think Paul might have referred to Adam and Eve as support or an example of verses 11 and 12?

2. Do you believe that the order of creation gives men permanent authority over women?

3. What are the difficulties with linking the bearing of children, "women continuing in love, holiness, and self-control," and salvation?

4. How might the worship of the goddess Artemis have influenced Paul to write these verses?

5. What difference does it make concerning how Christians interpret verses 13 and 14?

---

41. Lynn H. Cohick, *Women in the World of the Earliest Christians: Illuminating Ancient Ways of Life* (Grand Rapids: Baker Academic, 2009), 140.

What Does Paul Mean When He Directs Wives to "Submit" to Their Husbands?

On June 10, 1998, major newspapers throughout the United States reported that the Southern Baptist Convention had amended its essential statement of beliefs to include a declaration that a woman should "submit herself graciously" to her husband's leadership and that a husband should "provide for, protect and lead his family."[1] I remember that event became a "water cooler" conversation that year. Rev. Tim Owings of the First Baptist Church of Augusta, Georgia, proposed a revision to the statement that would have read, "Both husbands and wives are to submit graciously to each other as servant leaders in the home." He argued this was more biblically correct.[2] Who is right?

Biblical Text

Because Ephesians 5:21–33 is often used to answer this question, we'll focus on this passage. It reads:

> Submit to one another out of reverence for Christ.
> Wives, submit yourselves to your own husbands as you do to the Lord. For the husband is the head of the wife as Christ is the head of the church, his body, of which he is the

---

1. Gustav Nieber, "Southern Baptists Declare Wife Should 'Submit' to Her Husband," *The New York Times*, June 10, 1998.
2. Steve Kloehn, "Southern Baptists Approve Submissive Wives Doctrine," *Chicago Tribune*, June 10, 1998.

Savior. Now as the church submits to Christ, so also wives should submit to their husbands in everything.

Husbands, love your wives, just as Christ loved the church and gave himself up for her to make her holy, cleansing her by the washing with water through the word, and to present her to himself as a radiant church, without stain or wrinkle or any other blemish, but holy and blameless. In this same way, husbands ought to love their wives as their own bodies. He who loves his wife loves himself. After all, no one ever hated their own body, but they feed and care for their body, just as Christ does the church—for we are members of his body. "For this reason a man will leave his father and mother and be united to his wife, and the two will become one flesh." This is a profound mystery—but I am talking about Christ and the church. However, each one of you also must love his wife as he loves himself, and the wife must respect her husband.

Background

Historians continue to dig into ancient documents to learn more about the "household codes" referenced by Paul in Ephesians 5. From her research, Cynthia Westfall argues that the ethical, political, economic, and social structures in the ancient world were dependent on the behavior and subjugation of slaves and women. These people were considered inferior, and the Roman Empire's foundations were built on the backs of both groups of people. As a result, household codes were written to define how the members of households were expected to behave, especially in the areas of submission and obedience to authority.[3]

Glenn Hinson suggests a number of examples of household codes in ancient literature:

> Where did such materials come from? Are there parallels in earlier and contemporary writings? Yes, there are. First, extensive parallels may be drawn out of Stoic sources: Seneca (ca. 4 B.C.–A.D. 65), Epictetus (ca. A.D. 50–130), Diogenes Laertius (early third century), and others. Second, there are parallels in the writings of Hellenistic (but not Palestinian) Jews: Pseudo-Phocylides (after ca. A.D. 150), Philo (ca. 20 B.C.–ca. A.D. 50), and Josephus (ca. A.D. 37–100). Finally, there are parallels in other early Christian writings, including Paul's.[4]

---

3.   Cynthia Westfall, *Paul and Gender: Reclaiming the Apostle's Vision for Men and Women in Christ* (Grand Rapids: Baker Academic, 2016), 162.

4.   E. Glenn Hinson, "The Christian Household in Colossians 3:18–4:1," *Review and Expositor* 70 (1973): 496.

Typically, these codes followed a general pattern pairing up sets of people:

- How wives should behave toward husbands
- How children should behave toward fathers
- How slaves should behave toward masters

Heterarchs

Many heterarchs say they interpret Ephesians 5:21–33 through the historical lens of the household codes before they draw out principles and apply them today. Westfall argues that the Greco-Roman household codes focused on the obligations of household members to male authority, according to the cultural beliefs that, because men were superior beings, naturally inferior women and slaves should rightly obey them.[5]

But for Christians these codes were "inconsistent with the status of men and women in Christ. . . . Paul subverted these codes by changing the subordinate's motivations, and by changing the behavior of those in authority without directly challenging their authority."[6] Westfall believes that Paul didn't directly challenge Roman thinking concerning authority for "missional purposes,"[7] since the idea that in marriage women were partners and not property was completely foreign and countercultural and would have been scandalous. Philip Payne agrees, insisting that secular "household tables" served only the interests of the patriarch.[8] In contrast, Paul addressed all members of the body of Christ, and his goal was the nurture and Christlikeness of each member of the household.[9]

Thus, Paul writes only three verses of instruction solely to the wife and nine verses of instruction to the husband, illustrating the dramatic shift between the ancient family dynamics and Paul's new model of the Christian relationship between husband and wife. He emphasized the husband's sacrificial love for his wife while leaving out any mention of authority or leadership over her in instructions to husbands. Heterarchs argue that, as with all Scripture, the meaning of the codes should be interpreted with these ancient cultural realities in mind.

Other heterarchs emphasize verse 21 where Paul states, "Submit to one another out of reverence for Christ."[10] Payne insists that "Paul's use of the reciprocal pronoun in 5:21, 'submitting to one another,' indicates that he is not

---

5. Westfall, *Paul and Gender*, 162.
6. Westfall, *Paul and Gender*, 162.
7. Westfall, *Paul and Gender*, 162.
8. E.g., Aristotle, *Nichomachean Ethics* 8.1160b–1161a.
9. Philip B. Payne, *MWOC,* 271.
10. For a detailed analysis of Ephesians 5:21–33 see Lynn H. Cohick's chapter 10, "Loving and Submitting to One Another in Marriage, Ephesians 5:21–33 and Colossians 3:18–19," in *DBE*, 196–204.

endorsing hierarchical social structures."[11] Sarah Sumner disagrees that verse 21 means mutual submission. She says that nowhere in the Bible are husbands specifically commanded to submit to their wives. However, she contends that Paul equates submission with sacrifice, leading both to give up their own way for the benefit of the other. She insists that the text focuses on his sacrifice, and nowhere in the Bible do we find the words "lead, leadership, servant leadership or spiritual leader" in any passage on marriage; nor does the Bible say that the husband is "the head of the household." Instead, it says he is "the head of the wife," which is entirely different.[12] According to Sumner, the theme of Ephesians 5:21–33 is not about who's boss but about unity as reflected in verse 31, "For this reason a man will leave his father and mother and be united to his wife, and the two will become one flesh" (Gen. 2:24).

Sumner also makes the point that, grammatically, the Greek word for "submit" (*hypotassō*) is in the middle voice, showing that it's voluntary, something one does themselves and is never forced. It means "coming under" another in order to lift them up, and both husband and wife do this as she submits and he sacrifices.[13]

> The sacrifice of the husband is a full-time relational posture. For when the wife comes under the husband, thereby lifting him up, he sacrifices himself by giving up his advantage of being over her by exalting her to where he is. . . . [Both] participate together in a dynamic spiral of lifting each other up instead of putting each other down.[14]

Hierarchs

Hierarchs reach their interpretation of Ephesians 5:21–33 through the lens of their view of the creation order in Genesis 2 and their assertion that "God created male headship as one aspect of our pre-fall perfection."[15] They also insist that the term "head" means authority.[16]

> The instruction about wives and husbands found in Ephesians and Colossians, expressed in the key terms "be subject" for wives and "head" for husbands, teaches distinctive roles for

---

11. Payne, *Man and Woman*, 275.

12. See Question 21 for more on the question on the meaning of "head."

13. Sarah Sumner, *Men and Women in the Church: Building Consensus on Christian Leadership* (Downers Grove, IL: InterVarsity, 2003), 169–71.

14. Sumner, *Men and Women in the Church*, 171. For a full explanation of these concepts, see Sumner, "The Husband *Is* the Head."

15. Raymond C. Ortlund Jr., "Male-Female Equality and Male Headship: Genesis 1–3," in *RBMW*, 109.

16. See Questions 6 and 21 for more insight on Genesis 2 and the meaning of "head."

wives and husbands. . . . The fact that Paul appeals to the creation activity of God with reference to husbands and wives in
Ephesians . . . shows that the apostle regards these roles and
the pattern of the role relationship itself as divinely given.[17]

They also emphasize that marriage is an analogy of Christ and the church,
men picturing Christ and women picturing the bride of Christ, the church
(v. 32). In this analogy, hierarchs believe marriage pictures the authority of
Christ over the church, thus the authority of the husband over the wife. In
contrast, heterarchs tend to focus on what Christ did for the church through
his sacrifice on the cross (5:25–27) and on familial unity (5:31) to explain
Paul's analogy of marriage as Christ and the church.

John Piper offers his vision of the beauty of complementarity in the
opening chapter of *Recovering Biblical Manhood and Womanhood*. He contends that this biblical pattern where a husband leads like Jesus and a wife
responds like his bride results in a far more satisfying and beautiful pattern
of marriage than anything man could create. He defines biblical headship as a
divine calling to a man to take primary responsibility for leading, protecting,
and providing for his family, and biblical submission for a woman as her
calling to affirm, respect, and honor his leadership, and to help by using her
gifts.[18] He writes, "This is the way of joy. For God loves his people and he loves
his glory. And therefore when we follow his idea of marriage . . . we are most
satisfied and he is most glorified."[19]

Summary

We have just scratched the surface of the volumes of books and articles
written on this controversial topic. Should you want to know more, the related chapters and footnotes we provide will help you dig deeper. But in the
long run, like with many of these questions, gifted and sincere scholars with
various views begin with foundational issues and scaffold their ideas one
upon another, often building theologies that look radically different. As you
seek answers, ask God to guide you, apply your best thinking, and practice
humility and charity in your interactions with others.

17. George W. Knight III, "Husbands and Wives as Analogues of Christ and the Church:
Ephesians 5:21–33 and Colossians 3:18–19," *RBMW*, 177.

18. John Piper, "A Vision of Biblical Complementarity: Manhood and Womanhood Defined
according to the Bible," *RBMW*, 52–53.

19. Piper, "Vision of Biblical Complementarity," 52–53.

REFLECTION QUESTIONS

1. What is a "household code"?

2. What was the purpose of "household codes" in ancient cultures?

3. How was Paul's "household code" different?

4. How do you think Paul's "household codes" changed Christian marriages in the first century?

5. How do you think following Paul's instructions in these codes might affect marriages today?

What Does Peter Mean That the Woman Is the "Weaker Vessel"?

In 1 Peter 3:7, the apostle Peter called wives "weaker vessels," also translated as the "weaker partners." "Husbands, in the same way, treat your wives with consideration as the weaker partners and show them honor as fellow heirs of the grace of life. In this way nothing will hinder your prayers" (1 Peter 3:7 NET). The Greek word for vessel is *skeuos*, often referring to a container to hold liquid, like a jar or a household utensil. In 1 Thessalonians 4:4, Paul uses this word to refer to the physical body and sexual purity, denoting the idea that our bodies are like vessels containing a soul that God can use for good.

Traditional View

Some prominent early theologians wrote that Peter referred to women as weaker because they were naturally inferior to men. For instance, Thomas Aquinas (thirteenth century) considered women "naturally of less strength and dignity than man."[1] Reformer Martin Luther described women as "a creature somewhat different from man, in that she has dissimilar members, a varied form and a mind weaker than man."[2] And John Knox, writing shortly after Luther, said, "Woman in her greatest perfection was made to serve and obey man. . . . Nature I say, paints [women] further to be weak, frail, impatient, feeble and foolish: and experience has declared them to be inconstant, variable, cruel and lacking the spirit of counsel and regiment [or leadership]."[3]

---

1. Thomas Aquinas, *Summa Theologica* I, Q. 92, Art. 1, ad 2, https://www.newadvent.org/summa/1092.htm.
2. Martin Luther, *A Critical and Devotional Commentary on Genesis*, vol. 1, *Luther on the Creation*, trans. John Nicholas Lenker (Project Gutenberg Ebook, 2015), 2.6, "God's Work on the Sixth Day," 2.5.27b, https://www.gutenberg.org/files/48193/48193-h/48193-h.htm.
3. John Knox, *The First Blast of the Trumpet against the Monstrous Regiment of Women*, "The First Blast to Awake Women Degenerate," 2, "Causes Why Women Should Not Have

Hierarchs

Gotquestions.org, a popular parachurch website led by S. Michael Houdmann, seems to agree with some of the church fathers' insinuation that women are more easily deceived than men, when referring to wives:

> This is not a popular idea among many women or even many men. However, the Scripture tells us that the woman was deceived (1 Timothy 2:14), she is subject to her husband (1 Peter 3:1) and that she is a "weaker" vessel. That women are usually physically weaker is undeniable, but the implication of the fall is that by virtue of her being deceived by Satan, women *may* also sometimes be weaker in other ways. That definitely does not mean she is less valuable (Ephesians 1:6) or that she does not have equal access to grace (Galatians 3:28). Rather, it is a basis for a husband to treat his wife with understanding, tenderness, and patience.[4]

Wayne Grudem writes that wives are weaker in three ways: (1) physical strength (2) authority in the marriage, and (3) greater emotional sensitivity, thus making her more vulnerable and easily hurt by a self-centered or domineering partner. He cautions husbands not to take advantage of these weaknesses but rather to live with their wives in a considerate way.[5]

John Coe interprets this passage in terms of the husband's responsibility for the care of his wife: "The man is portrayed as being in some sense responsible for the wife in a way that she is not responsible for the man."[6] Tom Constable voices that responsibility this way:

> One of a husband's primary responsibilities in a marriage is caring for his wife. Caring requires understanding. If you are married, what are your wife's greatest needs? Ask her. What are her greatest concerns? Ask her. What are her hopes and dreams? Ask her. What new vistas would she like to explore? Ask her, and keep on asking her over the years!

Preeminence over Men" (1558; Project Gutenberg Ebook, 2003), www.gutenberg.org /files/9660/9660-h/9660-h.htm#kingdome.

4.   Question: "What does it mean that women are the 'weaker vessel' (1 Peter 3:7)?," Got Questions, https://www.gotquestions.org/weaker-vessel.html.

5.   Wayne Grudem, "Wives Like Sarah, and the Husbands Who Honor Them: 1 Peter 3:1–7," in *RBMW*, 207–8.

6.   John Coe, "Being Faithful to Christ in One's Gender: Theological Reflections on Masculinity and Femininity," in *Women and Men in Ministry: A Complementary Perspective*, eds. Robert L. Saucy and Judith K. TenElshof (Chicago: Moody, 2001), 206–7.

Her answers will enable you to understand and care for her more effectively.[7]

Heterarchs

Andrew Bartlett argues that when Peter writes that wives are weaker vessels, he is only comparing the muscle strength of men and women, with men obviously physically stronger. He bases his view on the meaning of the Greek word *skeuos*, which we defined earlier as "a container." Thus, he contends Peter's sole intention is to compare their human bodies, rather than any social advantage men may have over women either in marriage or in society. He also emphasizes that when Peter says "in the same way," he is referencing back to verse 4 where he instructs wives to behave toward their husbands with a "gentle spirit." He writes, "In the same way husbands should also be gentle, using their physical strength to serve their wives with kindness, not to coerce or mistreat them."[8]

Sandra Glahn explains why the term "weaker" would make more sense to Peter's audience than it does today, and she sees some social implications.

> Probably "weaker" simply means . . . weaker! Females on average have always had less muscle mass than men. This is less apparent to those of us living in a society in which we never hoist bags of grain, yank on mules' bits, or cultivate our own gardens. But everyone in Peter's audience would have been much more conscious of this differential than we are. Add to this the fact that childbirth was the number one cause of death for wives. Peter's audience would have been quite aware of females' physical strength relative to men's.[9]

She continues by explaining that the term "weaker vessel" should be interpreted in light of the rest of the verse: "Peter is elevating women. In his less-often-quoted but essential conclusion, he tells husbands to 'show them (wives) honor as fellow heirs of the grace of life. In this way nothing will hinder your prayers.' The instruction to the husbands is to view their beloveds not as deficient creatures, but as co-heirs."[10]

That "heir" language, focused as it is on inheritance, would have sounded radical to those in a world that limited women's ability to inherit and own

---

7. Tom Constable, "Dr. Constable's Notes on 1 Peter," 70, Sonic Light, Plano Bible Chapel, 2021, https://www.planobiblechapel.org/tcon/notes/html/nt/1peter/1peter.htm.

8. Andrew Bartlett, *Men and Women in Christ: Fresh Light from the Biblical Texts* (London: InterVarsity, 2019), 107.

9. Sandra Glahn, "Is Peter Insulting Women? Part 2," *Engage*, Bible.org, Dec. 10, 2013, https://blogs.bible.org/is-peter-insulting-women-part-2.

10. Glahn, "Is Peter Insulting Women?"

property. In Christ, not only is the wife granted an equal inheritance with her husband, but his treatment of her influences how their impartial judge hears his prayers.

Heterarchs believe that "Peter's picture, when lived out, then is of a family structure in which the man and woman grant each other honor and respect. She respects him; he honors her: two sides of the same coin. And their interaction foreshadows a future they will share as joint-heirs, equals, when Christ reigns on earth."[11]

Summary

Through the centuries, Christians usually interpreted the term "weaker vessel" in light of their already conceived perspectives on men and women. Early theologians believed Peter called women "weaker" because they were naturally inferior to men. Today hierarchs view women as physically weaker, and some write that women exhibit greater emotional sensitivity than men, making women more vulnerable and in need of men's care. Heterarchs argue that Peter was simply comparing men's and women's muscle mass, with men obviously being stronger.

REFLECTION QUESTIONS

1. What was your initial thought when you heard the term "weaker vessel"?

2. What does "weaker vessel" mean in Greek?

3. How did many early church theologians view women in light of this term?

4. What do you think the term "weaker vessel" actually means?

5. What was the consequence if husbands did not treat their wives well?

---

11. Glahn, "Is Peter Insulting Women?"

What Does the Bible Say About Who Makes Final Decisions in Marriage?

Every day Christian couples make millions of decisions concerning their own lives and the lives of their families. Many hierarchs tell wives that the Bible gives final authority regarding decision making to husbands, but heterarchs and even some hierarchs disagree. Does any passage give explicit insight on this question? The only passage that actually uses the Greek word "authority" (*exousia*) in the New Testament in relationship to marriage is 1 Corinthians 7:4–5. Thus, this text deserves attention as we consider the important question of authority in marriage.

1 Corinthians 7:4–5

The ESV Bible was translated by more than one hundred male scholars and pastors and endorsed by renowned male hierarchs including Wayne Grudem, John Piper, and Albert Mohler.[1] It reads:

> For the wife does not have *authority* [*exousia*] over her own body, but the husband does. Likewise the husband does not have *authority* [*exousia*] over his own body, but the wife does. Do not deprive one another, except perhaps by agreement for a limited time, that you may devote yourselves to prayer; but then come together again. (emphasis added)

The Common English Bible, 2011, was translated by more than 120 scholars, men and women, from twenty-four faith traditions in American, African,

---

1. "About the ESV," Esv.org.

Asian, European, and Latino communities.[2] Their translation of the same passage reads:

> The wife doesn't have *authority* [*exousia*] over her own body, but the husband does. Likewise, the husband doesn't have *authority* [*exousia*] over his own body, but the wife does. Don't refuse to meet each other's needs unless you both agree for a short period of time to devote yourselves to prayer. Then come back together again. (emphasis added)

Both versions seem to grant some sort of authority to both husband and wife over the other. Generally, heterarchs read these verses as Paul affirming equality and mutual submission in marriage. Many hierarchs refute that idea, claiming that the married couple's sexual relationship is a special exception. They don't interpret 1 Corinthians 7 as negating a husband's overall authority over his wife. Let's explore the different perspectives in more detail.

Hierarchs

Surprisingly, many hierarchs have little or nothing to say on this text. In *Women and Men in Ministry: A Complementary Perspective*, none of the authors in the fourteen chapters write anything concerning these verses and their application to marriage.[3] Neither do any of the authors in the twenty-six chapters of *Recovering Biblical Manhood and Womanhood*, except John Piper and Wayne Grudem, who write several paragraphs in response to the question: "Doesn't [1 Corinthians 7:3–4] show that unilateral authority from the husband is wrong?" They suggest that this text prevents husbands' "thoughtless sexual demands, or even lewd and humiliating erotic activity."[4] They continue,

> This text is not a license for sexual exploitation. . . . There is a wonderful mutuality and reciprocity running through this text from verse 2 to verse 5. . . . Do the call for mutual yielding to sexual need and the renunciation of unilateral planning nullify the husband's responsibility for general leadership in the marriage? We don't think so. . . . This text makes it crystal clear that leadership is not synonymous with having to get

2. "Explore," CommonEnglishBible.com.

3. Robert Saucy, "The Ministry of Women in the Early Church," in *Women and Men in Ministry: A Complementary Perspective*, eds. Robert L. Saucy and Judith K. TenElshof (Chicago: Moody, 2001).

4. John Piper and Wayne Grudem, "An Overview of Central Concerns: Questions and Answers," *RBMW*, 109.

one's way. This text is one of the main reasons we prefer to use the term *leadership* rather than *authority*.[5]

Two female hierarchs who write on marriage, Carrie Sandom[6] and Claire Smith,[7] also failed to address these verses in their books. In her five chapters on marriage, Smith doesn't mention 1 Corinthians 7. However, she does push back against Andrew Bartlett's criticism of her views in a book review entitled, "Another Unconvincing Case for Egalitarianism [Heterarchy]." She writes,

> Paul's comment about wives and husbands having authority over each other's bodies isn't a general statement about authority in marriage, but focuses on mutual *sexual* obligations in marriage. . . . In short, Bartlett has extended the application of the text beyond its scope, taking what is true for *part* of the marriage relationship and applying it to the whole.[8]

Therefore, Smith argues, mutual sexual obligations in marriage do not cancel the ordered relationships or hierarchy of authority that she and other hierarchs see in the Scriptures.

Heterarchs
 Bartlett takes an entirely different approach, beginning his argument on the Bible's teaching on the relationships of husbands and wives with a thorough treatment of 1 Corinthians 7. He believes this chapter contains one of the most extensive and detailed sections on this topic in the New Testament. He insists that 1 Corinthians 7 is the only place in the New Testament where there is an explicit statement about a husband's authority over his wife and the only explicit guidance on how decisions should be made in the marriage relationship.[9] He states, "So it would appear to be not merely a relevant passage but a rather obvious place to start."[10] He continues:

5. Piper and Grudem, "Overview of Central Concerns," *RBMW*, 109.
6. Carrie Sandom, *Different by Design: God's Blueprint for Men and Women* (Fearn, Scotland: Christian Focus, 2010).
7. Claire Smith, *God's Good Design: What the Bible Really Says about Men and Women* (Youngstown, OH: Matthias Media, 2012).
8. Claire Smith, "Another Unconvincing Case for Egalitarianism," *Gospel Coalition*, June 26, 2020, https://www.thegospelcoalition.org/reviews/unconvincing-case-egalitarianism.
9. Andrew Bartlett, *Men and Women in Christ: Fresh Light from the Biblical Texts* (London: InterVarsity, 2019), 18.
10. Bartlett, *Men and Women in Christ*, 18.

> The idea that these areas of married life are a special exception makes little sense. Physically, a couple's sexual relationship is the most intimate aspect of their marriage. . . . Spiritually, their prayers together are at the heart of their marriage. To make an exception in these two central matters would strike at the root of a hierarchical relationship. If there is equal authority and mutual submission at the physical and spiritual centres of the relationship, it would be strange indeed for there to be an overarching hierarchical relationship in less distinctive or less central matters.[11]

And he concludes: "In a society where men are usually in charge, and where in the worst cases wives are regarded as little more than a husband's property,[12] Paul's teaching is revolutionary."[13] Pierce and Kay add, "As evangelicals, we have wrongly neglected this text on many counts," asserting, "Paul's remarks here are three times longer than any gender-related passage in his other letters—in fact, roughly equal to the length of all of his other comments on this subject taken together."[14]

Philip Payne points out that in 1 Corinthians 7, Paul "specifies exactly the same conditions, opportunities, rights, and obligations for the woman as for the man regarding twelve distinct issues about marriage (vv. 2, 3, 4, 5, 10–11, 12–13, 14, 15, 16, 28, 32 and 34a, 33, and 34b)."[15] He continues: "1 Corinthians 7, then, presents a remarkable picture of Paul's vision of the equality of man and woman in marriage and in spiritual Christ-centered ministry."[16]

Practical Considerations and Evidence

With hierarchs and heterarchs coming to such vastly different conclusions on this question, is any current advice or research on marriage available to consider? Dr. Emerson Eggerich, counselor and internationally known public speaker on the topic of marriage, parenting, and communication,

---

11. Bartlett, *Men and Women in Christ*, 23.
12. Tom Holland in his book *Dominion* actually describes a party Nero threw where for one night any man could have any woman he wanted—the women had no choice to deny them (98). He says, "Sex was nothing if not an exercise of power" (99). From *Dominion: How the Christian Revolution Remade the World* (New York: Basic Books, 2021).
13. Bartlett, *Men and Women in Christ*, 24.
14. Ronald W. Pierce and Elizabeth A. Kay, "Mutuality in Marriage and Singleness: 1 Corinthians 7:1–40," *DBE*. For a more thorough discussion of this text from a heterarchical perspective, see pp. 108–25.
15. Philip B. Payne, *Man and Woman, One in Christ: An Exegetical and Theological Study of Paul's Letters* (Grand Rapids: Zondervan, 2009), 105. Payne lays out his reasoning regarding each example on pages 105–6. Bartlett, *Men and Women in Christ*, lays out these examples in detail at 25–26.
16. Payne, *Man and Woman*, 108.

developed the Love and Respect Marriage conferences. In an article entitled "Who Makes the Final Decisions When You Are Stalemated? (Part 2)," he asserts that the Bible clearly teaches that the husband, rather than the wife, is responsible to manage his household. He admits that this teaching may make many people uncomfortable. He exhorts husbands to make sure they reassure their wives of their love, and he does reprimand husbands who are unloving and abusive: "Let me send a warning to the husband who uses this information to his own advantage by unlovingly telling his wife he is in charge and making decisions his way without caring what she thinks or feels. Do you . . . think that your attitude will be ignored by the very Lord you seek to follow?"[17]

Regarding what to do if a stalemate threatens the survival of the marriage, Eggerich suggests that they bring in a third party from the church to weigh both sides of the disagreement and settle the dispute. He uses 1 Corinthians 6:5 to support his idea, quoting, "I say this to your shame. Is it so, that there is not among you one wise man who will be able to decide between his brethren?" (NASB 1995). We wonder, how likely it would ever be that this person chosen to settle the dispute would be a woman?

The Gottman Institute out of the University of Washington, led by Dr. John M. Gottman and his wife (also a doctor), has spent decades studying which practices are most likely to enable marriages to thrive and which are more likely to result in divorce. For example, in a scientific study of fifty couples married over sixteen years, they were able to predict whether the marriage would succeed or fail with a 91 percent success rate based on the couples' emotional intelligence and interactive principles that contributed to the long-term health of their marriage.[18]

One of these key principles that contributed to a successful marriage was "sharing power or allowing one's spouse to influence them."[19] He also found that men tended to struggle with sharing power more than women. According to Gottman, the benefits and the dangers of refusing to do so were fairly stark. In another long-term study of 130 newlywed couples, they found that "men who allowed their wives to influence them had happier relationships and were less likely to divorce," but that "when a man is not willing to share power with his partner there is an eighty-one percent chance that his marriage will self-destruct."[20]

In an article by Keith Gregoire, "Let's Look at the Evidence: Do Marriages Work Best If Men Make the Decisions?" a female reader commented:

---

17. Dr. Emerson Eggerich, "Who Makes the Final Decisions When You Are Stalemated? (Part 2)," Love and Respect, accessed May 20, 2021, https://www.loveandrespect.com/blog/who-makes-the-final-decision-when-you-are-stalemated-part-2.

18. John M. Gottman and Nan Silver, *The Seven Principles for Making Marriage Work* (New York: Harmony, 2015), 2–4.

19. Gottman and Silver, *Seven Principles*, 115.

20. Gottman and Silver, *Seven Principles*, 116.

I've heard this teaching all my life too, that somebody has to make the final decision. My two cents' worth from my own experience: There are other types of partnerships besides marriage, and in no full partnership do they give one partner the permanent, unchanging, back-pocket Decision-Making Badge. . . . Somehow they manage to come to a decision when one must be made—because they have to. . . . Two partners needing to come to agreement *can* do so—unless they themselves have decided on the shortcut of granting one of them the decision-making badge. . . . Marriage partners aren't special or unique in needing to come to agreement and make hard decisions with people they don't agree with from time to time.[21]

Summary

Again, hierarchs and heterarchs disagree based on their interpretations of what the Bible says about husbands' and wives' authority in marriage. It's been our observation, however, that what couples espouse as their view is often not lived out in the way their marriage actually functions.

Sheila Wray Gregoire, author of *The Great Sex Rescue*, echoes our own perspective:

God created male and female to be a picture of unity and intimacy. Let's spur one another on to love and good deeds. Let's work at knowing and loving each other more deeply every day. Let's study each other, learn about each other, excel in loving and serving each other. Let's truly "know" each other, and let's have that intimacy flow over into passion. That's what God wants for us, and we need to stop messing it up![22]

REFLECTION QUESTIONS

1. Who made final decisions in your family of origin, and how did it benefit or harm the marriage?

---

21. Keith Gregoire, "Let's Look at the Evidence: Do Marriages Work Best If Men Make the Decisions?," Men's Corner, Theology of Marriage and Sex, *To Love, Honor, and Vacuum*, January 28, 2020, https://tolovehonorandvacuum.com/2020/01/do-marriages-work-best-if-men-make-decisions.

22. Sheila Wray Gregoire, "Is Having the Husband Make the Final Decision a Harmful Shortcut in Your Marriage?," Resolving Conflict, *To Love, Honor, and Vacuum*, July 31, 2020, https://tolovehonorandvacuum.com/2020/07/should-husbands-make-final-decision.

2. How do you think 1 Corinthians 7:4–5 influences the decision on who, if anyone, should make final decisions in marriage?

3. If you are married, how have you determined to make final decisions with your spouse?

4. Do you believe that someone must make final decisions, or can a couple work out difficult decisions together?

5. What do you think the Bible teaches about who makes final decisions in marriage, and why?

If Women Cannot Teach Men, Should They Teach Children Who Are More Vulnerable?

Many Christians who grew up in the church treasure memories of Mrs. Jones or Miss Smith, devoted Sunday school teachers, who taught and encouraged them, and maybe even introduced them to Jesus. "Throughout the twentieth century, approximately sixty to seventy percent of church members in mainline denominations were nurtured through the Sunday school; in evangelical denominations (like the Assemblies of God and Southern Baptist), the percentage was even higher."[1] Ask any group of believers if the majority of their Sunday school teachers were women, and most would answer in the affirmative. Today this practice continues in many churches, though some restrict women from teaching teenage boys,[2] significantly impacting the spiritual formation and community life of millions. But should Mrs. Jones or Miss Smith be allowed to exercise this much influence over these impressionable and naïve little ones? This question raises others:

- Is she, a woman, more easily deceived, as some early church fathers insisted? Is this why she should not teach men? Should she then be trusted with the future lives of our children?

---

1. "Sunday School," Encyclopedia.com, May 17, 2018, https://www.encyclopedia.com/philosophy-and-religion/christianity/protestant-christianity/sunday-school.
2. Part of the impetus for Beth Allison Barr to write her book *The Making of Biblical Womanhood* (Grand Rapids: Brazos, 2021) was precisely because her Baptist church leaders decided that the Bible did not allow women to teach boys older than thirteen (67).

- If so, when should Mrs. Jones or Miss Smith hand over the boys in her class to a male teacher because they are now "men"? At what age does a boy become a man?
- Can she serve as a youth group leader? What if the class is co-led by a man?
- In the Industrial Revolution, as "keepers of the hearth," women in the Western world became largely responsible for the religious teaching of their sons in the home while their fathers exited to the public square.[3] This reality still exists in many homes today. If the Bible prohibits women from teaching men, should mothers resist teaching their sons once they reach a particular age?

Let's consider how hierarchs and heterarchs typically answer three of these questions:

- Are women more easily deceived than men?
- Where can women teach?
- When, if at all, should women stop teaching boys in the church?

Insight into these primary issues should help us make pertinent decisions in particular situations.

Are Women More Easily Deceived Than Men?

Hierarchs

Some hierarchs argue from 1 Timothy 2:13–14 that women are more easily deceived: "For Adam was formed first, then Eve. And Adam was not the one deceived; it was the woman who was deceived and became a sinner." For example, in his book *Evangelical Feminism and Biblical Truth*, Wayne Grudem entertains questions from heterarchs and then attempts to debunk their ideas. One such claim relates to the topic in this chapter: "Women today are not as easily deceived as in the first century; therefore, 1 Timothy 2:12–14 does not apply to us today." In response Grudem writes, "Paul makes no reference to his current culture, but to a characteristic of Eve that he sees as relevant for all women in all cultures."[4] He insists that this passage tells us something that is true of Eve and all women that is not true of Adam and all men, and this is one reason women should not teach or lead men.[5] Thus, he argues, this passage is transcultural or applicable for all time.

---

3. See Question 32 for more insight.
4. Grudem, *EFBT*, 296.
5. Grudem, *EFBT*, 295–96.

He further explains reasons different hierarchs give from this text that women are more easily deceived than men. Some, he says, fault Eve and thus all women because she usurped Adam's authority in their family and did not consult him when she made the decision to eat the forbidden fruit. Others "understand this to refer to a woman's 'kinder, gentler nature' that makes her less likely to draw a hard line when close friends are teaching doctrinal error and relationships need to be broken."[6] Grudem argues that whatever reason one takes, Paul is making a universal statement about women completely unrelated to the culture of the day.[7]

Heterarchs
Andrew Bartlett summarizes the view of heterarchs this way:

> Complementarians [hierarchs] who once put forward such a view [that women are more easily deceived] have usually withdrawn it, in the face of the rather obvious retorts that men cannot be proved to be less gullible than women, and that Paul regarded both as susceptible to deception (2 Cor. 11:3). If Paul had really thought women were disqualified from teaching because unduly gullible, he would hardly have instructed elsewhere that women should teach (Titus 2:3).[8]

In addition, argue some, historically and in the Scriptures, just as many men as women rebelled as false teachers, cult leaders, and addicts, illustrating equal vulnerability to deception. Heterarchs generally believe passages like 1 Timothy 2:12–14 only pertain to that particular situation in the text and should not be applied as a universal principle.[9]

According to Hierarchs, Where Can Women Teach?
Hierarchs hold a wide variety of views on this question, ranging from a total ban on women ever teaching men in any circumstance to giving women teaching and preaching opportunities as long as they are in some fashion "under" male leadership.

Tony Capoccia espouses a more "traditional" hierarchical view in answer to the following question: If women are not to teach, are they just not to teach classes with men in them, or not teach at all?

---

6. Grudem, *EFBT*, 296.
7. Grudem, *EFBT*, 296.
8. Andrew Bartlett, *Man and Women in Christ: Fresh Light from the Biblical Texts* (London: InterVarsity, 2019), 216.
9. See Questions 23–25 for further insight into the views of hierarchs and heterarchs on 1 Timothy 2.

> Actually, they are not to teach in the context of the church setting (worship/teaching services). The Scripture seems to indicate that women shouldn't teach because they are more easily deceived than men are (. . . 1 Timothy 2:14). Therefore, one would question the validity of women teaching any Bible Doctrine at all in the Church. Now the Bible does command older women to teach younger women, but to teach them to "love their husbands and children"—more of the practical application of the truth.[10]

He follows that advice with a few exceptions—women can teach children as long as male leaders or husbands are overseeing what they teach, both in the church and in the home.[11]

Regarding the question of when women should stop teaching boys in the church, the Gotquestions.org website concludes:

> Nowhere does the Bible specifically identify 20 or 18 or 13 or any other age as the age at which a boy becomes a man. The Bible is clear that the formal position of "teacher" in a church must be occupied by a male if adult males are among the students. . . . Most churches that hold to complementarianism have male teachers in classes for junior high and high school if boys are in those classes. This seems to be a good policy to follow, as it avoids any possible violation of the Bible's command concerning women shepherding men in the church.[12]

A Texas church's statement on women and ministry reflects the other end of the hierarchal spectrum. It begins:

> At IBC we recognize that God created both man and woman in His image, that He offers the same Holy Spirit to both men and women at salvation, and that the same spiritual gifts are available to both men and women for service. While the New Testament seems to imply that eldership is reserved for men, the elders of IBC affirm that women in all other roles are

---

10. Tony Capoccia, "If Women Are Not to Teach, Are They Just Not to Teach Classes with Men in Them, or Not Teach at All?," Bible Bulletin Board, https://www.biblebb.com/files/tonyqa/tc99-3.htm.
11. Capoccia, "If Women Are Not to Teach."
12. "When Should Women Stop Teaching Boys in the Church?," Jan. 4, 2022, Got Questions, https://www.gotquestions.org/women-teaching-boys.html.

scripturally qualified, spiritually blessed, and directly called
to use their spiritual gifts to build Christ's Kingdom.[13]

This large evangelical church encourages women to teach children, youth—
including boys and young men—and adults in a variety of venues, including
as part of a preaching team at the pulpit on Sunday morning. Their statement
concludes:

> The preponderance of biblical evidence indicates not only
> that God allows women to use their gifts without restriction
> in the local church, but that He actively calls them to do so.
> Therefore though the office of elder seems to be reserved for
> men, it seems good to us that, under the elders' authority and
> with their blessing, all other members of the Body, men and
> women included, can function in any role according to their
> giftedness.[14]

Summary

We have not found any reputable research that shows that women are more
easily deceived than men. If indeed women are more easily deceived than men,
it seems to us to logically follow that it would be wise for women not to teach
children or youth in the church, or even their own children, especially relating
to doctrine, since a strong doctrinal foundation sets a young person on the road
to a life rooted in faith and truth. However, if this is Paul's reasoning, it seems
inconsistent, for example, with the way he affirmed Priscilla when she and her
husband worked with Apollos, a gifted young preacher who needed corrective
doctrinal guidance (Acts 18:24–26) or when he trusted Phoebe (Rom. 16:1–2)
to deliver his letter to the church in Rome, a doctrinal masterpiece.

Also, common sense tells us that throughout the Bible, history, and current times, when given opportunity, women contribute value to society, including the academy, government, economics, science, health care, the home,
the church, and almost all other facets of a healthy and thriving world. If
they are easily deceived, we wonder if we would enjoy these significant
contributions.

---

13. "Women and Ministry at IBC," Irving Bible Church, Irving, TX, opening statement, http://
www.xpastor.org/wp-content/uploads/2012/12/irving_bible_women_ministry.pdf. In the
early 2000s, the elders entered a year-long process to discern God's direction, including
studying Scripture, reading books, sitting under the teaching of three seminary professors
with differing views, listening to audio messages on the subject, and meeting twice with
several godly women from inside and outside IBC to listen to their personal perspectives,
as well as carefully deliberating among themselves. The website statement is the result of
that process.
14. "Women and Ministry at IBC," 22.

In addition, for those of us who benefitted from the care, encouragement, and teaching of the fleets of Mrs. Joneses and Miss Smiths, discounting their influence on so many seems out of character with Jesus's teaching for all his followers to "go and make disciples of all nations, baptizing them in the name of the Father and of the Son and of the Holy Spirit, and teaching them to obey everything I have commanded you" (Matt. 28:19–20).

REFLECTION QUESTIONS

1. What effect did women teachers have on you when you were a child or a teenager?

2. Do you believe women are more easily deceived than men? If so, why?

3. What might be some benefits of having both men and women teachers in the lives of youth?

4. Where do you stand on women or mixed gender teams teaching children and teenagers in the church?

5. If you believe women should never teach men, at what age do you think a boy becomes a man, barring women from teaching them?

Women in Church History

What Does Church History Reveal About Women in Public Ministry? Part 1: Early Church to the Middle Ages

Dr. Cynthia Hester

What does church history from the ancient church through the Middle Ages reveal about women, leadership, and public ministry? Plenty! Evidence that alters our understanding of New Testament backgrounds—including online concordances of inscriptions, social-history findings, and discoveries in archaeology—provide reasons to reexamine the text.[1] New Testament professor Susan Hylen notes that interpreters in the past few centuries have assumed women played nonpublic roles in their communities, did not own or manage property, and were restricted to the household.[2] Yet, scholars continue to unveil new findings, including literary evidence illuminating that "women were active, just as men were, in the religious life of the Christian communities in all its different forms."[3] Here's a glimpse at women's ministries.

The Early Church

The church began at Pentecost with the Holy Spirit's descent. We know the apostles gathered with about 120 believers in an upper room, including women (Acts 1:13–15). Soon, all present were filled with the Holy Spirit (2:1, 4). Peter saw this as a fulfillment of Joel's prophetic word, "I will pour out my Spirit on

---

1. Sandra Glahn, "Theological and Biblical Foundations for Women in Ministry Leadership," unpublished class lecture notes for PM351 (Dallas Theological Seminary, Fall Semester, 2019); see also Sandra Glahn, ed., *Vindicating the Vixens: Revisiting Sexualized, Vilified, and Marginalized Women of the Bible* (Grand Rapids: Kregel Academic, 2017), 16.
2. Susan E. Hylen, *Women in the New Testament World* (New York: Oxford University Press, 2019), 164.
3. Ute E. Eisen, *Women Officeholders in Early Christianity: Epigraphical and Literary Studies* (Collegeville, MN: Liturgical, 2000), 1.

all people. Your sons and daughters will prophesy" (v. 17; Joel 2:29).[4] Women's public ministry in the early church began at Pentecost, when women, alongside their brothers, prophesied as a sign of the Holy Spirit's descent.

Women Prophets

God authorized women prophets, inspired by the Holy Spirit, to speak his word to others.[5] Luke names Anna (Luke 2:36), Elizabeth (1:42–45), Mary (vv. 47–55), and the four daughters of Philip (Acts 21:9) as prophets. The apostle Paul describes prophecy as providing instruction and encouragement (1 Cor. 14:31) for building up God's people (vv. 3–4). He ranked the gift of prophecy higher than the gift of teaching (v. 28). And Paul referenced women praying and prophesying in the gathered church (11:4–5; 14:23–24).[6] The early church had many women who were part of prophetic movements.[7]

Women Disciples

A disciple is a follower, and many women in the early church followed Jesus. Peter healed a woman named Tabitha, whom Luke praised for "continually doing good deeds and acts of charity," calling her "a disciple" (Acts 9:36 NET). The author of Acts mentions women disciples three times: those among a group of unnamed men and women (9:1–2), Tabitha (9:36), and Priscilla (18:23–26).[8]

Women Teachers, Leaders, and House Church Hosts

Paul highlighted and commended the faith of many women who served as teachers, leaders, and house church hosts. Lois and Eunice, the grandmother

---

4. See Questions 17 and 20.
5. See Question 11. Beginning with Miriam (Exod. 15:20), the other female prophets appearing in the Old Testament are Deborah (Judg. 4:4), Huldah (2 Kings 22:14), and Isaiah's wife (Isa. 8:3).
6. See Question 20.
7. Lynn H. Cohick and Amy Brown Hughes, "Perpetua and Felicitas: Mothers and Martyrs," in *Christian Women in the Patristic World: Their Influence, Authority, and Legacy in the Second through Fifth Centuries* (Grand Rapids: Baker Academic, 2017), 36. The authors noted, "The New Prophecy began in Asia Minor in the 160s. The movement stressed prophecy and was led by three key figures—a man named Montanus and two women, Priscilla and Maximilla—seen as inspired by the Holy Spirit. Asceticism was a prominent feature, as was an apocalyptic focus on the end of days. In time the New Prophecy (later known as Montanism) came to be regarded as heretical; its churches were desecrated, its shrines destroyed, and its writings burned. But in the early stages, from about the middle of the second to the early decades of the third century, its views fit within the broad definition of orthodoxy. Church writers such as Hippolytus and Tertullian confirmed that the New Prophecy was trinitarian and held to the saving work of Christ. Tertullian himself appears to have joined the New Prophecy in his hometown of Carthage, likely no later than 207" (36n39).
8. Robin Gallaher Branch, "Tabitha in the Bible: A Disciple Known for Doing Good," Dec. 23, 2021, Biblical Archaeology Society, https://www.biblicalarchaeology.org/daily/people-cultures-in-the-bible/people-in-the-bible/tabitha-in-the-bible. See also Question 14.

and mother of Timothy, Paul's protégé, forged Timothy's faith (2 Tim 1:5). Paul evangelized Lydia, a businesswoman, who with Paul planted a house church in Philippi (Acts 16:14–15, 40), which opened "a significant door for the advancement of the gospel into a new region of the world."[9] A married couple, Priscilla and Aquila, "explained" to Apollos, who needed correction, "the way of God more adequately" (Acts 18:26). They hosted churches at Ephesus and Rome in their home (1 Cor. 16:19; Rom. 16:3–5).[10] Paul affirmed Euodia and Syntyche, women in the church at Philippi. He wrote, "they have contended at my side in the cause of the gospel" (Phil. 4:3).

Woman Letter Carrier
    Paul commended Phoebe in his letter to the church at Rome (Rom. 16:1–2).[11] A significant reference to Phoebe in the book of Romans is the technical phrase "written through Phoebe" (*egraphē dia Phoibēs*), found in most ancient Greek manuscripts in the *subscriptio*, something written at the end of New Testament letters. The phrase "written through" specified the name of the letter carrier. Evidence indicates Phoebe carried this letter to the Roman Christians.[12] Paul charges the church to give Phoebe "any help she may need" in her ministry, which generally included carrying the letter and then explaining it.[13] Daniel Wallace, professor of New Testament Greek, notes that "the history of interpretation . . . argues decisively that the apostle Paul had no qualms with investing Phoebe, a woman, with this marvelous and sacred task." She "carried the most important letter written in Late Antiquity to its destination, so that we all might be the beneficiaries of her noble deed."[14] Jennifer Powell McNutt and Amy Peeler argue that after it was read aloud, Phoebe served as its first interpreter, meaning she probably served "as Paul's representative, to answer questions about Romans."[15]

---

9. Mary T. Lederleitner, *Women in God's Mission: Accepting the Invitation to Serve and Lead* (Downers Grove, IL: InterVarsity, 2018), 14. See also Question 20.
10. See Question 18.
11. See Question 19.
12. Daniel B. Wallace, "Medieval Manuscripts and Modern Evangelicals: Lessons from the Past, Guidance for the Future," *Journal of the Evangelical Theological Society* 60, no. 1 (2017): 5–34. See n58 for a list of Greek manuscripts.
13. Wallace, "Medieval Manuscripts," 17n39. See Jennifer Powell McNutt and Amy Beverage Peeler, "The First Interpreter of Romans," *Christianity Today*, November 2020, 57.
14. Wallace, "Medieval Manuscripts," 17.
15. McNutt and Peeler, "First Interpreter of Romans," 54–58. See also Denny Burk, "Engaging a Viral Interview with N. T. Wright," *The Council on Biblical Manhood and Womanhood (CBMW)* blog, February 25, 2020, https://cbmw.org/2020/02/25/engaging-a-viral-interview-with-n-t-wright-about-women-in-ministry. New Testament scholar N. T. Wright said, "Almost certainly in the ancient world, the person who delivers the letter is the person who will read it out. . . . And also—this isn't absolutely certain but it's a high probability—she [Phoebe] is the first person to explain when people [asked], 'What did Paul mean by that?'" In response, Peter M. Head writes, "I agree that Phoebe carried Romans; I agree that

Women Patrons

Client-patron relationships played a crucial role in Roman society. Patrons, male and female, provided clients with support ranging from food, finances, and legal services to introductions and favors.[16] In Greco-Roman times, wealthy women represented about one tenth of all patrons.[17] New Testament scholar Lynn Cohick notes, "Women had a voice and influence within society through the patronage system."[18] Jerome, a fourth-century biblical scholar who translated the Bible into Latin, had a patron named Paula. Employing her expertise in Greek and Hebrew, Paula assisted Jerome "with his biblical scholarship writing."[19]

Women Martyrs

The apostle Paul was celibate and preached on the value of celibacy, arguing that it enabled "undivided devotion to the Lord" (1 Cor. 7:32–35). Some early Christians following his lead emphasized celibacy over fertility and virginity over marriage.[20] Consequently, women as young as fifteen years old were martyred for refusing to revoke vows of virginity. Other believers, living in ways deemed threatening to the empire, were captured, brought before the emperor, and commanded to grant him imperial divine honors or worship Roman gods. Those who refused were imprisoned, tortured, and some were killed. Many died by beheading, and some by wild animals unleashed on them in arenas for sport.[21] In the first three centuries of Christianity, many men and women were martyred for their faith.

At the age of twenty-two, Perpetua, a young African wife and nursing mother, was imprisoned for her faith. She refused to recant, even as her father begged her to change her mind. Her diary describes her dark prison, her mistreatment from soldiers, and her dreams. In 203, she died a martyr in Carthage's arena, alongside her servant, Felicitas, who had just given

she was a 'deacon'. . . and I agree that she would have had a role in explaining the contents of Romans. . . . On the negative side it is not the case that letter carriers read letters to recipients" ("Letter Carriers and the Pauline Tradition," *Tychicus* [blog], November 27, 2012, https://tychichus.blogspot.com/2012/11/nt-wright-on-phoebe.html).

16. Lynn H. Cohick, *Women in the World of the Earliest Christians: Illuminating Ancient Ways of Life* (Grand Rapids: Baker Academic, 2009), 35.

17. Craig Keener, *NIV Cultural Backgrounds Study Bible* (Grand Rapids: Zondervan, 2016), 1761.

18. Cohick, *Women in the World*, 31.

19. Rosemary Ellen Guiley, *The Encyclopedia of Saints* (New York: Facts on File, 2001), 273; Kristin E. White, *A Guide to the Saints* (New York: Ivy, 1992), 306.

20. Katherine L. French and Allyson M. Poska, *Women and Gender in the Western Past*, vol. 1 (Boston: Houghton Mifflin, 2007), 106.

21. John Fox, "The Ten Primitive Persecutions," in *Fox's Book of Martyrs*, ed. William Byron Forbush, https://www.ccel.org/f/foxe/martyrs/home.html.

premature birth to a daughter.[22] Perpetua's diary, *Passion of Saint Perpetua*, is one of the rare surviving writings from early Christian women.

In his 1563 publication *The Book of Martyrs*, John Foxe recorded many martyrs' stories and deaths.[23] He admired the "constancy . . . of women and maidens," who publicly "gave their bodies to the tormentors, and their lives for the testimony of Christ, with no less boldness of spirit, than with the men."[24]

Widows

In 1976, a scholar in Belgium named Roger Gryson published a book titled *The Ministry of Women in the Early Church* that traced the clerical offices of widows and deacon[25] through the church's early centuries. He concluded, "One thing is undeniable: there were in the early Church women who occupied an official position, who were invested with a ministry, and who, at least at certain times and places, appeared as part of the clergy. These women were called 'deaconesses' and at times 'widows.'"[26] Up to the end of the nineteenth century, he noted, historians of the early church conflated the offices of deacon and widow.[27] And because in some locales mentions of women deacons did not appear until the third century, historians wrongly concluded that women deacons were a later development. These women are absent because the prominent office in that geographical location was labeled "widow." And the office of deacon looked different from the office of "widow" in the first centuries. Female clergy configurations were set up differently in different locations and according to the direction of local councils.[28]

In recent decades, historians have expanded their tools of analysis beyond church fathers' manuscripts and pronouncements by councils to

---

22. Cohick and Hughes, *Women in the Patristic World*, xix. See also Dan Graves, "The Prison Was Made a Palace for Me," Article 9, Christian History Institute, www.christianhistoryinstitute.org/incontext/article/perpetua.

23. Later editions give his name as John Fox.

24. John Fox, "Martyrdom of Eulalia," *The Book of Martyrs* (Liverpool: Nuttall, Fisher, & Dixon, 1807), 170.

25. Sandra Glahn explains that a female deacon was called a "deacon" and not a "deaconess" because, "There was no female form of the word 'deacon' in the early church and for some centuries to follow." In "Church History: What Do We Learn about Women in Public Ministry?," Bible.org, October 27, 2020, https://blogs.bible.org/church-history-what-do-we-learn-about-women-in-public-ministry.

26. Roger Gryson, *The Ministry of Women in the Early Church*, trans. Jean Laporte and Mary Louise Hall (Collegeville, MN: Liturgical, 1976), xi.

27. Gryson, *Ministry of Women in the Early Church*, 110.

28. Gryson, *Ministry of Women in the Early Church*, 22, 32–34. See also *Ordained Women in the Early Church: A Documentary History*, eds. Kevin Madigan and Carolyn Osiek (Baltimore: Johns Hopkins University Press, 2005), 4.

include liturgies and inscriptions, including tombstones. And the additional data has expanded our understanding of how women ministered in the early church.[29] In some locations the "widows" had to be sixty years old or older, and the virgins had to be younger. Tertullian (b. AD 160, N. Africa) ranked the widows among the clergy, and spoke of seats being reserved for them with the elders. In his work titled *De virginibus velandis* (9:2–3) he wrote with displeasure, "I know plainly that in a certain place a virgin of less than twenty years of age has been placed in the order of widows (*in viduatu*)!"[30] In this instance a "virgin" was not simply a maiden, but someone consecrated to Christ for vocational ministry.[31]

By the third century in the West, the office of widow was described as a thing of the past. Whenever the Alexandrians (Western church) mentioned women deacons or widows, they referred to these as offices of the past, no longer active. Both Clement and Origen wrote that women were placed in the service of the church in the time of the apostle Paul, but these men did not indicate that the office survived.[32]

In the fifth century, the *Testamentum Domini Nostri Jesu Christi*, probably from Syria (Eastern church),[33] devoted four long chapters to widows. It referred to the "ordination of widows" in two instances, using the same word for "ordain" that was employed for clerics in major orders.[34]

Epigraphic evidence, such as inscriptions on statues, tombstones, and coins, substantiates the ancient office of widows. For example, we find tombstones from the early centuries of the church describing women buried on church properties as "a widow of the church of [x] location."[35] A second-century Christian inscription at the Catacomb of Priscilla in Rome, "The widow Flavia Arcas, who lived eighty-five years," provides "the earliest epigraphical testimony" for an enrolled widow.[36]

Later in the East, the relationship between widows and deacons made a reversal, and widows, who had once supervised deacons, became subject

---

29. Glahn, "Theological and Biblical Foundations." I'm indebted to Dr. Glahn for her research on widows in the early church and her collaboration in summarizing Gryson's work.

30. Tertullian, "On the Veiling of Virgins," in *Ante-Nicene Fathers*, vol. 4, eds. S. Thelwall, Alexander Roberts, James Donaldson, and A. Cleveland Coxe (Buffalo, NY: Christian Literature Publishing Co., 1885).

31. Gryson, *Ministry of Women in the Early Church*, 21.

32. Gryson, *Ministry of Women in the Early Church*, 25.

33. "How the clergy was even configured varied by location (east as compared with west), century, and local council." In Glahn, "Church History," https://blogs.bible.org/church-history-what-do-we-learn-about-women-in-public-ministry.

34. Gryson, *Ministry of Women in the Early Church*, 44.

35. Ute E. Eisen, *Women Officeholders in Early Christianity: Epigraphical and Literary Studies* (Collegeville, MN: Liturgical, 2000), 146.

36. Eisen, *Women Officeholders in Early Christianity*, 143–44.

to deacons.[37] Eventually, offices in the East had the same labels as in the West, but in the West they were merely honorary. The East was actually more conservative and segregated, so we find more mentions of ministry focused exclusively on women. For men to have included women in their own ministries would have been considered an encroachment beyond their God-ordained boundaries. But as infant baptism eventually replaced adult baptism, the need for someone to assist with female adults being catechized and baptized (often nude to symbolize "rebirth")[38] disappeared. Other factors leading to the demise of the office were the rise of an all-male priesthood in the pattern of the Old Testament and a return to Old Testament temple practices, especially after Constantine, with church buildings and the clergy/laity divide. Factors leading to this demise included the exclusion of menstruating women from worship; the influence of Aristotle's views of women on influential men like Augustine and later Aquinas; and a later prevailing view that women were weak, fickle, lightheaded, of mediocre intelligence, and a "chosen instrument of the devil."[39]

Women Deacons

Heterarchs point out that, in the Bible, Phoebe is the only named deacon, male or female, connected to a specific church.[40] Substantial evidence for women deacons exists in historical documents including personal letters, Christian historians' writings, church council edicts, and references in the ecclesiastical laws of the *Apostolic Constitutions* (380).[41] In one example, seventeen fourth-century letters have been preserved between John Chrysostom, archbishop of Constantinople, and a woman, Olympias. Olympias built a monastery and presided over it as a deaconess, and it grew to include 250 nuns. The writings of Palladius and Sozomen, Christian historians, corroborate that Olympias was a deaconess.[42]

A review of records demonstrates that ecumenical councils, including the First and Second Council of Nicaea, the Ecumenical Council of Chalcedon, and the Council of Trullo, "endorsed the ordained diaconate of women for

---

37. Gryson, *Ministry of Women in the Early Church*, 62, 68–69.
38. Gryson, *Ministry of Women in the Early Church*, 113.
39. Gryson, *Ministry of Women in the Early Church*, 113.
40. See Question 33. She is the only named deacon (*diakonos*) connected to a specific church, "our sister Phoebe, a *diakonos* of the church in Cenchreae" (Rom. 16:1).
41. John Wijngaards, *The Ordained Women Deacons of the Church's First Millennium* (Norwich: Canterbury, 2011), 19. The *Apostolic Constitutions* detail the most ancient ordination rite for women deacons. Wijngaards also states, "The official status of the women's diaconate is also confirmed by detailed legislation under Emperor Justinian I of Constantinople (527–65), which attributed an equal legal position to men and women deacons" (19).
42. Gryson, *Ministry of Women in the Early Church*, 88–90.

over six centuries."[43] And numerous Greek inscriptions through the sixth century reveal women assigned the title of "deacon."[44]

The Middle Ages: Women Monastics

As holy men headed to the deserts or formed monastic communities in the mid-third century, women had a parallel but different development. Since it was considered unacceptable for women to take to the desert alone, wealthy older women, often widowed, would make space in their homes for holy younger women. Later they would will them their property. A young celibate woman dedicated fully to prayer in one's household became a person of respect. Eventually female monastic communities developed from this practice.[45]

By the Middle Ages, women served God vocationally as hermitesses, beguines, tertiaries, anchoresses, and nuns.[46] The flowering of monastic life allowed such women to obtain an education. Some women founded and ruled as abbesses over religious communities of men and women, called double monasteries. Jerome guided Paula (347–404), a wealthy woman and ascetic, as she founded a double monastery with her daughter Eustochium.[47] Hilda of Whitby (614–680) ruled as abbess for eight years over the double monastery of Heruteuas. Later she founded, built, and led as abbess over a double monastery at Whitby.[48] "Five future bishops were trained in her [Hilda's] community, and kings and rulers sought her advice."[49]

---

43. John Wijngaards, "Church Councils on Women Deacons," in Wijngaards Institute for Catholic Research, http://www.womendeacons.org/history-church-councils-women-deacons. See also Wijngaards, *Ordained Women Deacons*, 18–19.
44. Gary Macy, "The Ordination of Women in the Early Middle Ages," *Theological Studies* 61, no. 3 (2000): 481–507.
45. Susanna Elm, *Virgins of God: The Making of Asceticism in Late Antiquity* (Oxford: Clarendon, 1994), 45–47, 87–89, 92–93.
46. Ann K. Warren, "Five Religious Options for Medieval Women," *Christian History* 30 (1991): 10–13. Religious women called "beguines" lived in the eleventh to the fourteenth centuries. Having chosen a celibate life, they functioned outside of an order, and focused on doing good works. Two examples are Ivetta of Huy and Mary of Oignies. Tertiaries were members of Third Orders, an organization of laypeople associated with either the Dominicans or the Franciscans. One of the most famous anchoresses was Julian of Norwich. She lived a devoutly religious life and solitary life in her "cell," small living quarters connected to St. Julian's Church in Norwich, England, from which she dispensed ministry counsel to those visiting her cell window. Nuns were women who took vows, lived in a community (or convent) with other nuns, and were supervised by a superior.
47. French and Poska, *Women and Gender in the Western Past*, 128.
48. Beden Jarrett and Philip Hereford, *The Ecclesiastical History of the English People*, ed. Philip Hereford (London: Burns, Oates & Washborne, 1935), 104. See also H. E. Brown, *For God Alone: The Lives of the Early English Saints: St. Hilda and St. Elfleda of Whitby* (Phoenix: Leonine, 2016), 4–5.
49. Jeannette L. Angell, "Women in the Medieval Church: Did You Know?," *Christian History* 30 (1991): 2.

For hundreds of years women led monastic communities. Hildegard of Bingen, a twelfth-century woman, founded the Benedictine community in Germany and was its first abbess. She wrote hymns, commentaries on the Bible, and books, including *The Scivias*, a record of her spiritual visions.[50] Due to a calling she discerned from God, Hildegard preached across Germany on four extended trips, "often on horseback and sometimes accompanied by an armed guard because of the dangerous roads."[51]

Catherine of Siena (1347–1380), who lived during the era of the Black Plague, joined the Dominican's Third Order at age sixteen. Embracing a celibate life as a religious laywoman, she evangelized prisoners and nursed those with the plague in her hometown. The focus of her book *The Dialogue* presents Jesus as the bridge between God and humankind. The Roman Catholic Church canonized her and declared her a Doctor of the Church, one of four women including Hildegard of Bingen, Teresa of Ávila, and Thérèse of Lisieux.[52]

Prior to the Protestant Reformation, holy women's and men's biographies were incorporated into calendars and liturgies, for example, St. Valentine on February 14 and St. Patrick on March 17. Thus, holy people, men and women alike, became well known to Christians.

Summary

What does early church history reveal about women serving in public ministry? It shows women serving as prophets, patrons, disciples, house church hosts, teachers, preachers, martyrs, widows, deacons, and monastic leaders. From the time of the earliest Christians, women have served God and his people in a multiplicity of kingdom-building ways.

REFLECTION QUESTIONS

1. What was Phoebe's contribution to the early church, and what are the ramifications for today?

2. How active were women in the early church?

---

50. Elizabeth Gillan Muir, *A Women's History of the Christian Church: Two Thousand Years of Female Leadership* (Toronto: University of Toronto Press, 2019), 88. For additional information, see "Writings from Women in the Medieval Church," *Christian History* 30 (1991): 36.
51. Muir, *Women's History of the Christian Church*, 89.
52. Caroline T. Marshall, "Catherine of Siena," *Christian History* 30 (1991): 6–9. See also Mary T. Malone, *Four Women Doctors of the Church: Hildegard of Bingen, Catherine of Siena, Teresa of Avila, and Therese of Lisieux* (Maryknoll, NY: Orbis, 2017).

3. What was a "patron," and what role did women patrons play in early Roman society?

4. What kinds of leadership positions did women hold?

5. How have ancient inscriptions on tombstones, manuscripts, buildings, and statues, as well as social-historical findings and discoveries in archaeology, added to our understanding of women and ministry in the early church?

What Does Church History Reveal About Women in Public Ministry? Part 2: Reformation to the Twentieth Century

Dr. Cynthia Hester

What does church history from the Reformation to the twentieth century reveal about women in leadership who were preaching, pastoring, supervising, administering sacraments, and teaching?[1] In a word—lots. Despite the swirling mist of polarized theological views about what women *can* do, women *have been doing* public kingdom-building work for centuries.

Women in the Reformation

At the time of Martin Luther, the Roman Catholic Church had, in effect, made priests the mediators between God and humans. In contrast, Luther and the Reformers emphasized every Christian's direct access to God and each person's duty to understand and defend the faith. Luther wrote, "We are all consecrated priests through [believers'] baptism."[2] The priesthood of all believers, found in 1 Peter 2:9, teaches that all believers are part of a "royal priesthood" through faith in Christ. Two women influenced by this doctrine were Katharina Schütz Zell (1498–1562) and Marie Dentière (1495–1561).

---

1. Timothy Larsen, "Women in Public Ministry: A Historic Evangelical Distinctive," in *Women, Ministry and the Gospel: Exploring New Paradigms*, eds. Mark Husbands and Timothy Larsen (Downers Grove, IL: IVP Academic, 2007), 213.
2. Martin Luther, "To the Christian Nobility of the German Nation," 1520, quoted by Kristen Padilla in "Mothers of the Reformation," *Christianity Today*, November 12, 2018, https://www.christianitytoday.com/history/2018/november/mothers-of-reformation-women-ministry-luther-preaching.html.

Katharina, a Strasbourg native, felt that God called her to be a "fisher of people."[3] She married Matthias Zell, a former priest turned Protestant, in "an equal partnership founded on a shared religious commitment to the church."[4] A year later, she published a defense of clerical marriage and called for church reform, arguing that Catholic priests were paying the church taxes to keep mistresses.[5] The Zells frequently hosted Reformation theologians, and Katharina said of them, "They never withheld from me their conversation about holy matters, and they gladly (from the heart) heard mine. I devoted myself to that conversation about holy matters. . . . My desire, longing, and joy was always only to speak of and be busy with these same (holy) things."[6] Also, she wrote a series of letters and a devotional study, and edited a hymnbook, each with significant theological and pastoral elements.

Marie Dentière of Belgium entered an Augustinian convent as a young woman and became an abbess, the female head of a convent or monastery.[7] Luther's teaching, including the priesthood-of-all-believers doctrine, prompted her to leave monasticism. She married Simon Robert, a former priest, and they accepted a Reformed Church pastoral assignment. Later Dentière became a key advocate for church reform in Geneva.[8] John Calvin asked her to write a preface to one of his sermons on modesty.[9]

One hundred years later, Margaret Fell Fox, a Quaker, published *Women's Speaking Justified* to remind her readers of the many biblical examples of women publicly teaching women and men. She argued that the only women Paul intended to prohibit from preaching were the "busiebodies and tatlers" of Corinth.[10] These three women represent just a small sampling of many women during that time who were active for the cause of Christ.

---

3. Katharina Schütz Zell, *Church Mother: The Writings of a Protestant Reformer in Sixteenth-Century Germany*, ed. Elsie McKee (Chicago: University of Chicago Press, 2006), 484, quoted by Catherine Taeger Arnsperger, *Two Reformation Women and Their Views of Salvation: Katharina Schütz and Marie Dentière* (Dallas: Aspire, 2020), 13.
4. Arnsperger, *Two Reformation Women*, 3.
5. Arnsperger, *Two Reformation Women*, 4.
6. Arnsperger, *Two Reformation Women*, 4.
7. Arnsperger, *Two Reformation Women*, 7. See also Ann K. Warren, "Five Religious Options for Medieval Women," *Christian History* 30 (1991): 12.
8. Arnsperger, *Two Reformation Women*, 8.
9. Valerie Abraham, "Five Women of the Reformation," Roman Roads Media, Oct. 5, 2015, https://romanroadsmedia.com/2015/10/5-women-of-reformation.
10. Margaret Fell Fox, *Women's Speaking Justified, Proved, and Allowed of by the Scriptures, All Such as Speak by the Spirit and Power of the Lord Jesus* (London, 1666), located on the University of Pennsylvania website, https://digital.library.upenn.edu/women/fell/speaking/speaking.html.

Women in the 1800–1900s

In the nineteenth century and early twentieth century, many evangelical organizations and leaders supported women in public ministry. Let's review this time period to understand the various ways Asian women, African American women, early abolitionists, religious educators, and women in the missions movement pursued the Lord's call to grow his kingdom.

Bible Women in China

Women played a fundamental role in establishing the Christian church in China. Protestant women missionaries evangelized Chinese "Bible women" and discipled them to share the gospel with local women and children. Because many nineteenth-century Chinese women were preliterate, Protestant women taught the Bible women how to read Chinese characters, which enabled them to teach and disciple from the Mandarin Bible. By the 1880s, some Bible women publicly evangelized and taught the Bible to mixed-sex groups. Bible woman Dora Yu (1873–1931), an itinerant preacher to Korean women, led revival meetings. She evangelized Peace Lin and her son, Watchman Nee, who in turn became evangelists.

During the twentieth century, some Bible women received formal biblical and theological seminary education, and many served as pastors or co-pastors of Chinese churches.[11] Mary Stone (1873–1954) cofounded the Chinese Missionary Society and the Bethel Mission in Shanghai and presided over the Women's Christian Temperance Union in China as its first president.[12] Shortly after the 1924 General Conference of the Methodist Episcopal Church met in Massachusetts, the denomination decided "to permit women limited rights through ordination" and "five Chinese women were ordained as local preachers in the Foochow (Fuzhou) and Kiangsi (Jiangxi) Conferences."[13] The house church movement, in its infancy in the early 1900s, experienced rapid growth during the 1980s through the 1990s. And, in this time during the late twentieth century, most Protestant church members in China were women, and women leaders—pastors and evangelists—were the norm. One cannot

---

11. I interviewed Marlene Westergren (my maternal aunt) about Bible women. She and her husband, Cliff, served as Christian and Missionary Alliance missionaries in Cambodia (1956–65) and Hong Kong (1965–90). She described a Chinese church in Hong Kong that was co-pastored by two Bible women. Both were graduates of the Alliance Theological Seminary. The Westergrens often brought pastors they were mentoring to visit this church because of its administrative and pastoral excellence and its vibrant ministry. During a mission-related trip to China, she and her husband stayed overnight at a Bible woman's home, which was also the meeting place of a house church their host led there (secretly because Christian house churches were illegal).

12. Alexander Chow, "The Remarkable Story of China's 'Bible Women,'" *Christianity Today*, March 16, 2018, 3, https://www.christianitytoday.com/history/2018/march/christian-china-bible-women.html.

13. Chow, "China's 'Bible Women,'" 4.

tell the story of Christianity in China "without acknowledging the female evangelists and pastors who built the Chinese church."[14]

African American Women Clergy

Elizabeth, known only by her first name, held her first prayer meeting at the beginning of the nineteenth century (1808). She was the earliest known Black female preacher in America. Born a slave in Maryland to devout parents, Elizabeth embraced faith in Christ at age twelve. She sought strength through faith, with prayer as a refuge, after her owner sent her to work at a different farm from that of her family and refused all her pleas to let her visit them. A freedwoman at age thirty, she received visions of traveling and preaching. But twelve years would pass before, at the age of forty-two, she felt the Holy Spirit confirm her calling. She described it, saying, "The message which had been given to me I had not yet delivered, and the time had come."[15] Though at times she risked enslavement, Elizabeth preached across the States for almost fifty years. Upon retiring, she lived with Quakers in Philadelphia.[16]

Jarena Lee (1783–1849), the second known Black female preacher, was an official itinerant preacher in the African Methodist Episcopal Church. In her 1836 autobiography, *The Life and Religious Experience of Jarena Lee, A Coloured Lady, Giving an Account of Her Call to Preach the Gospel*, she described how the Holy Spirit urged her with the message "Go, preach the Gospel!" She balked, "No one will believe me." Again, the Spirit urged her, "Preach the Gospel; I will put words in your mouth, and will turn your enemies to become your friends."[17] Though denying her a license, Lee's bishop invited her to preach in Pennsylvania churches.[18] She also preached in Canada, New England, and across the mid-Atlantic states.[19]

Describing Julia A. J. Foote, a Black woman preacher, Alexander Walters, a bishop in the African Methodist Episcopal Zion Church, said, "She was a great preacher, an uncompromising advocate of holiness, and [one] who practiced the gospel she preached."[20] For many years, Mrs. Foote had firmly believed only men should preach, and she had openly spoken against women preaching. But after discerning God calling her to preach, she prepared herself for certain opposition ahead and committed wholeheartedly to her call,

14. Chow, "China's 'Bible Women,'" 2.
15. Bettye Collier-Thomas, *Daughters of Thunder: Black Women Preachers and Their Sermons, 1850–1979* (San Francisco: Jossey-Bass, 1998), 42.
16. Collier-Thomas, *Daughters of Thunder*, 42.
17. Eric Washington, "Jarena Lee," *Christianity Today*, May 23, 2017, https://www.christianity-today.com/history/people/pastorsandpreachers/jarena-lee.html.
18. Collier-Thomas, *Daughters of Thunder*, 45.
19. Washington, "Jarena Lee." See also Collier-Thomas, *Daughters of Thunder*, 45.
20. Quote by the bishop in his book *My Life and Work*, as quoted in Collier-Thomas, *Daughters of Thunder*, 57.

which she pursued for the next fifty years. As an itinerant evangelist and preacher, Foote spoke "at camp meetings, revivals, and churches in California, the Midwest, the Northeast, and Canada."[21] In 1895, the African Methodist Episcopal Zion Church ordained Julia A. J. Foote as their first woman deacon. Four years later, they ordained her as their second woman elder.[22] These three denominations ordained women ministers between the late 1800s and the mid-1950s: the African Methodist Episcopal Zion, the African Methodist Episcopal, and the Colored Methodist Episcopal.[23]

During the early 1900s, Black women preachers in the American Methodist Episcopal Church and Baptist denominations included Mary Evans, Ella Whitfield, Ruth Dennis, and Mrs. Raiff. Quinceila Whitlow and Mrs. F. E. Redwine preached in the Colored Methodist Episcopal Church.[24] And during the 1920s, Rosa Horn, Ida Robinson, and Rosa Edwards preached in the Holiness, Pentecostal, and Spiritual movements.

Citing sexism and the refusal of some Black denominations to ordain women pastors, some Black women established independent churches, many of which still exist. Rosa Horn founded the Pentecostal Faith Church for All Nations in Harlem.[25] Ida Johnson founded a new denomination, the Mount Sinai Holy Church of America, and presided as bishop.[26]

In 1977, the Protestant Episcopal Church ordained Pauli Murray in Washington, DC, their first ordained Black female priest. An author, attorney with three law degrees, and a distinguished university law professor, Murray served until the mandatory retirement age of seventy-two.[27] Twelve years later, the Episcopal Church in Massachusetts ordained Barbara Harris as its first female bishop.[28]

These preaching women believed in their divine call to preach at the Holy Spirit's commissioning. And they overcame obstacles such as rejection, ridicule, travel challenges, and possible enslavement. Pew Research has noted that African American women stand among the most religiously committed

---

21. Collier-Thomas, *Daughters of Thunder*, 59.
22. Collier-Thomas, *Daughters of Thunder*, 59.
23. Sandra L. Barnes, "Whosoever Will Let *Her* Come: Social Activism and Gender Inclusivity in the Black Church," *Journal for the Scientific Study of Religion* 45, no. 3 (Sept. 2006): 373.
24. Thomas, *Daughters of Thunder*, 3.
25. "Rosa Artimus Horn," Oxford African American Studies Center, December 1, 2006, https://www.oxfordaasc.com/view/10.1093/acref/9780195301731.001.0001/acref-9780195301731-e-41715. See also Thomas, *Daughters of Thunder*, 278.
26. Collier-Thomas, *Daughters of Thunder*, 278. See also David Michel, "Ida Bell Robinson," Oxford African American Studies Center, May 31, 2013, https://www.oxfordaasc.com/view/10.1093/acref/9780195301731.001.0001/acref-9780195301731-e-37762.
27. Collier-Thomas, *Daughters of Thunder*, 223.
28. Rosemary Skinner Keller and Rosemary Radford Ruether, eds., *In Our Own Voices: Four Centuries of American Women's Religious Writing* (Louisville: Westminster John Knox, 1995), 310.

Protestants, with eight in ten ranking religion as very important.[29] In Black Protestant churches today, women represent 16 percent of religious leaders.[30] Church history reveals many Black women served in public ministry as evangelists, church founders, and preachers.

First-Wave Feminists

Many of first-wave feminism's roots were Christian. Black and White women abolitionists like Angelina Grimké Weld, Sojourner Truth, and Harriet Tubman considered slavery a moral and spiritual transgression. Thirty years before the Civil War broke out, Weld, who was raised Episcopalian but became a Quaker, published a pamphlet, *An Appeal to Christian Women of the South*, imploring women to join the abolitionist movement.[31] And much of the same philosophy that undergirded their belief in the equality of all played itself out in the suffrage movement.

One Christian denomination played an outsized role in this movement: the Religious Society of Friends, or Quakers. They have provided an equal role for women since their founding in sixteenth-century England. And Quakers were highly influential in bringing together the hundreds of women and a few men who met in Seneca Falls, New York, for the first Women's Rights Convention. This was where the right to vote was first mentioned on paper. Frances Willard, national president of the Women's Christian Temperance Union (WCTU), advocated for temperance, women's rights, and suffrage. She was influential in the fight for the passage of the Eighteenth and Nineteenth Amendments to the United States Constitution.[32]

Women Religious Educators, Pastors, and Preachers

Frances E. Townsley (1849–c. 1913) received a theological education from Wheaton College. After sensing a call to ministry, she taught men in Sunday school and preached at Congregational and Baptist churches. In the late 1880s, she served as the senior minister at Fairfield Baptist Church in Nebraska. A Baptist council made up of representatives from fourteen churches voted unanimously to ordain her.[33] Three decades earlier, Antoinette Brown (Blackwell), a Congregationalist, was ordained in a Baptist church,

---

29. "A Religious Portrait of African-Americans," Pew Research Center: Religion and Public Life, January 2009, https://www.pewforum.org/2009/01/30/a-religious-portrait-of-african-americans.

30. "Gender of Religious Leader," Association of Religion Data Archives, 2018–2019, https://www.thearda.com/ConQS/QS_8.asp.

31. Debra Michals, "Angelina Grimké Weld," National Women's History Museum, 2015, https://www.womenshistory.org/education-resources/biographies/angelina-grimke-weld.

32. "The Journal of Frances E. Willard, 1855–96," National Historical Publications and Records Commission, https://www.archives.gov/nhprc/projects/catalog/frances-willard-journal.

33. Larsen, "Women in Public Ministry," 223.

the first woman ordained in a recognized US denomination.[34] Townsley and Brown were among the "numerous evangelical Baptist women who were ordained and served as senior ministers" in churches in the United States in the late nineteenth and early twentieth centuries.[35]

Janette Hassey, in *No Time for Silence: Evangelical Women in Public Ministry around the Turn of the Century*, wrote about Bible institutes that recruited women as students, and hired female administrators and professors. The Bible Institute of the Chicago Evangelization Society, founded by Dwight L. Moody in 1889 and renamed Moody Bible Institute (MBI) the following year, purposed to train women and men for public teaching and preaching.[36] In its first forty years, MBI exhibited "a clear commitment to the equal training and utilization of women along with men in church ministry."[37] Their women graduates served in evangelical churches in a variety of denominations "as pastors, evangelists, pulpit supply preachers, Bible teachers, and even in the ordained ministry."[38]

Gordon Missionary Training School, founded also in 1889, welcomed all races of men and women,[39] and "in its earliest years had an equal number of women and men professors."[40] Its founder, A. J. Gordon, a Baptist, "linked every great spiritual revival in church history with women's public ministry."[41]

The Christian and Missionary Alliance (C&MA), founded within the same decade by A. B. Simpson, encouraged women's participation and leadership. Female students were required to practice preaching in chapel alongside male students. Simpson "included women on the executive board committee, employed them as Bible professors, and supported female evangelists and branch officers (the early C&MA equivalent to a local minister)."[42]

Helen Barrett Montgomery's church, Lake Avenue Baptist Church in Rochester, New York, credentialed her as a licensed minister in 1892.[43] From 1921–22, Montgomery served as the Northern Baptist Convention's president,

34. Keller and Ruether, *In Our Own Voices*, 226.
35. Larsen, "Women in Public Ministry," 224.
36. Janette Hassey, *Evangelical Women in Public Ministry around the Turn of the Century: No Time for Silence* (Minneapolis: Christians for Biblical Equality, 1986), 36–37.
37. Hassey, *Evangelical Women in Public Ministry*, 45.
38. Hassey, *Evangelical Women in Public Ministry*, 31.
39. "A. J. Gordon," Past Presidents, Gordon College, https://www.gordon.edu/president/ajgordon.
40. Aída Besançon Spencer, Donna F. G. Hailson, Catherine Clark Kroeger, and William David Spencer, *The Goddess Revival: A Biblical Response to God(dess) Spirituality* (Eugene, OR: Wipf & Stock, 1995), 180. See also Nathan R. Wood, *A School of Christ* (Boston: Halliday, 1953), 25–27, 34–35.
41. Hassey, *Evangelical Women in Public Ministry*, 107.
42. Hassey, *Evangelical Women in Public Ministry*, 16.
43. William H. Brackney, "The Legacy of Helen B. Montgomery and Lucy W. Peabody," *International Bulletin of Missionary Research* 14, no. 4 (1991): 174–78.

the first woman president of a national Protestant denomination.[44] Two years after her term ended, the New York Bible Society published her translation of the New Testament from Greek into English, *The New Testament in Modern English*.[45] Four decades later, the Southern Baptists ordained their first woman pastor in the Southern Baptist Convention—Addie Davis.[46]

Henrietta Mears ministered in the mid-1900s as a gifted Bible teacher, Christian education director, publisher, and founder of the National Sunday School Association. The Presbyterian Sunday school class she taught became the largest in the world. William "Bill" R. Bright, founder of Campus Crusade for Christ, described Mears as "truly one of the great women of the twentieth century and one of the greatest influences of my life. . . . Her life was a life of spiritual multiplication."[47] Other notable people who sat under her teaching were the not-yet-an-evangelist Billy Graham; Jim Rayburn, Young Life founder; and Howard Hendricks, distinguished Dallas Theological Seminary professor. The *Handbook of Women Biblical Interpreters* says that "four hundred young men entered full-time ministry as a result of her teaching."[48]

Women in the Missions Movement

A zeal for missions swept across the Protestant church in America in the nineteenth century. And women were being allowed to evangelize, teach, and pastor on the mission field, though they were restricted from doing so in their home churches. At first, women only served as leaders on the mission field as wives of missionaries. And single women only served as caretakers for missionary couples' children. But in time, females from a cross-section of ethnicities and social classes, including some born free and some held as slaves, embraced opportunities "scarcely imaginable in the very countries that sent the women out,"[49] and they carried the gospel across nations.

Lilias Trotter, born into a wealthy British family, prayed for a heart for the unreached. Soon she heard of the spiritual need in North Africa and felt God calling her to share the gospel there. Trotter moved to Algeria, learned Arabic, lived among Arab people, and traveled into unreached regions establishing what she called ministry stations. Over time, she translated the New Testament

---

44. Brackney, "Legacy of Helen B. Montgomery," 176.
45. Spencer et al., *Goddess Revival*, 180.
46. Walter B. Shurden, *The Struggle for the Soul of the SBC: Moderate Responses to the Fundamentalist Movement* (Macon, GA: Mercer University Press, 1993), 130.
47. Esther S. Brinkley, "An Instrument of Calling: Henrietta Mears," Fuller Theological Seminary, *Theology, News and Notes* 42, no. 2 (June 1995): 5–7, 22. See also Arlin C. Migliazzo, *Mother of Modern Evangelicalism: The Life and Legacy of Henrietta Mears* (Grand Rapids: Eerdmans, 2020).
48. Marion Ann Taylor, ed., *Handbook of Women Biblical Interpreters: A Historical and Biographical Guide* (Grand Rapids: Baker Academic, 2012), 356.
49. Timothy C. Tennent, *Invitation to World Missions: A Trinitarian Missiology for the Twenty-First Century* (Grand Rapids: Kregel Academic, 2010), 270.

into Algerian Arabic; wrote devotional leaflets, books, and apologetic materials; and kept journals in which she painted exquisite watercolor pictures alongside her reflections about God. Trotter was the first Protestant woman to found and lead a mission society, the Algiers Mission Band. At the time of her death, the society had thirteen mission stations and thirty workers.[50]

Significantly, many male evangelical leaders of the day—D. L. Moody, A. B. Simpson, A. J. Gordon, Fredrik Franson, and others—encouraged, recruited, shared platforms with, and sent women to serve in public ministry roles. The China Inland Mission founder, J. Hudson Taylor, "expected women, both single and married, to carry out all the missionary duties, including preaching and teaching."[51] By the turn of the twentieth century, forty denominational women's missionary societies had formed, "paying the salaries of indigenous female evangelists and sending single women as missionary doctors, teachers, and evangelists." Women outnumbered men on the mission field by two to one.[52]

Summary

God preserved women's speech for all to read in his holy Word. The words of fifty-one women speak in the Old Testament and twenty women in the New Testament.[53] And in that tradition, women have continued in public ministry. Historian Timothy Larsen writes, "Women in public Christian ministry is a historic distinctive of evangelicalism. It is historic because evangelical women have been fulfilling their callings in public ministry from the founding generation of evangelicalism to the present day and in every period in between."[54]

REFLECTION QUESTIONS

1. What woman from the Reformation to the twentieth century did you find most inspiring, and why?

2. Which religious institutions and denominations affirmed and developed female scholarship, teaching, and leadership?

---

50. Miriam Huffman Rockness, *A Passion for the Impossible: The Life of Lilias Trotter* (Grand Rapids: Discovery House, 2003).

51. Marguerite Kraft and Meg Crossman, "Women in Mission," in *Perspectives on the World Christian Movement*, 4th ed., eds. Ralph D. Winter and Stephen C. Hawthorne (Pasadena, CA: William Carey Library, 2009), 295–96.

52. Kraft and Crossman, "Women in Mission," 296.

53. Lindsay Hardin Freeman, *Bible Women: All Their Words and Why They Matter*, 2nd ed. (Cincinnati: Forward Movement, 2015), 465–68.

54. Larsen, "Women in Public Ministry," 213.

3. How active were women in this time period and what kinds of ministries did they take part in?

4. What kinds of leadership positions did women hold?

5. What did you learn about first-wave feminists, their religious affiliation generally, and what kinds of rights they were asking for?

How Did Western Culture Influence Women in the Home, Society, and the Church?

Dr. Cynthia Hester

In the previous chapters, we reviewed what the early church through the twentieth century reveals about women, leadership, and public ministry. In contrast, this chapter will consider three historical periods in the Western world—the Protestant Reformation, Enlightenment, and Industrial Revolution—and their influence on women in the home, society, and the church.

Protestant Reformation

In 1517, Catholic priest Martin Luther posted ninety-five talking points on the doors of Castle Church in Wittenberg, Germany. A century before him, theologian John Hus had expressed similar concerns regarding Catholic Church doctrine and clergy authority. A new invention, the printing press, meant Luther's words were translated, distributed, and discussed across Europe within days. This event birthed the Protestant Reformation that ultimately diminished the influence of the Catholic Church and led to the creation of new variations of Christian churches.

As the Reformation reduced the authority of popes, cardinals, and priests, it heightened male authority in the home, church, and political realm.[1] Both the English Puritans and Protestant Reformers taught that women, though created in God's image and saved through faith, were subordinate to men.[2]

---

1. Merry E. Wiesner-Hanks, *Women and Gender in Early Modern Europe*, 4th ed. (New York: Cambridge University Press, 2019), 314.
2. Wiesner-Hanks, *Women and Gender in Early Modern Europe*, 39.

They embraced pagan Aristotle's view that "the female is a misbegotten male."[3] The Reformers believed "all women are born that they may acknowledge themselves as inferior in consequence to the superiority of the male sex."[4]

Before the Reformation, singleness had been considered the Christians' highest estate, but the Reformers taught that marriage was a woman's highest calling. Katharina von Bora (Katie Luther), a former nun, bore Martin Luther nine children. Due to her renowned expertise as a hostess, many coveted a seat at the Luthers' dinner table. Her husband "extolled the virtues of Martha, the sister of Lazarus, who stayed in the kitchen, prepared the food, and oversaw the household."[5] Luther opposed educating girls beyond the basics, saying, "There is no dress that suits a woman as badly as trying to become wise."[6]

Prior to the Reformation a significant number of women in Europe lived in convents, leading spiritually focused lives with access to education unavailable anywhere else.[7] But Luther and his followers emptied monasteries of their nuns and priests; and marriage—rather than celibacy—became the preferred marital status for ministers and other holy people.[8] Soon, women's economically viable options narrowed to marriage. Legal regulations required parental consent for marriage in many Protestant territories,[9] and married women were legally dependent on their husbands.[10] Municipal authorities in "every Protestant territory passed a marriage ordinance that stressed wifely obedience."[11]

Some resisted such thinking. Influential people, including Margaret Fell Fox and the Quakers, appealed to the Scriptures to challenge the emphasis on women's inherent weakness. Nevertheless, the ideas prevailed.

During this same period, new data in the fields of mathematics, physics, astronomy, biology (including human anatomy), and chemistry transformed

3. Frank A. James, "Thomas Aquinas on Women," Carolyn Custis James (blog), August 6, 2013, https://carolyncustisjames.com/2013/08/06/thomas-aquinas-on-women. See also Terrence E. Cook, "'Misbegotten Males'? Innate Differences and Stratified Choice in the Subjection of Women," *The Western Political Quarterly* 36, no. 2 (1983): 194–220.

4. John Calvin, *Commentary on 1 Corinthians*, quoted by Marg Mowczko, "Misogynistic Quotations from Church Fathers and Reformers," MargMowczko.com, January 24, 2013, https://margmowczko.com/misogynist-quotes-from-church-fathers.

5. Katherine L. French and Allyson M. Poska, *Women and Gender in the Western Past*, vol. 1 (Boston: Houghton Mifflin, 2007), 219.

6. Merry Wiesner, "Luther and Women: The Death of Two Marys," in *Disciplines of Faith: Studies in Religion, Patriarchy, and Politics*, eds. Raphael Samuel, James Obelkevich, and Lyndal Roper (London: Routledge, 1987), 300, as quoted in French and Poska, *Women and Gender in the Western Past*.

7. Jennifer Powell McNutt, "No Simple Story," *Christian History Magazine* 131 (2019): 7.

8. French and Poska, *Women and Gender in the Western Past*, 221.

9. Wiesner-Hanks, *Women and Gender in Early Modern Europe*, 314.

10. Wiesner-Hanks, *Women and Gender in Early Modern Europe*, 317.

11. French and Poska, *Women and Gender in the Western Past*, 221.

societal views about nature. A growing focus on intellectual inquiry contributed to the Scientific Revolution.

Enlightenment

From Western Europe to the American colonies, thought leaders argued for employing human reasoning, through the lens of logic and science, to understand humanity, society, religion, and the natural world.[12] This time, 1685–1850, became known as the Age of Reason, or the Enlightenment, and topics of debate included the nature of government, religion, "social functions of the family," and the "biological and psychological differences between the sexes."[13]

Regarding faith, Enlightenment thinkers theorized that religions were human inventions created by religious leaders to preserve their own interests. Human thought no longer centered on God and the Bible. And over time, many linked religions to superstitious thought.[14]

The debate about the differences between the sexes led to differing conclusions. Certain eighteenth-century anatomists believed differences between women and men extended beyond their reproductive organs. For example, Marie Geneviève Thiroux d'Arconville (1720–1805), a wife and author, believed the female body's highest use was childbearing. In contrast, philosopher René Descartes believed men's and women's bodies differed in sexual organs only. So, he concluded, women's intellect was not inferior. John Locke's advocacy for individual rights and ensuing attacks on the monarchy as a "patriarchal model of political authority" unintentionally supported women's participation in politics.[15]

Descartes's defense of the intellect of women led many to reject the long-held Aristotelian view of the female body as a deformed male body. D'Arconville, and other anatomists, viewed the female womb "as an amazing organ, instead of the source of hysteria and confusion advanced by Aristotle."[16] Subsequently, many acknowledged women's capability for rational thought. Both d'Arconville and Descartes held in common this new view of women's bodies: that they "differed fundamentally from men's and were not inferior versions of them."[17]

Historian Barbara Welter noted that writers at that time often used the term "true womanhood" to describe the ideal woman. She held "a fearful obligation, a solemn responsibility" to uphold "four cardinal virtues—piety,

---

12. Barbara Taylor, "Feminism and the Enlightenment, 1650–1850," *History Workshop Journal*, no. 47 (Spring 1999): 261–72.
13. Taylor, "Feminism and Enlightenment," 265.
14. Alister McGrath, *Christian Theology: An Introduction*, 5th ed. (Malden, MA: Wiley-Blackwell, 2011), 428.
15. Taylor, "Feminism and the Enlightenment," 265.
16. French and Poska, *Women and Gender*, 263.
17. French and Poska, *Women and Gender*, 262–63.

purity, submissiveness, and domesticity."[18] Whereas public virtue had once been a valued male trait, now women, not men, were held to the virtues of piety. Women were also perceived as needing to pursue purity because they held the primary responsibility to keep men, "being by nature more sensual," from sexual sin.[19]

And thus, many justified educating men differently from women. To help women reach their full potential as future wives and mothers, they could receive an education, but only on topics restricted primarily to the domestic realm. In contrast, a male needed his education to prepare him for the public realm of commerce and politics.[20]

Industrial Revolution (1780–1830 in America)

Advances in transportation and manufacturing utilizing water and steam power, rather than animal strength, ushered in the Industrial Revolution. It began in England and spread across Europe to America. Industrialization rapidly changed the nature of work, the economy, and the home, shifting food and home-produced goods to production outside the home. Whereas in agrarian cultures, family and business often occupy the same space, the Industrial Revolution, with factories and specialized tasks, created a private/public divide. In doing so, it redefined faith and family as private, and business and industry as public.[21]

The gradual changes moved the center of life from farms to cities. America began importing a variety of goods from Britain, and consumption skyrocketed. Instead of trading or bartering, people paid for products with money. And in this cash-centered economy, the standard of living for most Americans improved. Middle- and upper-class families in the cities could afford luxury items. And rural families could opt to purchase essential goods from peddlers.[22]

The Industrial Revolution had a profound effect on the family. Work moved outside the home. The agrarian society as it had been known, which had consisted of husband, wife, children, and hired hands laboring together to provide mutual sustenance, ended. Earned wages defined work. Men were no longer present on a regular basis in the home. And fathers spent less time with their children, no longer helping "educate them, enforce regular discipline, or train them in adult skills and trades."[23]

---

18. Barbara Welter, "The Cult of True Womanhood: 1820–1860," *American Quarterly* 18, no. 2 (1966): 151–74.
19. Welter, "Cult of True Womanhood," 153.
20. French and Poska, *Women and Gender in the Western Past*, 263.
21. Nancy Pearcey, *Total Truth: Liberating Christianity From Its Cultural Captivity* (Westchester, IL: Crossway Books, 2004), 327.
22. Catherine A. Brekus, *Strangers and Pilgrims: Female Preaching in America, 1740–1845* (Chapel Hill: University of North Carolina Press, 1998), 234.
23. Pearcey, *Total Truth*, 330.

How did the Industrial Revolution affect women? Despite the amount of hard work at home, housewives' labor was considered less valuable because it did not reap wages. So, rather than productively contributing to the family's economic well-being as printers, weavers, artisans, and other small business proprietors, as these types of work moved outside the home, many wives became dependent on their husbands' wages. Additionally, "women's work" that had proved interesting to them in the home—from candle-making to canning to trading in textiles—moved with the men to factories. Socially isolated from other adults, women carried the primary responsibility for children. Consequently, most women experienced a "drastic *decrease* in the range of work available to them in the home" and "a dramatic *increase* in responsibility for the narrow range of tasks that remained."[24]

As family farms and homes produced fewer goods, it became a mark of a family's status when they could afford for the wife and children to stay in the home rather than go out to earn wages.[25] Thus, in some middle- and most upper-class families, women were ideally home, mothering and educating their children. Of course, lower-class families could not achieve this new "ideal." Women in these families, unable to contribute alongside their husbands, worked long hours in factories, or they earned wages as seamstresses, milliners, laundresses, tavern and innkeepers, and domestic servants.

Yet, the wages paid to women were "only half as much as men for their labor."[26] In this new cash-driven economy, the market valued women's work less than it did men's. James Mitchell, a factory commissioner, argued for paying women lower wages than men because "the low price of female labor makes it the most profitable as well as most agreeable occupation for a female to superintend her own domestic establishment, and her low wages do not tempt her to abandon the care of her own children."[27]

In the nineteenth century, these women could not vote, initiate a divorce, sign a contract, make a will, or have or exercise control over any property. If a husband denied or restricted access to their children, the wife had no legal recourse. Women "effectively held the legal status of children."[28]

Alarmed by what they saw as injustices concerning women, hundreds of men and women, many driven by Christian conviction, gathered in Seneca Falls, New York, in 1848, for the first Women's Rights Convention. Prior to

24. Pearcey, *Total Truth*, 331, emphasis original.
25. "Changes in Gender Roles and Family Life," US History 1, Lumen Learning, https://courses.lumenlearning.com/suny-ushistory1ay/chapter/changes-in-gender-roles-and-family-life.
26. Brekus, *Strangers and Pilgrims*, 237.
27. Joyce Burnette, *Gender, Work and Wages in Industrial Revolution Britain* (Cambridge: Cambridge University Press, 2008), 134, quoted in Beth Allison Barr, *The Making of Biblical Womanhood* (Grand Rapids: Brazos, 2021), 164.
28. "Women's Rights in Antebellum America," US History 1, Lumen Learning, https://courses.lumenlearning.com/suny-ushistory1ay/chapter/womens-rights-in-antebellum-america.

that convention, a smaller group of men and women drafted a Declaration of Sentiments. Alluding to the Declaration of Independence, this document began with "We hold these truths to be self-evident: that all men *and women* are created equal." It listed fifteen grievances along with eleven resolutions advocating for women's civil rights. The fifteen grievances included:[29]

- He has compelled her to submit to laws, in the formation of which she had no voice.
- He has withheld her from rights which are given to the most ignorant and degraded men—both natives and foreigners.
- He has made her, if married, in the eye of the law, civilly dead.
- He has taken from her all right in property, even to the wages she earns.
- He has created a false public sentiment by giving to the world a different code of morals for men and women, by which moral delinquencies which exclude women from society, are not only tolerated but deemed of little account in man.

Sixty-eight women and thirty-two men signed the Declaration of Sentiments, inaugurating almost a century of advocacy for women's rights.[30]

Summary

Society considered woman's highest calling prior to the Reformation to be celibacy for the purpose of devotion to God. But Reformers viewed marriage as the best and highest call for women. Enlightenment thinkers viewed women as physically and intellectually weak. The Industrial Revolution resulted in the prioritized private/public split of home and work, and valuing women as domestic guardians of the home. These changing viewpoints, which resulted in the subjugation of women, derived their foundation not completely from Scripture but from the economic and social changes stemming from the Reformation, the Enlightenment, and the Industrial Revolution.

These issues led to the second wave of feminism in the 1960s and to Christian hierarchs and heterarchs waging war over many of the questions that we cover in this book that divide the Christian church today.

---

29. Elizabeth Cady Stanton, "Declaration of Sentiments: Women's Grievances Against Men," July 19, 1848, https://achievethecore.org/content/upload/Text%20and%20Text_ Dependent_Questions%20with%20writing%20prompt%20(Motter).pdf.
30. "Women's Rights in Antebellum America," US History 1, Lumen Learning, https://courses. lumenlearning.com/suny-ushistory1ay/chapter/womens-rights-in-antebellum-america.

REFLECTION QUESTIONS

1. What effect did the changes brought on by the Reformation have on women?

2. How did the Enlightenment change the place and priority of God in everyday life?

3. What catastrophic impact did the Industrial Revolution have on families?

4. How were upper-class, middle-class, and lower-class families differently affected?

5. How were the seeds of feminism planted in the Industrial Revolution?

Current Issues

Can Women Be Deacons?

Many churches include the position of *deacon* as an official office where a male lay person has the opportunity to be involved in assisting elders or professional clergy. Women are allowed to serve in this capacity in some churches and not in others. To help you decide which approach is more biblical, let's consider where the role of deacon originated, key biblical texts, and the different perspectives on this question.

What Do Deacons Do?

Deacons were first appointed due to a conflict that arose in Jerusalem in the first church. As organizations grow, the need for quality administration increases—and this infant church was experiencing meteoric growth. The church provided for widows lacking male assistance because they had little opportunity to meet their own financial needs (1 Tim. 5:1–16). But a controversy erupted between the Greek and Hebrew Christians. The first group complained that their widows were being overlooked in the daily distribution of food in favor of the second.

As a result, the twelve apostles called everyone in the church together and asked them to choose seven worthy men to take over running the ministry of food distribution so that the Twelve could focus on "prayer and the ministry of the word" (Acts 6:4). Here we observe the adoption of wise administrative principles such as delegation of tasks and including everyone in the process of decision-making.

Over time, early church history tells us that the kinds of church tasks assigned to deacons were broadened and women were also chosen to serve in these capacities. For example:

> The third-century "Didascalia Apostolorum" ("Teaching of the Apostles") refers to deaconesses and tells bishops they should honor these women "as the Holy Spirit is honored."

A later chapter describes the activities of deaconesses in some detail. They can, for example, freely visit the homes of women who are sick, without causing scandal. They also played a major role in the baptism of women. In antiquity, new Christians were baptized naked, and many were baptized as adult converts. Since the clergy were male, deaconesses safeguarded the modesty of women, taking them into the water and completing the anointing that had been ceremonially begun by the bishop.[1]

What Does the Bible Say About Women Deacons?

While heterarchs see scriptural support for women deacons, hierarchs disagree with one another on what they think Scripture says about women deacons.

1 Timothy 3:11

Paul wrote this letter to Timothy, his son in the faith and a leader in the Ephesian church, to help him combat the false teaching erupting from within (1 Tim. 1:3–7) and the resulting chaos (1 Tim. 2:1–2). In 3:1–13, Paul laid out the qualifications for elders (or overseers) and deacons, but in verse 11, he expressed what God expects of women leaders. However, some scholars believe Paul refers here to the wives of deacons while others believe he was giving the church the qualifications for female deacons. Verse 11 says: "In the same way, the women [or wives] are to be worthy of respect, not malicious talkers but temperate and trustworthy in everything."

The word "women" here is translated as "wives" in some Bibles. The Greek word is *gynaikas*, which can be translated either way. Hierarch Thomas Schreiner argues that if Paul meant "wives" he would have added the word "their," to mean the deacons' wives. But because "their" is absent, he believes a more honest rendition, "women," is in view.[2] This perspective opens the door to the possibility that Paul approved of women deacons.

Hierarch Tom Constable comes to the same conclusion but for different reasons:

- First, there is nothing about the office as such that would exclude a woman.
- Second, it would be unusual for Paul to prescribe qualifications for wives of deacons but not for wives of elders.

1. Mike Aquilina, "Special Report: Can There Be Women Deacons?," *Angelus*, February 22, 2019, https://angelusnews.com/voices/special-report-can-there-be-women-deacons.
2. Thomas Schreiner, "Does the Bible Support Female Deacons? Yes," The Gospel Coalition, February 19, 2019, https://www.thegospelcoalition.org/article/bible-support-female-deacons-yes.

- Third, the fact that he inserted special qualifications for women—in the middle of his list of *deacon qualifications*—seems to indicate that he considered these women to be "deacons" (i.e., "deaconesses").[3]

Verse 11 is nestled among Paul's qualifications for male elders and male deacons:

Verses 1–7	Qualifications for Male Elders
Verses 8–10	Qualifications for Male Deacons
Verse 11	Qualifications for Female Deacons or Deacon's Wives
Verse 12	An Additional Qualification for a Male Deacon

It does seem strange that Paul would only mention qualifications for deacons' wives but leave out qualifications for elders' wives. If he had been consistent, the passage would look like this:

Verses 1–7	Qualifications for Male Elders
(Missing)	Qualifications for Elders' Wives
Verses 8–10	Qualifications for Male Deacons
Verse 11	Qualifications for Deacons' Wives
Verse 12	An Additional Qualification for Male Deacons

Thus hierarchs Schreiner and Constable agree that Paul may well have been listing the qualifications for female deacons in the early church, affirming historical records.

Romans 16:1–2

"I commend to you our sister Phoebe, a deacon [or a servant?] of the church in Cenchreae [the port of Corinth]. I ask you to receive her in the Lord in a way worthy of his people and to give her any help she may need from you, for she has been the benefactor of many people, including me." These verses begin the conclusion of Paul's treasured theological letter to the churches in Rome where he personally greets his dear friends there. But first he commends Phoebe for her part in delivering the letter to the Romans. Most scholars agree that Paul commissioned Phoebe to make the dangerous trip from Corinth to bring them this letter, trusting her fortitude, courage, and reliability.

He calls her "a *diakonos* of the church in Cenchreae." This word can be translated as "deacon" or as "servant." Interpreters must determine which meaning

---

3. Dr. Tom Constable, "Notes on 1 Timothy," Sonic Light, Plano Bible Chapel, 2021, 78–79, http://planobiblechapel.org/tcon/notes/pdf/1timothy.pdf.

Paul meant. Bible translators make different choices, often according to their presuppositions. For example, when referring to males in 1 Timothy 3:8, 12, and Philippians 1:1, the word is almost always translated as "deacon," but when referring to a woman, Phoebe, the translators often choose "servant."[4] The King James Version of the Bible was the first to translate *diakonos* here as "servant."

Let's see if further details in the text help us. First, we know that Paul is "commending" her and calling her "our sister." In 2 Corinthians 3:1, Paul writes, "Or do we need, like some people, letters of recommendation to you or from you?" Clearly, writing letters of recommendation was a common custom, and at the end of Romans, Paul commends Phoebe to the Roman Christians to ensure she will receive the honor and care due her.

In verse 2, Paul describes her as a "benefactor of many," including himself. Patrons or benefactors were people of means who championed others, usually providing finances and lending their prestige as a testimony to the worthy character of their protégé. The women who traveled with Jesus were described this way (see Question 13).

> For all its faults (noted by the ancients themselves), the institution of patronage was in many respects gender-blind. As such, it allowed a freedom of movement at most social levels for women to participate in the social, economic, and political environment without any cultural condemnation. Thus while a woman might otherwise be stigmatized for speaking or acting publicly on economic, religious, or political matters, a patroness had liberty to exercise her ideas and interests with society's blessings.[5]

With these details in mind, you must decide what you think Paul meant when he described Phoebe as "a *diakonos* of the church in Cenchreae." Is it deacon or servant?

Arguments for "Deacon"

Hierarch Thomas Schreiner believes that Phoebe was an official deacon in the Corinthian church. Phoebe is the only named *diakonos* in the Bible that is connected to a named church. He contends, "The addition of the words 'the church in Cenchreae' suggests an official capacity."[6] Greek scholar R. C. H. Lenski agrees:

---

4. Of the major English versions, the ESV, CSB, NASB, KJV, NET, CEB, and NKJV all chose "servant," while "deacon" was used in the NIV, NLT, RSV ("deaconess"), and NRSV.
5. Lynn H. Cohick, *Women in the World of the Earliest Christians: Illuminating Ancient Ways of Life* (Grand Rapids: Baker Academic, 2009), 320.
6. Schreiner, "Does the Bible Support Female Deacons?"

This is the first mention of women deacons in the church. . . . While we lack information we must, nevertheless, say that, since the arrangement of having male deacons in Jerusalem had proven highly beneficial at the very start, the appointment of women was the next logical step. The ministration of the first deacons consisted in the distribution of food to widows. But, surely, it must soon have become apparent that, for instance, in cases of sickness and of poverty and of loneliness, especially of poor widows and orphans, a need had arisen for the alleviation of which men could not be used; only competent women could serve in this capacity. Voluntary efforts would accomplish much, and in many churches they, no doubt, sufficed as they still do; but at least in Cenchreae we see the forward step, the addition of duly appointed deaconesses.[7]

Arguments for "Servant"

Hierarch Guy Waters argues that women cannot be deacons because as they serve in this official capacity they may make decisions that carry some kind of authority. He bases his thinking on 1 Timothy 2:8–15. To be sure, the context of Paul's statement is the church gathered in worship, and particularly the work of preaching (1 Tim. 2:8–15). Paul's statement, however, is not limited to the preaching of the Word in public worship. Paul here forbids women from exercising any authority in the church. Because the offices of elder and deacon entail the possession and exercise of authority in the church, Paul forbids women from holding either office.[8] Therefore, argues Waters, women cannot be deacons and the word *diakonos*, when referring to Phoebe or any woman, should be translated "servant."[9]

Evidence from Church History

With today's scholars disagreeing, a look at early church history may provide direction and clarity. In AD 112, we find a reference to "women deacons" in a letter from Roman author and lawyer Pliny the Younger to the Emperor Trajan. Pliny compiled his huge collection of private letters into books before he died. These letters provide us with intimate details concerning public and private life during that time in the Roman Empire. In one of his letters, Pliny revealed that while investigating Christians, he tortured two Christian

---

7. R. C. H. Lenski, *The Interpretation of St. Paul's Epistle to the Romans* (Minneapolis: Augsburg, 1936), 899–900.
8. Guy Waters, "Does the Bible Support Female Deacons? No," The Gospel Coalition, February 19, 2019, https://www.thegospelcoalition.org/article/bible-support-female-deacons-no.
9. Waters, "Does the Bible Support Female Deacons?"

women that he identified as *ministrae*, or deaconesses in Latin. Heterarchs argue that Phoebe is the only named deacon, male or female, connected to a specific church.

Substantial evidence for women deacons exists in historical documents including personal letters, Christian historians' writings, church council edicts, and references in the ecclesiastical laws of the *Apostolic Constitutions* (380).[10] In one example, seventeen fourth-century letters have been preserved between John Chrysostom, archbishop of Constantinople, and a woman, Olympias. Olympias built a monastery and presided over it as a deaconess, and it grew to include 250 nuns. The writings of Palladius and Sozomen, Christian historians, corroborate that Olympias was a deaconess.[11]

A review of records demonstrates that ecumenical councils, including the First and Second Council of Nicaea, the Ecumenical Council of Chalcedon, and the Council of Trullo, "endorsed the ordained diaconate of women for over six centuries."[12] And numerous Greek inscriptions through the sixth century reveal women assigned the title "deacon."[13]

Origen (c. 185–c. 254) refers to deacons in his writings, summarized here by Catherine Kroeger:

> The text teaches with the authority of the Apostle that even women are instituted deacons in the Church. This is the function which was exercised in the church of Cenchreae by Phoebe, who was the object of high praise and recommendation by Paul. . . . And thus this text teaches at the same time two things: that there are . . . women deacons in the Church, and that women, who by their good works deserve to be praised by the Apostle, ought to be accepted in the diaconate.[14]

In AD 325, the first ecumenical council of the Christian church, the Council of Nicaea, met. By looking at documents coming out of that important

---

10. John Wijngaards, *The Ordained Women Deacons of the Church's First Millennium* (Norwich: Canterbury, 2011), 19. The *Apostolic Constitutions* detail the most ancient ordination rite for women deacons. Wijngaards also states, "The official status of the women's diaconate is also confirmed by detailed legislation under Emperor Justinian I of Constantinople (527–65), which attributed an equal legal position to men and women deacons" (19).

11. Gryson, *Ministry of Women in the Early Church*, 88–90.

12. John Wijngaards, "Church Councils on Women Deacons," *Wijngaards Institute for Catholic Research*, http://www.womendeacons.org/history-church-councils-women-deacons. See also Wijngaards, *Ordained Women Deacons*, 18–19.

13. Gary Macy, "The Ordination of Women in the Early Middle Ages," *Theological Studies* 61, no. 3 (2000): 481–507.

14. Catherine Kroeger, "The Neglected History of Women in the Early Church," in *Christian History* 17, no. 1 (1988): 11.

gathering, we know that "women deacons were well known and active in the Byzantine [Eastern] part of the Church. . . . At the end of the 4th century, forty women deacons ministered at the Hagia Sophia [Cathedral] in Constantinople [Turkey], some of whom we know from literary sources by had been ordained by John Chrysostom, such as Olympias and Amproukla."[15] Also, many tombstone inscriptions carry the term "deaconess."[16]

Hierarch Wayne Grudem argues that the real issue is not whether or not women were ever deacons. Instead, what matters is whether or not the office of deacon in a specific church includes the governing and teaching authority that is reserved for elders. These leadership roles are not open to women, whatever the label.[17]

Summary

Some hierarchs and all heterarchs agree that today women can serve as deacons. For example, Saucy concludes that today women are "appointed along with men to the recognized function of deacon, giving leadership to the church's ministry of mercy, and probably also a wide variety of other tasks complementing and supporting the ministry of the elders."[18]

We believe churches have the choice to commission women to serve in the office of deacon according to their biblical beliefs and practices. And, where appropriate, that choice would go far in communicating to women that they are valued.

Former Southern Baptist Convention pastor, thought leader, and writer Jim Denison offered a wise perspective when he challenged his Baptist denomination to consider making this practice the norm in their churches:

> I believe that women should be ordained as leaders and deacons for the following strategic and practical reasons. First, ordination to the ministry or diaconate is the most significant way most churches recognize congregational leaders. While we know that other roles are vitally important (i.e., Sunday school teachers and officers, worship leaders, trustees, committee chairs and members), no other roles carry congregational endorsement and recognition equal to that of minister

15. John Wijngaards, "The Ancient Deaconesses—Women Who Were Ordained Deacons," Wijngaards Institute, https://www.womendeacons.org/history-canon19-council-nicea.

16. John McKinley, "Can Women Be Deacons?," The Good Book Blog, Talbot School of Theology, Biola University, https://www.biblestudytools.com/bible-study/explore-the-bible/can-women-be-deacons.html.

17. Grudem, *EFBT*, 263–66.

18. Robert Saucy, "The Ministry of Women in the Early Church," in *Women and Men in Ministry: A Complementary Perspective*, eds. Robert L. Saucy and Judith K. TenElshof (Chicago: Moody, 2001), 176.

or deacon. To deny godly women such affirmation seems wrong to me, especially given the strong evidence for this affirmation in the Bible, and in Christian and Baptist history. The signal we send is that our churches do not value the servant leadership of women as fully as it affirms men.

Second, when ministers and deacons serve in public roles (as in helping administer the Lord's Supper and leading in congregational business), many see the absence of women as indication that the church devalues their place in ministry. . . .

Third, I believe women serving as ministers and deacons will help churches fulfill our Great Commission purpose more obediently. Their insights and experiences will help them formulate the most effective strategies for congregational and community ministry. . . . In these crucial days, churches need the spiritual engagement of the entire congregation as they assault the gates of hell together (Matthew 16:18).[19]

Wendy Alsup adds her plea on behalf of women deacons:

I am hopeful that having female deacons will become the norm among conservative evangelical churches once again. We need to cultivate the spiritual gifts of women and then use those gifts in the ways that God intends. We need to value the particular aspects of HELP (in the strongest sense of the word *ezer*) that God created women to bring to the table in His image. If we deny women the office of Deaconess when God hasn't, we can push women toward accepting either feminism or chauvinism. We haven't given them a biblical norm.[20]

For too long, many conservative churches have focused on what women can't do in the church and home instead of considering what they can do. One consequence is that women, especially young women, are the largest demographic exiting churches today.[21] A healthier, and less costly, perspective,

19. Jim Denison, "Should Women Serve as Deacons? Seeking the Word and Will of God," Denison Forum, January 4, 2011, https://www.denisonforum.org/resources/should-women-serve-as-deacons-seeking-the-word-and-will-of-god.

20. Wendy Alsup, "The Case for Women Deacons," The Gospel-Centered Woman, https://gospelcenteredwoman.com/the-case-for-women-deacons.

21. George Barna, "20 Years of Surveys Show Key Differences in the Faith of America's Men and Women: Part 3: Gender Differences," Barna.com, Aug. 1, 2011, https://www.barna.com/research/20-years-of-surveys-show-key-differences-in-the-faith-of-americas-men-and-women.

instead of setting up barriers for women, would be to examine Scripture thoroughly, look honestly for limitations on women, and push for women to do everything they possibly can biblically—never less. Alsup writes, "If we go past Scripture from a liberal end or refuse to move up to it from the conservative end, we have capitulated to culture either way. Particularly troubling in the conservative response is that we have denied women the use of their gifts in the Church as God allows."[22]

One way to focus on what women can do would be to consider whether the office of deacon is actually open to women, and if so, to make it common practice by reconstructing church governments to reflect this biblical norm. Imagine how this new observance might change the church culture and ethos and encourage godly women to use their spiritual gifts to build up the body. Volunteerism might soar as women realize they have a place at the table to contribute and serve alongside their brothers.

REFLECTION QUESTIONS

1. How would you summarize the evidence from church history that women served as deacons in the early church?

2. What are the arguments for and against this practice?

3. Why do you think women deacons might be helpful in a church?

4. Why do you think women deacons might be harmful to a church?

5. How would you feel about women serving as deacons where you worship?

---

22. Alsup, "Case for Women Deacons."

Can Women Be Priests?

Exploring the qualifications for priesthood involves the broader issue of ordination. Those asking, "Can women be priests?" are essentially asking, "Can women be ordained to church office?" Observers of the church's debate on ordination rightly point out that the Bible does not mention ordination at all. The word isn't in there. The closest we get to the principle of ordination in the Old Testament is Aaron's investiture as high priest (Exod. 28–29), and in the New Testament, the laying on of hands in Acts 6:1–7 for the seven men chosen to lead the church through service. But these occasions are not referred to as "ordination."

"Ordination" generally refers to a process by which church leaders recognize a person's calling to ministry. Priests, deacons, and ministers of the gospel are typically ordained into their roles upon affirmation that they indeed have been called and have demonstrated fitness for their new role. In this chapter, we explore the role of priest/minister of the gospel in the Protestant tradition.

What the Priesthood in the Church Is Not

When we consider the question "Can women be priests?" we must realize that we are not discussing the Levitical priesthood of the Old Testament. Some scholars will compare the Christian priesthood and Jewish priesthood, but the offices are not the same. Neither are the requirements. Why not?

When God gave his law to the nation of Israel at Mount Sinai (Exodus 20), he included instructions on who would lead his people spiritually. He chose the tribe of Levi to carry out sacrificial rites and care for the tabernacle. Only male Levites without blemish or disability could serve as priests. No other Israelite was qualified for that task.

No Christian priest—whether Catholic, Protestant, or Eastern Orthodox, the three major branches of the universal church—must be a descendant from Levi. The church is not Israel, our priests are not sons of Aaron, and Christ united Jew and Gentile through the cross. Yet some strains of Christendom continue to require that an ordained priest—or pastor—be male. What are their arguments?

Protestant and Catholic Reasoning

We realize that most of our readers will approach this book from a Protestant perspective. And perhaps when you hear "priest" you likely think of Catholics. But Eastern Orthodox and several Protestant mainline denominations (e.g., Anglican and Episcopalian) are led by ordained priests. One of the most fascinating issues is that Catholics approach the question using completely different reasons than do Protestants. What do we mean?

Protestants tend to ask, "Does Scripture prohibit women from leading men?" Answers will rely on various perspectives on Genesis 1–3, 1 Timothy 2, and the sorts of conversations found in the rest of this book. Hierarchs oppose women's ordination to the priesthood, and heterarchs support it.

Catholics and Christians in the Eastern Orthodox Church ask instead, "What is the tradition of the church?" and "Is the priest male as Jesus was male?" Disagreements between Catholics and Orthodox center on whether the priest acts, while presiding over communion, in one of two ways: Is he *in persona Christi*—representing Christ to the church—or *in persona ecclesiae*, praying on behalf of the congregation and representing the church to God?

Catholic and Orthodox Concerns

Arguments for Male-Only Priesthood

Through most of church history, church leaders considered women to be intellectually and morally inferior to men. Because of these beliefs, they allowed only men to lead. This thinking prevailed even as biblical imagery or symbolism became the dominant reason for male-only ordination.

- Biblical imagery used of God is masculine: we call God "he," therefore men share somehow more directly in his image.[1]
- Just as the Old Testament priesthood was exclusively male, due to the priest being God's representative, so only males can be priests in the church.
- Jesus was a male.
- Jesus chose only male apostles, and since apostolic authority came through them, only males can lead the church as their successors.[2]

---

1. William Witt, *Icons of Christ: A Biblical and Systematic Theology for Women's Ordination* (Waco, TX: Baylor University Press, 2020), 269.
2. Catechism of the Catholic Church, 2.2.3.6.6, https://www.vatican.va/archive/ENG0015/__P4X.HTM, accessed July 24, 2021.

Arguments Against Male-Only Priesthood
Proponents for female ordination refute each of the points listed above.

- God is not male. When the biblical writers called God "he," they referred to the Trinity. Male humans do not somehow more fully represent or image God, per Genesis 1:27: "So God created mankind in his own image, in the image of God he created them; male and female he created them."
- Israelite priests could only be men so as to fulfill the purity codes of the law (women's menstrual cycles would have been problematic for fulfilling the regular duties of a priest).[3] Those codes were set aside when Gentiles were admitted to the church—we are not bound by Jewish law. Jesus, our High Priest, is not even of the tribe of Levi, but is our high priest in a completely different and superior way (Heb. 3:1–6; 4:14–5:10).
- The critical aspect of the incarnation is not that Jesus came as a male, but that he became human. "The Word became flesh" (John 1:14). A human savior who happens to be male saves all humans, male and female.
- That Jesus chose male apostles reflects the same reasoning he chose twelve Jewish apostles: they represented the twelve sons of Jacob and the tribes of Israel descended from them. But he had other followers who were women, whom he empowered to disciple, evangelize, and lead.[4] By fixating only on the sex of the apostles, other characteristics are ignored: Why can more than twelve Gentiles carry on the apostolic traditions, and yet they must still only be men?

The Catholic and Orthodox churches remain firmly entrenched in their male-only leadership structure. The key issue for Catholic and Orthodox ordination remains the question of representation: Is the priest, while presiding over the Eucharist during Mass, representing Christ to the people, or the people to God? Catholic theology affirms that priests perform their duties as representatives of Christ—*in persona Christi*.[5] Orthodox theology, similarly, identifies the priest as a living "ikon of Christ"—bearing the spiritual image of Christ so that worshippers may draw near to God through his role in worship. Thus

---

3. Witt, *Icons of Christ*, 180.
4. Consider Mary Magdalene, the first to see the risen Jesus (John 20) and commissioned to "go and tell" the male disciples that the savior was alive. Women also received the Holy Spirit at Pentecost (Acts 2) and were empowered and gifted by the Spirit with such gifts as teaching, prophecy, and tongues (1 Cor. 12)—all used to benefit the church.
5. Catechism of the Catholic Church, 1.2.3.9.4, https://www.vatican.va/archive/ENG0015/__P2A.HTM#-15W.

far in the eyes of the churches' leaders, only an ordained male can perform this duty.

Protestant Concerns
The Anglican Communion, of which the Episcopal Church is the primary American branch, is the only Protestant denomination to call their clergy "priests" rather than "pastors." Anglicanism is rooted historically in the English Reformation, when King Henry VIII, angry at the Pope for not allowing him to divorce his wife and remarry, effected an ecclesial coup and declared himself Defender of the Faith, taking over the churches (heretofore all Catholic by default, as it was the only Western Christian church).

Henry did not intend to change the churches' theology or structure, other than separating them from papal authority. But under his daughter Elizabeth I, Protestant doctrine began to dominate while regular worship styles and functions remained largely the same. Even today, the liturgies of Anglican churches retain many of the aspects of the Roman Catholic Mass.

Theologically, Anglicans look to the Bible as their authority, rather than the traditions of church history. They consider the priest to represent the congregation (*in persona ecclesiae*), a servant leader among fellow lay "priests"—referring to the Protestant doctrine of the priesthood of all believers, which is based on 1 Peter 2:9 ("But you are a chosen race, a royal priesthood, a holy nation, a people for his possession," CSB). Each Protestant denomination must work through its understanding of biblical arguments for and against women in leadership. The subject matter of the rest of this book, barring the current chapter, informs Anglican theology just as it does a Baptist or Methodist church.

Though organized hierarchically from local parish up through diocese and archdiocese, most of the denominations within the Anglican Communion nevertheless adhere to a heterarchical theology of women. Women priests were first ordained in the Episcopal Church in 1974, but the church had begun ordaining deaconesses in 1855. The Church of England ordained its first woman priest in 1994.

Summary
Priests are found in all three of the major Christian faith traditions. Whether a woman is affirmed as a priest depends upon which tradition she belongs to and how that tradition understands the priesthood's purpose. Catholic and Orthodox doctrine emphasizes the maleness of Jesus, making a man the only proper representative of Christ presiding over the Table, the Eucharist. Anglicans instead tend to focus on the Bible's discussion of authority, with most denominations within their Communion affirming women as priests.[6]

---

6. For a more thorough study of this topic, we encourage you to consult William Witt's *Icons of Christ*.

REFLECTION QUESTIONS

1. How are priests in the Old Testament and the New Testament different?

2. In what sense are all Christians priests today, according to 1 Peter 2:9–10?

3. What is one major responsibility of Christian priests, according to 1 Peter 2:9–10?

4. How does Romans 12:1–2 help you understand your role as a priest?

5. Do you believe women should occupy the office of priest in churches today?

Can Women Be Pastors or Elders?

Cynthia Westfall speaks for many Christian women who desire to serve the Lord:

> A man knows that his calling is based on who God has created him to be in terms of his personality and spiritual gifting/skills, where he has been, and where he is now in his life journey. A woman's sense of calling can be regarded with suspicion and hostility if, for example, she has a leadership personality and/or a significant set of leadership skills and abilities. The starting point for a man's call is his own discernment. . . . However, a woman's discernment, emotion, and experience must be tested and qualified against possible prohibitions. A man can approach spiritual gifts as spiritual possibilities, but a woman may be unsure of what she is allowed to do. She becomes immobilized.[1]

The answer to this chapter's question, "Can women be pastors or elders?," is more than academic to Westfall and millions of other women like her. In this brief chapter, we will attempt to clarify terminology and show the array of ways the words "elder" and "pastor" are defined by scholars. The question is also complicated by the variety of organizational structures within different denominations. We'll give you several related perspectives and provide you with resources for further study.

---

1. Cynthia Westfall, *Paul and Gender: Reclaiming the Apostle's Vision for Men and Women in Christ* (Grand Rapids: Baker Academic, 2016), 218–19.

Definitions

"Elder"

The Hebrew term for "elder" means "beard" and refers to a respected older man who oversees a family, clan, or tribe—a leader of a community. By Exodus 24, at least seventy elders had been chosen and were helping Moses oversee the Israelites.

In the New Testament, the Greek terms *presbyteros* and *episkopos* are sometimes used to refer to the same group of people (see Acts 20:17 and 28, and Titus 1:5–9). Generally, *presbyteros* appears in English as "elder," and *episkopos* as "overseer." Luke informs us that "Paul and Barnabas appointed elders for them in each church and, with prayer and fasting, committed them to the Lord, in whom they had put their trust" (Acts 14:23). Paul lays out the qualifications for overseers in 1 Timothy 3:1–7 and Titus 1:5–9.

"Pastor"

The Greek word for pastor is *poimēn*, which means "shepherd," and Peter encouraged church leaders in 1 Peter 5:2–4 to do the work of shepherding their flocks:

> Be shepherds [*poimanate*] of God's flock that is under your care, watching over them—not because you must, but because you are willing, as God wants you to be; not pursuing dishonest gain, but eager to serve; not lording it over those entrusted to you, but being examples to the flock. And when the Chief Shepherd appears, you will receive the crown of glory that will never fade away.

Are the Terms "Pastor" and "Elder" Interchangeable?

Some hierarchs believe that the terms "pastor" and "elder" refer to different offices. According to Harold W. Hoehner, "Scripture consistently maintains a distinction between the office and the gift. Eldership is an office, whereas pastor-teacher is a gift."[2] In his detailed treatment of the topic, Hoehner concludes:

> A woman, then, may have the gift of pastor-teacher, apostle, evangelist, and prophetess (as Philip's four daughters—Acts 21:9), while, scripturally speaking, she cannot hold the office of an elder or bishop. The aforementioned gifts are sovereignly bestowed on her, and it is her duty and privilege to

---

2. Harold Hoehner, "Can a Woman Be a Pastor-Teacher?," *Journal of the Evangelical Theological Society* 50, no. 4 (December 2007): 763.

exercise them. This is completely different from appointment to the office of elder, which the Scriptures specify only for men who meet the qualifications for that office.[3]

He continues,

> By distinguishing between office and gift, 85–90% of the problems raised about women's ministry would be resolved. ... By making this distinction between office and gift, it allows our local churches to recognize fully the gifts that women have received from God. All too often this has not been the *modus operandi* in evangelical churches. It is imperative that gifted women should and must be encouraged to minister inside and outside the local church. ... Male overseers should encourage *all* in the body of Christ to develop and use the gifts that God has given to them. This includes women.[4]

Other hierarchs disagree, among them Denny Burk, president of the Council on Biblical Manhood and Womanhood.[5] He concludes that his former professor is mistaken about the Bible's teaching on pastoral leadership. He insists that "the New Testament uses three terms to refer to one office—pastor/overseer/elder. That one office of leadership is limited to men as qualified by Scripture. This is a good and necessary boundary."[6]

Burk contends that Hoehner and others misunderstand the ideas of gifts versus offices on the basis of Ephesians 4:11–13: "Christ himself gave the apostles, the prophets, the evangelists, the pastors and teachers, to equip his people for works of service, so that the body of Christ may be built up until we all reach unity in the faith ... and become mature, attaining to the whole measure of the fullness of Christ." Burk argues that what Christ gave the church was not a list of gifts but a list of gifted persons, and thus these were not Spirit-given ministries but persons, men, who fulfilled offices in the church.[7]

Does the Bible Teach That Only Men Should Be Pastors or Elders?

Many hierarchs defend gender-based hierarchy on the basis of their interpretations of Scripture. For example, John Piper and Wayne Grudem state

3. Hoehner, "Can a Woman Be a Pastor-Teacher?," 769.
4. Hoehner, "Can a Woman Be a Pastor-Teacher?," 771.
5. CBMW is an evangelical Christian organization promoting a complementarian view of gender issues.
6. Denny Burk, "Can Women Be Pastors but Not Elders?," 9Marks, Dec. 11, 2019, https://www.9marks.org/article/can-women-be-pastors-but-not-elders.
7. Burk, "Can Women Be Pastors but Not Elders?" For additional insight, read Hoehner and Burk, and compare their ideas concerning church leadership.

in *Recovering Biblical Manhood and Womanhood*: "We are persuaded that the Bible teaches that only men should be pastors and elders. That is, men should bear *primary* responsibility for Christlike leadership and teaching in the church. So it is unbiblical, we believe, and therefore detrimental, for women to assume this role."[8] Thomas Schreiner bases the same conviction on 1 Corinthians 11:3, "But I want you to realize that the head of every man is Christ, and the head of the woman is man, and the head of Christ is God," and 1 Timothy 2:8–15.[9] Douglas Moo agrees and states:

> We think 1 Timothy 2:8–15 imposes two restrictions on the ministry of women: they are not to teach Christian doctrine to men and they are not to exercise authority directly over men in the church. These restrictions are permanent, authoritative for the church in all times and places and circumstances as long as men and women are descended from Adam and Eve.[10]

Heterarchs counter with passages like Galatians 3:26–28, "So in Christ Jesus you are all children of God through faith, for all of you who were baptized into Christ have clothed yourselves with Christ. There is neither Jew nor Gentile, neither slave nor free, nor is there male and female, for you are all one in Christ Jesus." Although hierarchs claim that these verses only apply to salvation, heterarchs insist that our salvation has sociological implications that give women freedom to serve in any capacity according to their spiritual gifts and abilities. Christians for Biblical Equality list the following as one of their core values: "The unrestricted use of women's gifts is integral to the work of the Holy Spirit and essential for the advancement of the gospel in the world."[11]

Qualifications for Elders

Some heterarchs argue that the Greek texts of 1 Timothy 3:1–12 and Titus 1:5–9, where we find the qualifications for church offices, do not contain a single male pronoun. Yet, the hierarch-leaning ESV translation uses the male pronouns "he" or "his" ten times in 1 Timothy 3:1–7. Even the more "gender language inclusive" translations like the NRSV and the 2011 NIV

---

8. John Piper and Wayne Grudem, "An Overview of Central Concerns: Questions and Answers," *RBMW*, 60–61.

9. Thomas R. Schreiner, "Head Coverings, Prophecies, and the Trinity: 1 Corinthians 11:2–16," *RBMW*, 124–39.

10. Douglas Moo, "What Does It Mean Not to Teach or Have Authority over Men? 1 Timothy 2:11–15," in *RBMW*, 180.

11. CBE International, Mission and Values, https://www.cbeinternational.org/content/cbes-mission. To evaluate the different views on these statements and on 1 Corinthians 11:3 and 1 Timothy 2:9–15, see Questions 22–25.

include eight and ten masculine pronouns respectively, while there are none in the original Greek. Instead, Paul uses the generic *tis*, correctly translated "whoever" or "anyone." Thus, they insist, the qualifications in Timothy should begin, "Whoever aspires to be an overseer desires a noble task." Philip Payne charges that by their introductions of male pronouns where there are none in the original Greek text, modern English translations give the misleading impression that Paul is claiming that church leaders must be male.[12]

In response, hierarchs can counter by claiming that such evidence is irrelevant and potentially misleading to the reader. Although it is true that male pronouns are not used, the passage contains about twenty masculine nouns, adjectives, and participles. Thus, the broader contextual use of the masculine gender, along with use of the term *anēr* ("man," v. 2), implies that the subject is masculine.

Grudem points to 1 Timothy 3:2, *mias gynaikos andra*, translated as "husband of one wife" (KJV, ESV), "married only once" (NRSV), and "faithful to his wife" (NIV), insisting this is the reason only men can qualify as elder.[13]

Heterarch William Witt counters that "the qualifications for church office in the Pastoral Epistles are moral qualifications, not job descriptions, and not gender qualifications."[14] Witt, along with Payne, argues that to insist otherwise would mean only the husband of one wife could be a leader in the church, eliminating the possibility that singles, divorced, or widowed people could ever serve as leaders. Such a requirement would mean that Paul, a number of the first apostles who were itinerant missionaries, later church leaders, and even Jesus could never qualify. Witt and Payne insist that generally the church has never applied this ultra-restrictive view of 1 Timothy 3:2 and that women should not be excluded on this basis.[15]

Summary

As you can see, gifted and godly scholars disagree on whether women can lead in church. Hierarchs believe "pastor" is a church office and is restricted to qualified men. Heterarchs believe "pastor/shepherd" is a spiritual gift and therefore open to women. However, the question of women on church staff is more than an academic issue. Before I (Sue) was invited to teach in the academy, I led a ministry to women in a megachurch where the senior pastor and all the elders were men, and still are. However, these godly men decided to call the staff "pastors," to reflect the Greek meaning of "pastor," shepherd. Women were given titles like "pastor to children," "pastor to adults," and I

---

12. Philip B. Payne, *Man and Woman, One in Christ: An Exegetical and Theological Study of Paul's Letters* (Grand Rapids: Zondervan, 2009), 445–59.
13. Grudem, *EFBT*, 80.
14. Witt, *Icons of Christ*, 327.
15. Read Witt, Payne, and Grudem for their detailed arguments.

was called the "pastor to women." I taught women the Bible weekly, raised up and unleashed a team of women leaders, and together we ministered to the women in the church and community. Many women came to faith and grew strong in the Lord.

Women leaders in other churches were often labeled "directors," and some were envious that I served in a church where what I did actually reflected my title. I was also paid the same as my male counterparts on staff, while many of these other women leaders were paid a fraction of my salary. I was regarded as a sister in Christ by my brothers in the church, and my voice counted. When I was called to the academy, the women in the church took over the ministry and it didn't skip a beat. In the academy, God has used this wonderful experience to help me prepare both men and women for future ministry.

However, I've also experienced judgment from some Christians strictly on the basis that I was once called a "pastor." They make assumptions based on that word, and I learned that one church across the country refused to use any of my Bible studies as a result. Now when asked, I sometimes simply say I was a "minister to women" to skirt the controversy and possibility of misunderstanding. I love people on both sides and dream of the day that we will all stand united to show our world the wonders and beauty of knowing Christ and living for him.

Keep wrestling with these questions, brothers and sisters, because they affect individuals, families, churches, communities, and ultimately the cause of Christ in the world. We have a common enemy, and it's not one another.

REFLECTION QUESTIONS

1. What does the term "elder" mean?

2. What does the term "pastor" mean?

3. What are your thoughts on Hoehner's argument that "elder" is an office but "pastor" is a spiritual gift?

4. Do you tend to side with hierarchs or heterarchs on this issue? Why?

5. What are some ways to disagree amicably with your brothers and sisters in Christ?

Should Women Leaders Be Called "Directors" or "Pastors" in the Church?

Before answering the question of what women leaders should be called in the church, we need to define these two terms—"pastor" and "director."

Definitions

The Greek word *poimēn* that we translate as "pastor" actually means "shepherd." Originally, it's unlikely that this word was intended to refer to a job title or professional office, since church staffs did not exist in the first century. New Testament churchgoers probably never called the overseers in their house churches "Pastor James" or "Pastor John." The only place where *poimēn* is usually translated as "pastor" instead of "shepherd" is Ephesians 4:11–12: "So Christ himself gave the apostles, the prophets, the evangelists, the pastors and teachers, to equip his people for works of service, so that the body of Christ may be built up." This passage lists the spiritual gifts available to all believers. In all other texts, the noun *poimēn* describes the shepherd who tenderly cares for the flock—feeding, protecting, leading, teaching, and loving the sheep. The Scriptures paint a metaphorical picture of "pastors" as dutiful leaders who, like shepherds, feed, protect, guide, teach, love, and care for the believers entrusted to them.

In contrast, the term "director" is not found in the Bible but hails from the corporate business world. A director in a company is a supervisor or a manager. These people organize, coordinate, and produce plans and projects. They are sometimes defined as a people or members of a group who control or govern the affairs of an institution or corporation. They oversee people, directing them to implement the vision and mission of the corporation. They supervise and lead but usually without the nurture, protection, and tender care that accompanies the ministry of a shepherd.

Does a Title Matter?

Now, back to our question: Should women leaders be called "directors" or "pastors" in the church? What about women who are hired onto multichurch staffs where they serve under the guidance and direction of male senior leaders? Does a title influence a person's ability to be effective in their job? Jennie Kitchin writes,

> There is a lot of debate around the importance of job titles. Some feel they represent your skills and expertise, and some are of the opinion that they are irrelevant and it's your accomplishments that define your role. Job titles have obvious relevance in terms of company hierarchy. . . . They can also inspire confidence and a sense of status amongst employees. There are levels of compensation and remuneration associated with titles that can motivate and encourage a great work ethic. But how much sway should a headline really have?[1]

Hierarchs and Heterarchs

Hierarchs and heterarchs tend to answer this question based on their views of biblical passages like 1 Timothy 2:11–15, although ministry titles for women vary even in hierarchical churches.[2] John Piper, former pastor of Bethlehem Baptist Church in Minneapolis and chancellor of Bethlehem College and Seminary, expressed the perspective of many hierarchs in an interview entitled "Should We Call Female Leaders Pastors?" Piper begins by addressing a question he received from a church member that frames the current issue. This fellow wrote:

> My church is changing its view on the use of the word *pastor* to include women, saying Ephesians 4:11 is the only place in the Bible where the Greek word for *pastor* is ever used, and that it doesn't have any specific qualifications there. Women could fill this role and still be under male headship and a male elder board, almost more like a deacon or deaconess who leads specific ministries in the church—like a pastor over worship, or a pastor over women's ministry. But would this change in title be in line with other parts of Scripture?[3]

1.   Jennie Kitchin, "Do Job Titles Really Matter?," Aquent, July 16, 2019, https://aquent.co.uk /blog/do-job-titles-really-matter. Aquent is a thirty-year-old company described as the largest creative and marketing recruiter, with thirty-eight offices in seven countries.
2.   See Questions 23–25 for chapters related to 1 Timothy 2:11–15.
3.   John Piper, "Should We Call Female Leaders 'Pastors'?," Ask Pastor John, episode 1428, Desiring God, January 31, 2020, https://www.desiringgod.org/interviews/ should-we-call-female-leaders-pastors.

This gentleman attends a multi-staff church where the Women's Ministry Director will now hold the title Women's Pastor and the woman who oversees the children's ministry will now be called the Children's Pastor instead of Director of Children's Ministries. This man wants to know if this change is biblical.

Piper answers that this change is not biblical or wise, and he insists it's misleading, for the four reasons below:

1. The English word "pastor" ordinarily refers to someone who preaches and occupies an official governing position like a lead elder or overseer. Therefore, Piper argues, "This title should not be given to any lay person in the church because they don't hold that kind of an official leadership role."[4] However, Piper's answer doesn't address this gentleman's actual situation but seems to assume that all churches have only one paid senior pastor and everyone else serves in volunteer roles. The question concerns women who are not lay volunteers but are part of the paid staff.

2. The Greek uses the same word for "shepherd" and "pastor"—*poimēn*. Piper argues that the term almost always describes the nonauthoritarian role of one who tends sheep. "That noun [*poimēn*] is used eighteen times in the New Testament, one of which is sometimes translated *pastor*—namely, Ephesians 4:11—where Christ has appointed pastors and teachers in the church. But the ESV, for example, translates this 'shepherds and teachers.' And if we do that, then the word *pastor* never occurs in the entire English Bible."[5] Thus, contends Piper, we cannot look back into first-century practices to make a decision to determine whether or not women should be called "pastors" today.

3. Only elders and overseers shepherd the flock. Piper says, "My third argument for why it is unwise and misleading and ill-founded to call laypeople pastors is the observation that when the New Testament does describe its church leaders as doing the work of a shepherd (with the verb *poimainō*, which has the same root as the noun *poimēn*), they were thought of not as laypeople, but as elders and overseers."[6] Piper's argument fits well for churches where women only serve as volunteers and the only person who carries the title of "pastor" is the senior pastor. However, again, he doesn't address the question at hand, which relates to larger churches where both genders have been hired to oversee particular ministries under the leadership of the senior pastor.

---

4. Piper doesn't address what to do when women are hired to serve under the direction and leadership of a senior pastor, elders, or whatever governing structure that church embraces.
5. Piper, "Should We Call Female Leaders Pastors?"
6. Piper, "Should We Call Female Leaders Pastors?" For the three passages that Piper contends illustrate this third point, see the full interview. Piper continues to ignore the issue of what women are called in multi-staffed churches.

4. Calling a woman a "pastor" would undermine what the Bible teaches concerning church leadership. Piper argues that giving a woman the title of pastor will inevitably lead to young people in the church as well as newcomers mistakenly believing it's proper and biblical for women to fill the role of shepherding the flock. Therefore, the practice is unbiblical, unwise, and misleading.

Most other hierarchs don't address the question we've been considering. If they hire women in leadership positions, they simply offer those positions with the title "director." A few use the title "minister" for women who lead ministries.[7]

In contrast, heterarch-led churches generally use the title of "pastor" for women leaders.

A Female "Director" Speaks

Carolyn Taketa, Executive Director of Small Groups at Calvary Community Church in Westlake Village, California, recalls a breakfast meeting with one of the elders at her church. "When the check came, I reached across the table to pay. But he refused and said, 'I have a policy that I always pay for the pastor.' I laughed. 'But I am not a pastor,' I said, using air quotes. He responded, 'Yes you are. That may not be your title, but it is what you do.' In that poignant moment, I felt both affirmed and empowered."[8]

Taketa reveals that when she meets with other women leaders, the topic of titles sometimes comes up. The "directors" conversations are usually peppered with emotions of hurt, confusion, and anger, as they share how being called a director when men in similar positions are called pastors affects them and their ability to function well in their ministry.

Taketa speaks of women directors routinely left out of pastors' gatherings where important decisions were made and where valuable mentoring occurred.[9]

> Another woman director with an advanced seminary degree who led a thriving ministry for two decades as a director expressed her hurt and dismay when she noticed a double standard. Whenever young men joined the church staff, they were automatically given the title of "pastor"—regardless of their job, level of education, or ministry experience.[10]

---

7. Sue worships at Northwest Bible Church in Dallas, Texas, led on the senior level by male senior and executive pastors and male volunteer elders. However, women are given titles like Minister to Women, Family Life Minister, Early Childhood Minister, and Worship Leader.
8. Carolyn Taketa, "Pastor or Director: Does Title Matter? An Honest Look at What Our Titles Communicate," WomenLeaders.com (blog), *Christianity Today*, November 19, 2015, https://www.christianitytoday.com/women-leaders/2015/november/pastor-or-director-does-title-matter.html.
9. Taketa, "Pastor or Director: Does Title Matter?"
10. Taketa, "Pastor or Director: Does Title Matter?"

Women's titles often reveal a lot about a church's culture, and women directors sometimes don't receive the same respect, resources, ministry budget, or paycheck that male pastors on the same leadership level receive.[11] "According to the 2016–2017 Church Law and Tax Compensation Handbook, full-time male senior pastors received 27 percent more in compensation and benefits than females—a $15,000 difference."[12]

Three Groups of Women Leaders and Their Titles

1. The first group is composed of hierarchal women leaders. For them, the issue of their title is irrelevant because they agree with the biblical and theological interpretation that women should never be called "pastors."
2. For the second group, the issue is also irrelevant. These women serve in churches where anyone who oversees a ministry as a shepherd is called a "pastor" and anyone who organizes, coordinates, or produces plans and projects is called a "director." The titles fit their functions.
3. The third group is composed of women leaders who function as *pastors* but are called "directors." These women must determine whether or not they want to serve there. If they become resentful, they must discern whether it's rooted in their own pride or ego. If God has called them to shepherd a particular group of people, he may want them to serve there, regardless of the title. If so, they must lead without a wounded spirit or a hidden agenda. If they find they cannot, wisdom dictates they relocate to a place that's a better fit for them.

Taketa sums it up well:

> I also consider whether my title or lack thereof limits what God has called me to do or negatively affects our ministry as a whole (e.g., resources, priorities, visibility, decision-making influence). If that's the case, it requires further thought and perhaps a tough conversation. Positional titles do matter when they impact our ministry effectiveness, devalue our contribution, limit our leadership capabilities, or put obstacles in the way of our calling. And yet, we can't lose sight of the bigger picture of the kingdom of God. It's more

---

11. Taketa, "Pastor or Director: Does Title Matter?"
12. Ashley Emmert, "The State of Female Pastors," WomenLeaders.com (blog), *Christianity Today*, October 15, 2015, https://www.christianitytoday.com/women-leaders/2015/october/state-of-female-pastors.html.

important to lead through spiritual influence than an organizational title.[13]

Summary

The question of women's titles is often complicated and messy and can depend on the church's organizational structure. If you hold a hierarchical view
of women in ministry, you will likely agree with Piper that a woman should
never serve as senior pastor. But your decision gets sticky when a woman
serves *under* the senior leadership of men. She's lower on the organizational
chart, titled a "director," but functions in a position like a shepherd. She feeds,
protects, guides, counsels, encourages, teaches, and cares for those she's called
to serve. Her title obviously doesn't reflect what she actually does.

In addition, outsiders may look at this woman's title and make assumptions
about how the church actually values and treats women, affecting whether or
not that unbeliever would consider Christianity as a faith that truly reflects
the values of a loving God. Checking out ministry titles of women on church
staffs can sometimes provide insight into whether a church operates under a
hierarchical or heterarchical structure, as well as how women are viewed and
valued—but not always.

When one of my (Sue) female interns graduated from our seminary, she
took a position as Pastor to Women in a large New England church. They
recently had moved from a long history as a hierarchical church to a heterarchical structure, adding several women to their elder board for the first
time. My student wrestled with whether or not to take the position since she
wasn't sure that carrying the title "pastor" fit well with her theological convictions. Most of all, she desired to serve where she would be given a voice at
the leadership table, the resources to create a vigorous and biblical ministry
with women, and an opportunity to be a respected member of a leadership
team. After a rigorous interview process and much prayer, she accepted the
position.

However, although the church professed to listen to women leaders and
include them in decisions that impacted the women in the congregation, my
student found that, in reality, this wasn't her experience. After four years, she
left to pursue another calling.

Although a heterarchical structure tends to give women a more authentic
voice at the leadership table, as my student learned, it's no guarantee. The core
issue is about respect, women's value, and a belief that God created men and
women to serve together as brothers and sisters in God's family and church.
This can occur in either hierarch or heterarch churches.

When women leaders have a voice and are valued, this perspective trickles
down into every aspect of a church ethos, including whether women in the

---

13. Taketa, "Pastor or Director: Does Title Matter?"

congregation are treated well. However, women leaders mustn't serve to earn a title. We serve to glorify God as under-shepherds of Jesus Christ, as do men. But God also delights when all people are treated with dignity and individual justice, whatever their gender.

REFLECTION QUESTIONS

1. What do you think titles reflect concerning the value of women in your church?

2. How much do you think titles should be taken into consideration when someone desires to serve in a ministry?

3. What are the benefits of having your title reflect what you actually do?

4. How do you think outsiders feel if they see that women don't seem to be valued or have a voice?

5. Do you think women should carry the same or different titles from men who serve in equivalent staff position levels in a church?

Are Men by Design Better Leaders Than Women?

Before we address the question of whether men are by design better leaders than women, we need to define leadership and then set out several parameters.

What Is Christian Leadership?

Definitions abound, but the best comes from the mouth of our Lord Jesus in the upper room on the evening before he went to the cross:

> A dispute also arose among them [the Twelve] as to which of them was considered to be greatest. Jesus said to them, "The kings of the Gentiles lord it over them; and those who exercise authority over them call themselves Benefactors. But you are not to be like that. Instead, the greatest among you should be like the youngest, and the one who rules like the one who serves. (Luke 22:24–26)

In light of Jesus's mandate, we should add the word "servant" to the word "leadership" if we desire leadership to be Christian instead of secular. We must not mistakenly draw our leadership models as the world often does from secular business, the military, or sports. Nevertheless, someone has to be out front leading for any group to make forward progress. Does God wire and gift men to be more effective at moving groups forward than women?

Did God's First Instructions to Men and Women Involve Leadership?

In the creation account, we read: "So God created mankind in his own image, in the image of God he created them; male and female he created them. God blessed them and said to them, 'Be fruitful and increase in number; fill the earth and subdue it. Rule over the fish in the sea and the birds in the sky and over every living creature that moves on the ground'" (Gen. 1:27–28).

God gave both men and women the mandate to "rule over," which involves overseeing or leading. We know that many men make great leaders. They've led through history in the church and in secular society. But clearly from this Genesis text, women are also called to lead in some capacity. What might women bring to the table that could complement men or even make some women great individual leaders?

Our Suppositions

To answer our chapter's question—are men by design better leaders than women?—we first need to articulate several suppositions that many hierarchs and heterarchs generally agree on as a premise for our discussion.

1. Scripture makes no gender distinctions regarding spiritual gifts. Thus, spiritual gifting isn't an issue in the gender debate.
2. Our answer should be grounded in reliable research rather than people's anecdotal opinions.
3. We believe God has designed men and women physically and biologically different, and they also exhibit additional differences that can be supported by valid research studies. We reject the idea that all gender differences are sociologically constructed, and people are free to choose their gender.
4. However, we believe that stereotypes, a fixed and oversimplified image or idea about all men and all women, are not helpful since many are not based on reliable research but on anecdotal and sometimes biased opinions. Also, these stereotypes can and have led to gender confusion. Some individuals who don't fit these stereotypes have become uncertain as to their gender identity. Thus, stereotypes have been the source of immeasurable harm and hurt in people's lives.

Research on Gender Differences

Some differences are physical but have implications for how men and women respond to life situations. For example:

*   Girls' hearing is substantially more sensitive than boys', especially in the 1000- to 4,000-Hz range.[1]
*   The male retina is substantially thicker than the female retina. As a result, women see rich textures and variances in colors, while most

---

1. For more information about hearing differences, see "Sex Differences in the Auditory System," Dennis McFadden, www.tandfonline.com/doi/abs/10.1080/87565649809540712?journalCode=hdvn20.

males are insensitive to these variances and are drawn to motion. Researchers at Cambridge University found girl babies would respond first to a young woman's face while boy babies looked first at a mobile.[2] This ability allows many women to be more observant of people's faces and emotional expressions, helping women read what others are feeling. This ability can help women lead people effectively.

Other typical differences relate to brain function:

- Women often navigate using landmarks while men are more likely to use maps. Neuroscientists have learned that the different genders typically use different areas of the brain when navigating. Females use the cerebral cortex and males use the hippocampus.[3] However, these are only tendencies. When I (Sue) was studying for my doctorate in Boston, I spent weekends with two female colleagues touring the northeast. Two of us navigated using landmarks, making us useless getting around large cities and subways, but one of us was a master with maps. We made her our permanent driver.
- A Harvard study using MRI imaging sought to understand how emotion is processed in the brains of children. Children process emotions in the amygdala, a primitive area deep in the brain far from the cerebral cortex where language is processed. Seven-year-olds often can't tell why they are feeling sad. But as girls mature, brain activity associated with emotion moves out of the amygdala and into the cerebral cortex—in girls, but not in boys. In fact, even in adult men, much of the brain activity associated with emotion remains in the amygdala, making it difficult and uncomfortable for many men to tell how they feel.[4] This ability makes many women skilled at leading people.
- Boys fight twenty times as often as girls do, but after the fight, boys usually end up better friends and are more likely to play together. Girls seldom fight, but when they do, bad feelings last.[5] These tendencies affect how each gender typically resolves conflict, a vital leadership skill.
- Women tend to make moral decisions on the basis of whom it might help and whom it might hurt. Men tend to make moral decisions on

2. Jennifer Connellan and Simon Baron-Cohen, "Sex Differences in Human Neonatal Social Perception," *Infant Behavior and Development* 23 (2000): 113–18.
3. Georg Gron and Matthias Riepe, "Brain Activation during Human Navigation: Gender-Different Neural Networks as Substrate of Performance," *Nature Neuroscience* 3 (2000): 404–8.
4. William Killgore, Mika Oki, and Deborah Yurgelun-Todd, "Sex-Specific Developmental Changes in Amygdala Responses to Affective Faces," *NeuroReport* 12 (2001): 427–33.
5. Janet Lever, "Sex Differences in the Games Children Play," *Social Problems* 23 (1976): 478–87.

the basis of right and wrong, regardless of how it impacts others.[6] Gilligan's groundbreaking research led the way for scientists to begin studying women separate from men. Before, women were simply classified as an aberration. This study helps us understand why, in Genesis 1:27–28, God mandated that men and women oversee the world together. In ministry we need both. Effective leaders make decisions based on what's right, but also take into account how their decisions impact the people they lead.

What Advantages Might Women Bring to Ministry Leadership?

In 1998, Cindy Simon Rosenthal analyzed data from 291 state legislative committee chairs, both men and women. Before that, these kinds of studies focused more on male leadership styles. She found that the women legislators tended to lead in a much more inclusive style, contradicting the typical male perspective in which leadership is more transactional and competitive. Instead, she noted that the women focused on collaboration, consensus, and problem-solving with others.[7]

Her findings agree with Sally Helgesen, who documented the leadership activities and practices of four highly successful female executives to find the strategies they shared:[8]

- Inclusive organizational forms that celebrate points of contact among people from all organizational levels and specializations.
- Communication methods that are driven by personality, not only by mission.
- Recognition of employee relationships as familial more than hierarchical.[9]

In her second book, *The Web of Inclusion*, Helgesen coined that title phrase, and she concluded that women lead most comfortably when sharing power and influence with other leaders.[10] Alice Mathews writes, "Such a style is especially advantageous for Christian women because it more closely resembles

6. Carol Gilligan, *In a Different Voice* (Cambridge, MA: Harvard University Press, 1982), 64–105.
7. Cindy Simon Rosenthal, *When Women Lead: Integrative Leadership in State Legislatures* (New York: Oxford University Press, 1998).
8. The four leaders were Frances Hesselbein, Executive Director of the Peter Drucker Institute; Barbara Grogan, President of Western Industrial Contractors; Nancy Badore, Director of Ford Motor Company's Executive Development Center; and Dorothy Brunson, President of minority-owned Brunson Communications.
9. Sally Helgesen, *The Female Advantage: Women's Ways of Leadership* (New York: Doubleday, 1995), front jacket.
10. Sally Helgesen, *The Web of Inclusion: A New Architecture for Building Great Organizations* (New York: Doubleday, 1995).

the apostle Paul's image of the body and Jesus' description of the behavior of those who follow him."[11]

Mary Chapman describes the typical differences between male and female leadership styles using the analogy of an octopus and a goose. She contends men often lead like the octopus who has one central brain and many arms to do its bidding, representing a top-down style. In contrast, female leadership is like the goose, who "sniffs fall in the air and shares the vision of the South with the gaggle. Once in the air, the leader of the V-formation breaks the wind resistance for the flock. Eventually, the lead goose tires and goes to the end of the V, with another goose taking its place."[12]

Summary

So, are men by design better leaders than women? We would answer "no," in agreement with Leonard Sax, who asks and answers a similar question in his book *Why Gender Matters*. "The tired argument about which sex is more intelligent or which sex has the 'better' brain is about as meaningful as arguing about which utensil is 'better,' a knife or a spoon. . . . A knife is better than a spoon if you want to cut through a piece of meat, while a spoon is better if you're facing a bowl of chicken broth."[13]

Both men and women bring valuable insights and tendencies to the leadership table, and when both are invited to participate, they provide a delicious feast for everyone. What leadership positions they should hold will depend on whether you favor a hierarchical or a heterarchical leadership structure. But because women represent over half of the church in the majority of congregations,[14] women's input can only serve to strengthen ministries' goals to evangelize the lost, equip believers, and bring glory to God. We are all called to work together as brothers and sisters in God's eternal family. Michelle Lee-Barnewall concludes:

> The corporate identity of the church, not individual rights or personal power and position, provides a more fitting perspective for understanding gender. The goal of the church as

11. Alice P. Mathews, *Preaching That Speaks to Women* (Grand Rapids: Baker Academic, 2003), 131.

12. Mathews, *Preaching That Speaks to Women*, 129. This analogy was presented by Mary Chapman, corporate trainer at Moody Bible Institute, during a seminar at the National Broadcaster's Midwest Convention, 1998.

13. Leonard Sax, *Why Gender Matters* (New York: Broadway, 2005), 32. We recommend the first six chapters and the extra material in the back to learn more about gender differences, especially relating to learning differences.

14. "Christian Women Today, Part 1 of 4: What Women Think of Faith, Leadership and Their Role in the Church," Barna.org, August 13, 2012, https://www.barna.com/research/christian-women-today-part-1-of-4-what-women-think-of-faith-leadership-and-their-role-in-the-church.

Christ's body and bride is to be wholly dedicated to him and through the Spirit to live in holiness and loving and sacrificial relationships with one another. The orientation is not simply toward the benefits or rights of women and men in the new age. Rather believers are called to become a community that pursues holiness, submission, and devotion to God through the Spirit in imitation of Christ.[15]

REFLECTION QUESTIONS

1. How do you define leadership?

2. How did Jesus define leadership?

3. In what sense did God command both men and women to be leaders?

4. What did you learn about some of the different tendencies that make both men and women strong leaders?

5. How can stereotyping, as well as assuming all gender is sociologically constructed, harm people?

---

15. Michelle Lee-Barnewall, *Neither Complementarian nor Egalitarian: A Kingdom Corrective to the Evangelical Gender Debate* (Grand Rapids: Baker Academic, 2016), 177. For additional insight into this important idea of ministering together, consider Sue Edwards, Kelley Mathews, and Henry J. Rogers, *Mixed Ministry: Working Together as Brothers and Sisters in an Oversexed Society* (Grand Rapids: Kregel, 2008).

How Can Women Appropriately Use Leadership and Teaching Gifts?

Taylor and Morgan, a married couple with teens, lead the college ministry at their church. On any given Sunday evening, Taylor and Morgan have cooked food and cleaned their home in preparation for the group, who enjoy conversation and food before transitioning to teaching time. Taylor strums a worship song on the guitar, then opens with prayer. Finally, Morgan walks up and says, "Let's open our Bibles" to begin teaching the lesson.

Depending on your understanding of the Bible's teaching on leadership, you may have instinctively identified Morgan as the husband in the couple. But does it have to be? Can Taylor be the husband who takes the supporting role while his wife, Morgan, teaches the lesson?

That God gifts women and men alike with various skills, talents, and abilities has never been in question. Where, when, and how a woman uses her gifts in line with the Bible's instruction remains a disputed issue.

Heterarchs

Heterarchs believe that both women and men are only limited in how they serve the church by their spiritual gifts and abilities. To them, gender is a non-issue when it comes to what Christians are allowed to do. Cynthia Westfall maintains,

> Women receive their appointments to build up the body of Christ exactly the same way that men do and with the same criteria. . . . The Spirit is supposed to have full control in the distribution of spiritual gifts to believers. There cannot be artificially constructed rules or biblical principles that override

and restrict the Spirit's work in terms of whom he will use in various functions to edify the church.[1]

So, in heterarch-led churches, what is the appropriate way for women to use their gifts of leadership and teaching? They serve in consultation with leaders, obeying the prompting of the Holy Spirit, filling a need within the church body that fits with their gifting and passion. If they have a gift of teaching, heterarchs say they should teach, regardless of gender. If they are gifted leaders, heterarchs believe they are free to consider any church-wide role open to them as circumstances, opportunity, and wisdom allow. This can include such activities as writing curriculum, leading small-group classes, mentoring, teaching the Bible, preaching, becoming a deacon, priest, or pastor, or joining church staff in a pastoral vocation, as a business administrator, or in human resources.

What about formal training? Kristen Padilla, author of *Now That I'm Called*, encourages women called to vocational service to consider seminary: "We need seminary training because the Bible will never mean something today that it didn't mean in its original context. . . . We need the right tools to help us faithfully interpret Scripture. . . . Just like Paul tells Timothy, continue in what you have learned. A serious calling requires serious study of Scripture."[2] According to heterarchs, women participating in church leadership is not a new phenomenon. For examples of women throughout history who led, taught, and served in the church, read the three chapters in our historical section.

Hierarchs

Hierarchs also affirm a woman's ability to serve the church with her gifts, but they limit how teaching and leadership gifts are used based on gender. Churches differ in how they determine which offices or positions are open to women because of the wide variety of denominational policies, informal church traditions, and individual churches' theological convictions. In other words, walk into any two churches of differing denomination or background and you will likely encounter two different sets of rules for women in leadership.

How Will You Know a Church's Stance on Women Using Their Gifts?

A common method of learning about a church or ministry is to examine its website. Does it include a doctrinal statement? Are women included on the pastoral staff? If so, what sorts of positions do they hold? Do they ordain women, or do women serve in any official offices or capacities? Is the church

---

1. Cynthia Long Westfall, *Paul and Gender: Reclaiming the Apostle's Vision for Men and Women in Christ* (Grand Rapids: Baker Academic, 2016), 157, 159.
2. Kristen Padilla, *Now That I'm Called: A Guide for Women Discerning a Call to Ministry* (Grand Rapids: Zondervan, 2018), 158–59.

part of a denomination or alliance of churches? These and other investigative clues will help you determine how that church might react to a woman seeking to use leadership and teaching gifts there. But appearances don't always tell the whole story.

Sandra Glahn illustrates where various churches draw the line at women in leadership and how such limitations might appear in church life:

1. *At the bishop level.* They may believe the bishop must be male, but they don't necessarily have elders in their structure. The bishop might not even reside in their town. So the church may function with what looks like complete gender equality. But they still have that one position that must be filled by a male.
2. *At the elder level.* They believe women can preach with men present, as long as women are not elders. The elder board is the ruling board. They may emphasize that pastor/preacher is a spiritual gift, not an office. So women may "exercise their gift of pastoring or teaching" as long as they speak "under the authority" of male elders and there are no female elders.
3. *At women preaching.* They believe anyone who lets a woman preach with men in the room must be egalitarian (some exceptions are made for women who are famous).[3]

According to Hierarchs, What Positions Are Open to Women?

Hierarchs, even the most conservative ones, believe that women with teaching and leadership gifts can use them by leading and teaching women and children. Many women thrive under the shepherding of a spiritually mature woman who can mentor, teach, and counsel in specific ways that men are unable to fulfill. Healthy women's ministries cultivate a community of truth-seeking, others-loving, spiritually maturing women. For such ministries to flourish, they need church leadership to encourage and equip *their own* gifted, qualified women to teach and lead their female congregants.

Children's ministries also attract many women leaders. The Bible does not speak directly to such service, but hierarchs see children's ministry as a natural extension of a woman's nurturing, mothering qualities. Of course, not all who volunteer or lead in children's ministries are mothers (or even women—many men join this critical aspect of church life to the betterment of the kids), but the leadership positions in this area of church life are usually open to women.

Youth ministry remains a gray area: different churches have different convictions on when a boy becomes a man. Some will allow women to teach and

---

3. Sandra Glahn, "Eight Views of Women in the Church, Home, and Society within the Inerrancy Camp," *Engage* (blog), Bible.org, Sept. 11, 2018, https://blogs.bible.org/eight-views-of-women-in-the-church-home-and-society-within-the-inerrancy-camp.

lead any youth in the program, while others will limit women to only leading girls. Women wishing to minister to youth should do diligent research before seeking a place on that staff.

Summary

"A manifestation of the Spirit is given to each person for the common good: to one is given a message of wisdom through the Spirit, to another, a message of knowledge by the same Spirit, to another, faith by the same Spirit. . . . One and the same Spirit is active in all these, distributing to each person as he wills" (1 Cor. 12:7–9, 11 CSB). Spiritual gifts are given by the Holy Spirit without regard to gender but rather according to God's purpose and for the common good of the church body. Women whom God gifts with teaching or leadership abilities have multiple options to use them within the church. Churches vary greatly in how they understand the Bible's teaching on women, which can lead to confusion in what a woman leader/teacher feels she is "allowed" to do. Once a woman understands her own convictions about God's will for women, she must decide whether to work within her own church's policies or seek a church home that fits her view more closely.

Wherever you sit on the spectrum of views, we encourage you to respect your church leadership as you seek to use the gifts God has given you. Remember that they were given "for the common good"—not one person's.

REFLECTION QUESTIONS

1. What did your initial interpretation of the introductory story reveal about your views regarding women leading and teaching?

2. Do you tend to agree more with heterarchs or hierarchs on this question?

3. What are some reasons women leaders are confused about where it would be wise for them to serve in a leadership or teaching position?

4. What are some ways to assess a church's or ministry's stance on what women can do there?

5. What are the benefits and drawbacks of women teaching and leading in ministry?

How Does One's View of the Trinity Shape Relationships Between Men and Women?

In the 1100s, a Scot, Richard of St. Victor, articulated the beauty of a Triune God. He wrote that if God were just one Person, he could not be in essence loving because before creation, he would have had no one to love. And if God were two Persons, he could be loving but in an unhealthy, excluding way, not willing to share that love with others. But when two people are secure in their love they rejoice to share that love with others.[1] Michael Reeves explains: "Being perfectly loving, from all eternity the Father and the Son have delighted to share their love and joy with and through the Spirit. It is not, then, that God *becomes* sharing; being triune, God *is* a sharing God, a God who loves to include. Indeed, that is why God will go on to create. His love is not for keeping but for spreading."[2]

The Doctrine of the Trinity

You will not find the word "Trinity" in the Bible, yet the three Persons of the Godhead appear throughout. Scholars through the centuries have attempted to study the whole of the Scriptures and then articulate a correct, orthodox, theological doctrine in the form of creeds and confessions. Such creeds and confessions are the work of the church fathers throughout history, who hammered out these doctrines together concerning this mysterious yet important doctrine. Below are a sampling of the creeds and confessions that may help you discern where the church stood on this doctrine through the ages, as well as evaluate the various views that relate to men and women today.

---

1. Michael Reeves, *Delighting in the Trinity: An Introduction to the Christian Faith* (Downers Grove, IL: IVP Academic, 2012), 31.
2. Reeves, *Delighting in the Trinity*, 31.

The Nicene Creed (Fourth Century)

> We believe in one Lord, Jesus Christ, the only Son of God, eternally begotten of the Father, God from God, Light from Light, true God from true God, begotten not made, of one being with the Father. Through him all things were made. For us and our salvation he came down from heaven, by the power of the Spirit he was incarnate of the Virgin Mary and became man.

The Athanasian Creed (Fifth Century)

> The Godhead of the Father, of the Son, and the Holy Spirit is all one: the glory equal, the majesty co-equal. Such as the Father is, such is the Son, such is the Holy Spirit. . . . The Father is Lord, the Son is Lord, and the Holy Spirit is Lord. And yet there are not three Lords, but one Lord. . . . In the Trinity none is before or after, none is greater or less than another. But the whole three persons are co-eternal and co-equal.

The Belgic Confession of 1561 (Article 8)

> All three are co-eternal and co-essential. There is neither first nor last: for they are all three one, in truth, in power, in goodness, and in mercy.[3]

The Second Helvetic Confession of 1566 (Clause 3)

> This statement condemns "all heresies and heretics who teach . . . that there is something created and subservient, or subordinate to another in the Trinity, and that there is something unequal in it, a greater or a less."[4]

The Evangelical Theological Society (1949–Present)

> God is a Trinity, Father, Son, and Holy Spirit, each an uncreated person, one in essence, equal in power and glory.[5]

---

3. Belgic Confession, Christian Reformed Church, art. 8, https://www.crcna.org/welcome/beliefs/confessions/belgic-confession#toc-article-8-the-trinity.

4. Second Helvetic Confession (1566), chap. 3, "Of God, His Unity and Trinity," *The Voice*, Christian Resource Institute, http://www.crivoice.org/creed2helvetic.html.

5. Evangelical Theological Society Constitution, art. 3, https://www.etsjets.org/about/constitution#A3.

The Subordination Debate

What can we clearly know about the eternal relationships between members of the Godhead? Should these eternal relationships legitimately be used as a model for how men and women should interact here on earth, and if so, how? In this chapter, we will explore how hierarchs and heterarchs answer those questions differently.

Hierarchs

The Father is the supreme member of the Godhead, and the Son is subordinate, or submissive, and obedient to the Father eternally and not just during his time on earth when Jesus, while still fully God, became fully man. The Father planned and set in motion the Trinity's purposes through this obedience of the Son and Spirit. Some apply this thinking to the relationship between husbands and wives and to men and women working together in ministry. This supports their view of order that they believe God ordained in the garden before the fall. Thus, like the Father, the husband is the head and authority and, like the Son, the wife is submissive and obeys him.[6]

Heterarchs

Heterarchs reject the social parallel that some hierarchs make and instead argue that the Son's obedience to the Father was limited to the time during his earthly ministry, to accomplish redemption. Therefore, the idea that Jesus is eternally subordinate to the Father who is eternally supreme is flawed.[7]

This difference of perspectives is called the "Subordination Debate."

Historical Context

The Subordination Debate isn't new, but it has reemerged recently. In the fourth century, leaders debated this issue and wrote the Nicene Creed as a result. The primary proponent of one major view was Arius. He argued that the Son was not quite God in the way that the Father was God because God created or "begot" him at a later time and therefore had authority over him. In the end, at the Council of Nicaea in 325, the church determined that Arianism was not consistent with biblical revelation and therefore must be declared heresy. Heterarchs today insist that the Father and Son possess equal authority if they are both to be understood as fully divine, and they accuse some hierarchs of promoting a kind of Arianism.

---

6. Grudem, *EFBT*, 405–32.
7. Kevin Giles provides an excellent overview of both sides of the Subordination Debate in "The Trinity Argument for Women's Subordination: The Story of Its Rise, Ascendancy, and Fall," in *DBE*, 3rd ed., 351–71.

Deeper Consideration of the Two Views

This theological conversation is complex and requires more than we can provide here. If you want to learn more, study the resources provided in the footnotes. Nevertheless, let's hear directly from leaders of each of these factions to give you an overview.

Hierarchs

Wayne Grudem insists,

> There is substantial testimony in Scripture that the Son was subject to the Father before He came to live on earth. Scripture frequently speaks of the Father-Son relationship within the Trinity, a relationship in which the Father "gave" His only Son (John 3:16). . . . But if the Father shows His great love by the fact that He gave His Son, then he had to *be* Father *before* He could give His Son. . . . The idea of giving His Son implies a headship, a unique authority.[8]

On the basis of this and many other Bible passages, Grudem argues that the "parallel between the Son's submission to the Father, together with their equality in attributes and deity and honor, still provides an excellent parallel to the relationship between a husband and wife in marriage."[9] According to this perspective, Grudem claims it logically follows that the Father represents the husband, who like the Father is head and authority, while the wife represents the submissive Son.

J. Scott Horrell affirms an eternally ordered social model of the Trinity "while insisting on equality of the divine nature" but also affirming "distinction of roles within the immanent Godhead."[10] He goes on to describe the Trinity as "the generous preeminence of the Father, the joyous collaboration of the Son, and the ever-glorifying activity of the Spirit,"[11] but he adds in a footnote,

> The author recognizes that he has not explicitly defended these divine roles but only the structure in which greater refinement can be made. Nor, given divine reciprocity, does he wish to imply that each member of the Godhead *exclusively* assumes

---

8. Grudem, *EFBT*, 406. For an explanation of additional verses that Grudem says support eternal subordination in the Trinity, see pages 403–56, where he answers multiple heterarch claims that his view is flawed.

9. Grudem, *EFBT*, 455.

10. J. Scott Horrell, "The Eternal Son of God in the Social Trinity," in *Jesus in Trinitarian Perspective: An Intermediate Christology*, eds. Fred Sanders and Klaus Issler (Nashville: B&H Academic, 2007), 76.

11. Horrell, "Son of God in the Social Trinity," 76.

these roles. Those who on the basis of a hierarchical model of the Trinity justify . . . autonomous masculine rulership in familial and ecclesiastical settings do not grasp the self-sacrificing nature of the Father as well as the Son and the Spirit.[12]

Again, differences of opinion like this exist between these two hierarchs and many others when attempting to make social parallels between the Trinity and the relationships between men and women in marriage and ministry.

Heterarchs

Millard Erikson calls his view the equivalence view: "For it holds that the Father, Son, and Holy Spirit are eternally equal in authority. A temporary functional subordination of the Son and the Holy Spirit to the Father has been established for the purpose of carrying out a particular mission. But when that mission is completed, the three persons' full equality of authority will resume."[13]

McGrath writes that Arius came to flawed conclusions because he used a "proof text" approach: "One of the outcomes of the Arian controversy was the recognition of the futility, even theological illegitimacy, of biblical 'proof-texting'—the simplistic practice of believing that a theological debate can be settled by quoting a few passages from the Bible."[14] He argues Athanasius, for whom the Athanasian Creed (fifth century) was named, came to a correct conclusion because he looked for "the overall pattern disclosed by these texts."[15]

Kevin Giles insists, "The Scripture associates distinctive works with each divine person, for example, the Father creation, the Son salvation, and the Spirit sanctification, yet they also make clear that the divine persons always work *as one*. In the Bible, no divine act, work, or operation is ever depicted as the work of one divine person in isolation of the other two."[16] He cites a number of passages to support his argument, including Colossians 1:15–19:

> The Son is the image of the invisible God, the firstborn over all creation. For in him all things were created: things in heaven and on earth, visible and invisible, whether thrones or powers or rulers or authorities; all things have been created through him and for him. He is before all things, and in him all things hold

12. Horrell, "Son of God in the Social Trinity," 76–77.
13. Millard J. Erikson, *Who's Tampering with the Trinity? An Assessment of the Subordination Debate* (Grand Rapids: Kregel Academic, 2009), 18.
14. Alister McGrath, *Heresy: A History of Defending the Truth* (San Francisco: Harper One, 2010), 143.
15. McGrath, *Heresy*, 143.
16. Kevin Giles, *The Rise and Fall of the Complementarian Doctrine of the Trinity* (Eugene, OR: Cascade, 2017), 93.

together . . . so that in everything he might have the supremacy.
For God was pleased to have all his fullness dwell in him.

Giles goes on to argue against using the mysterious and unexplainable nature of
the Trinity to support any social agenda on earth. He warns heterarchs against
drawing parallels between the equality in the Godhead and equality of men and
women just as he chastises hierarchs who conclude that because they believe
the Trinity is hierarchically ordered, relationships between men and women on
earth should also be ordered hierarchically. "The Bible never makes divine relations in eternity prescriptive for human relationships on earth."[17]

Summary

Some hierarchs argue that the Trinity is a model for human relationships
between men and women: The Father is the Supreme member of the Godhead,
and the Son is subordinate, or submissive, and obedient to the Father eternally and not just during his time on earth when Jesus, while still fully God,
became fully man. Thus, like the Father, the husband is the head and authority
and, like the Son, the wife is submissive. Other hierarchs disagree.

Heterarchs reject the social parallel that some hierarchs make and instead
argue that the Son's obedience to the Father was limited to the time during his
earthly ministry, to accomplish redemption. Giles expresses his hope for rec-
onciliation in the future between those who disagree as they listen and learn
from each other. We share his optimism. "It seems to me that we have exciting
times ahead. . . . In this process we can hope that old divisions and misunder-
standings that for too long have painfully and sharply divided brothers and
sisters in Christ can be resolved and overcome for the sake of the gospel."[18]

REFLECTION QUESTIONS

1. Since the word "Trinity" is not in the Bible, how do we know that God is
   a "Trinity"?

2. How would you explain the Trinity to someone who doesn't understand it?

3. What did the creeds generally teach about the Trinity?

4. Explain the two sides of the "Subordination Debate."

5. Do you tend to side with hierarchs or heterarchs on this debate, and why?

---

17. Giles, *Rise and Fall*, 102.
18. Giles, *Rise and Fall*, 114.

How Can We Make Churches and Other Ministries Safer for Women?

Misty Hedrick

In her 2019 memoir *What Is a Girl Worth?* Rachael Denhollander describes her story of sexual abuse within the microcosm of USA gymnastics. Team doctor Larry Nassar had abused her for years (continuing through attempted cover-ups by coaches and USAG authorities) under cover of providing medical treatment. Her public accusation led to hundreds of other gymnasts coming forward with similar accusations. As late as summer 2021, more gymnasts were testifying, some before the US Congress, of Nassar's abuse.

Sadly, Denhollander relates her experience against the backdrop of four local churches. Preferring to keep issues like sexual abuse concealed, two churches avoided the issue that consumed her life at the time.[1] But two others opened their doors and arms to comfort, encourage, and support the Denhollanders as they fought for justice for more than a hundred abuse survivors throughout a tumultuous case.

In her book, Denhollander writes candidly about her struggle to maintain faith in a church culture so focused on the victimizer that the victim often goes unacknowledged. In fact, in the case of the latter, church leaders often focus only on the injured party's need to avoid bitterness and prematurely forgive rather than heal brokenness and seek justice.[2]

What Does It Mean for a Church to Be *Safe*?

Church safety involves more than protecting members from gun violence, hate crimes, or other physical threats. The church must also protect

---

1. Rachael Denhollander, *What Is a Girl Worth? My Story of Breaking the Silence and Exposing the Truth about Larry Nassar and USA Gymnastics* (Carol Stream, IL: Tyndale Momentum, 2019), 220.
2. Denhollander, *What Is a Girl Worth?*, 99.

congregations from dangers within, such as emotional, spiritual, domestic, and sexual abuse. As Henry Cloud and John Townsend point out, "The church is not a totally safe place, and it does not consist of only safe people. . . . The walls of the church do not make it safe from sin. In fact, the church by definition is composed of sinners."[3] Paul recognized this fact as he spoke to the leaders of the Ephesian church in Acts 20:28–31:

> Pay careful attention to yourselves and to all the flock, in which the Holy Spirit has made you overseers, to care for the church of God, which he obtained with his own blood. I know that after my departure fierce wolves will come in among you, not sparing the flock; and from among your own selves will arise men speaking twisted things, to draw away the disciples after them. Therefore be alert, remembering that for three years I did not cease night or day to admonish every one with tears. (ESV)

Fierce wolves. Not sparing the flock. Twisted words. The passage describes more than false teachers. Paul's point is that evil comes from both within the church and from outside, and that leaders should be on guard.

What Can We Do to Keep a Church Safe?

Educate

Churches can invest in education for pastors and lay leaders to equip them as trauma-informed shepherds. Entities such as GRACE (Godly Response to Abuse in the Christian Environment) offer church safety training and certification geared toward protecting everyone in the congregation.[4] Church leaders can also learn to recognize and respond to various types of abuse and learn the terms, such as knowing the differences between abuse and assault.

Where physical and emotional safety reign, spiritual safety often thrives. But if a church lacks physical or emotional safety, spiritual safety is unlikely. Spiritual abuse happens when someone in a position of authority uses his or her influence to coerce behavior modification. Authors Scot McKnight and Laura Barringer point out that fear-based church cultures begin when "powerful pastors become associated too easily with God in the minds of the congregation," and people seek the pastor's approval, which they equate with God's approval.[5]

---

3. Henry Cloud and John Townsend, *Safe People: How to Find Relationships That Are Good for You and Avoid Those That Aren't* (Grand Rapids: Zondervan, 1995), 160.
4. "Protect Your Faith Community," GRACE, https://www.netgrace.org/safeguarding-initiative.
5. Scot McKnight and Laura Barringer, *A Church Called Tov: Forming a Goodness Culture That Resists Abuses of Power and Promotes Healing* (Carol Stream, IL: Tyndale House, 2020), 35.

In power- and fear-based cultures, McKnight and Barringer point out, secrecy reigns with only insiders knowing about decisions and judgments. And those "in the know" use power and fear to control and silence people.[6] Often spiritual abusers use Scripture out of context as well. Preventing spiritual abuse is difficult because tangible evidence remains elusive. But one effective way to combat spiritual abuse is to encourage biblical literacy. When believers know the Word of God for themselves, they are better able to detect false teaching, including false teaching that seeks to influence behavior or misuse authority.

Listen

Abuse and trauma affect many in congregations, whether the abuse occurs within the church or not. In the United States, nearly one in four women has been sexually assaulted,[7] and one in four has experienced domestic violence.[8] In many cases, a pastor or lay leader could be the first person a woman tells—often doing so only after many years have passed. While it is vital to equip male pastors and leaders to listen to women, it is equally vital to have a female minister available. Of course, while it's not acceptable to convict innocent people, leaders must also take a stance of believing victims while investigating the circumstances.

"Telling a secret like this is belittling, scary, and traumatic," writes Mary DeMuth, Christian writer and sexual abuse survivor. "False reports are rare. In order to ensure someone isn't retraumatized by our responses, we should listen without judgment, asking clarifying questions when necessary, and offering extreme empathy."[9] Keeping a list of qualified counselors available also helps leaders who may not have the training necessary to counsel long-term. As DeMuth also points out, "Someone traumatized is not thinking linearly—they need support, not advice. . . . Sexual abuse is traumatic. If you haven't walked through it yourself, don't assume you know how soul crushing it is."[10]

Protect the Victim, Not the Abuser

DeMuth stresses that it's more important to protect survivors than it is to protect reputations. She reminds leaders that "the church will grow when it brims with truth, not when it covers up misdeeds."[11] Psychologist and trauma expert Diane Langberg delves into the motivations underlying an abusive use of power, but she also explores the motivations behind concealing abuse.

6. McKnight and Barringer, *Church Called Tov*, 37–39.
7. "Sexual Violence Is Preventable," Centers for Disease Control and Prevention, July 12, 2022, https://www.cdc.gov/injury/features/sexual-violence/index.html.
8. "Statistics," National Coalition Against Domestic Violence, https://ncadv.org/STATISTICS.
9. Mary E. DeMuth, *We Too: How the Church Can Respond Redemptively to the Sexual Abuse Crisis* (Eugene, OR: Harvest House, 2019), 168.
10. DeMuth, *We Too*, 172.
11. DeMuth, *We Too*, 175.

She writes: "The revelation of sexual abuse exposes the heart of the abuser, not the heart of the victim. The refusal to help exposes those asked, not the victim. The asking exposes the courage of the victim."[12] Then she flips the coin, showing that "withholding power in the face of sin, abuse, and tyranny is also a wrong use of power."[13]

Research shows that one in ten church attenders under the age of thirty-five have left a church because of how the church handled cases of sexual abuse,[14] and almost one-third of churchgoers believe the church has more scandal to uncover.[15] Langberg stresses the urgency of victim care rather than victim shaming: "We are called to be a sacred place for the vulnerable. We have often chosen to be a safe place for the powerful and have deceived ourselves into believing that God would call that good."[16]

In *Mixed Ministry*, we argue that hiding sin "ultimately makes the church vulnerable to *more—not less*—sin, especially sexual sin."[17] Abuse is about power, and one way that people exert power is by trying to cover up even criminal abuse, often in the name of protecting Jesus's reputation. But while spiritual abuse and emotional abuse are bad, physical and sexual abuse are *crimes*. As such, they should be reported to the proper authorities immediately.

Internal investigations are inappropriate in the face of sexual or physical abuse because the church is simply not equipped to carry out such an investigation. McKnight and Barringer assert that a church's response to accusations of abuse—whether the leadership commits to seeking the truth or instead takes a defensive posture—reveals whether or not that church's culture is toxic.[18]

Love

Langberg points out that church leaders must keep a careful watch on their own walks with Christ. She notes that leaders must first be followers, stating, "Your value as a shepherd depends on your life as a lamb."[19] The prophet Ezekiel declared that shepherds who do not serve their sheep well would be removed, and God would rescue his sheep from their lack of care

12. Diane Langberg, *Redeeming Power: Understanding Authority and Abuse in the Church* (Grand Rapids: Brazos, 2020), 71.

13. Langberg, *Redeeming Power*, 12.

14. Kate Shellnutt, "One in Ten Young Protestants Have Left a Church over Abuse," *Christianity Today*, May 21, 2019, https://www.christianitytoday.com/news/2019/may/lifeway-protes-tant-abuse-survey-young-christians-leave-chur.html.

15. Aaron Earls, "Churchgoers Split on Existence of More Sexual Abuse by Pastors," Lifeway Research, May 21, 2019, https://lifewayresearch.com/2019/05/21/churchgoers-split-on-existence-of-more-sexual-abuse-by-pastors.

16. Langberg, *Redeeming Power*, 38.

17. Sue Edwards, Kelley Mathews, and Henry J. Rogers, *Mixed Ministry: Working Together as Brothers and Sisters in an Oversexed Society* (Grand Rapids: Kregel, 2008), 157.

18. McKnight and Barringer, *Church Called Tov*, 41.

19. Langberg, *Redeeming Power*, 150.

(see Ezekiel 34). When a church is well tended, it functions as a close community, a family of believers who treat each other with respect and love, as siblings in Christ.

In *Mixed Ministry*, we write: "Personal relationships require love, peace, patience, kindness, gentleness, self-control—the fruit of the Spirit. They demand wisdom as we create an ethos of care and respect. A family ethos is a supernatural ethos, superintended by the Holy Spirit. But life transformation and exciting spiritual adventure are the norm in a supernatural ethos and that's the kind of place where Jesus shows up and works wonders."[20] But shepherds do more than show affection to the sheep—they also vigorously protect the sheep.

Summary

Cloud and Townsend note, "We have to experience trustworthy love before we can deal with an untrustworthy world. If we have no place to learn about dependable, safe people, we will never be able to sustain ourselves."[21] Too many people need but cannot find safe places and safe people. In the time of #metoo and #churchtoo, the church has an opportunity to shed light on and purge itself of hidden abuses, and to bring healing for the vulnerable and broken. As McKnight and Barringer point out, "When the voices of women become customary, common, expected, and accepted, the church becomes more inviting, more inclusive, more empathetic, more compassionate, safer, and more secure—for everyone."[22]

REFLECTION QUESTIONS

1. What role do the leaders play in creating a safe church or ministry?

2. How would you assess whether a church or ministry is safe?

3. Do you naturally tend to sympathize with the victim or the accused? Why?

4. Why is it important that a church or ministry make sure that the process of keeping everyone safe is both legal and just?

5. What is your opinion of Mary DeMuth's statement that it is more important to protect survivors than it is to protect reputations?

---

20. Edwards, Mathews, and Rogers, *Mixed Ministry*, 83.
21. Cloud and Townsend, *Safe People*, 62.
22. McKnight and Barringer, *Church Called Tov*, 111.

Select Bibliography

Barr, Beth Allison. *The Making of Biblical Womanhood*. Grand Rapids: Brazos, 2021.

Bartlett, Andrew. *Men and Women in Christ: Fresh Light from the Biblical Texts*. London: InterVarsity, 2019.

Bauckham, Richard. *Gospel Women: Studies of the Named Women in the Gospels*. Grand Rapids: Eerdmans, 2002.

Beck, James R., and Craig L. Blomberg, eds. *Two Views on Women in Ministry*. 2nd ed. Grand Rapids: Zondervan, 2005.

Belleville, Linda L. *Women Leaders and the Church: Three Crucial Questions*. Grand Rapids: Baker, 2000.

Cohick, Lynn. *Women in the World of the Earliest Christians: Illuminating Ancient Ways of Life*. Grand Rapids: Baker Academic, 2009.

Cohick, Lynn, and Amy Brown Hughes. *Christian Women in the Patristic World: Their Influence, Authority, and Legacy in the Second through Fifth Centuries*. Grand Rapids: Baker Academic, 2017.

DeMuth, Mary. *We Too: How the Church Can Respond Redemptively to the Sexual Abuse Crisis*. Eugene, OR: Harvest House, 2019.

Denhollander, Rachael. *What Is a Girl Worth? My Story of Breaking the Silence and Exposing the Truth about Larry Nassar and USA Gymnastics*. Carol Stream, IL: Tyndale Momentum, 2019.

Doriani, Dan. *Women and Ministry: What the Bible Teaches*. Wheaton, IL: Crossway, 2003.

Edwards, Sue, Kelley Mathews, and Henry J. Rogers. *Mixed Ministry: Working Together as Brothers and Sisters in an Oversexed Society*. Grand Rapids: Kregel, 2008.

Epp, Eldon Jay. *Junia: The First Woman Apostle*. Minneapolis: Fortress, 2005.

Freedman, R. David. "Woman, a Power Equal to Man: Translation of Woman a 'Fit Helpmate' for Man Is Questioned." *Biblical Archaeology Review* 9, no. 1 (Jan./Feb. 1983): 56–58.

Garn, Elizabeth. "What Women Need to Know about Being Image-Bearers of God." The Gospel Coalition. July 19, 2017. https://www.thegospelcoalition.org/article/what-women-need-to-know-about-being-image-bearers-of-god.

Glahn, Sandra. "The First-Century Ephesian Artemis: Ramifications of Her Identity." *Bibliotheca Sacra* 172 (Oct.–Dec. 2015): 450–69.

_____. "The Identity of Artemis in First-Century Ephesus." *Bibliotheca Sacra* 172 (July–Sept. 2015): 316–34.

_____, ed. *Vindicating the Vixens: Revisiting Sexualized, Vilified, and Marginalized Women of the Bible*. Grand Rapids: Kregel, 2017.

Grudem, Wayne. *Evangelical Feminism and Biblical Truth: An Analysis of More Than 100 Disputed Questions*. Wheaton, IL: Crossway, 2012.

Hamner, Curt, John Trent, Rebekah J. Byrd, Eric L. Johnson, and Eric Thoennes. *Marriage: Its Foundation, Theology, and Mission in a Changing World*. Chicago: Moody, 2018.

Köstenberger, Andreas J., and Margaret E. Köstenberger. *God's Design for Man and Woman: A Biblical-Theological Survey*. Wheaton, IL: Crossway, 2014.

Köstenberger, Andreas J., and Thomas R. Schreiner. *Women in the Church: An Interpretation and Application of 1 Timothy 2:9–15*. 3rd edition. Wheaton, IL: Crossway, 2016.

Lee-Barnewall, Michelle. *Neither Complementarian nor Egalitarian: A Kingdom Corrective to the Evangelical Gender Debate*. Grand Rapids: Baker Academic, 2016.

McKnight, Scot, and Laura Barringer. *A Church Called Tov: Forming a Goodness Culture That Resists Abuses of Power and Promotes Healing.* Carol Stream, IL: Tyndale House, 2020.

Ortlund, Raymond. "Male-Female Equality and Male Headship: Genesis 1–3." In *Recovering Biblical Manhood and Womanhood: A Response to Evangelical Feminism.* Wheaton, IL: Crossway, 2021.

Payne, Philip B. *Man and Woman, One in Christ: An Exegetical and Theological Study of Paul's Letters.* Grand Rapids: Zondervan, 2009.

Peppiatt, Lucy. *Rediscovering Scripture's Vision for Women: Fresh Perspectives on Disputed Texts.* Downers Grove, IL: IVP Academic, 2019.

Pierce, Ronald W., Cynthia Long Westfall, and Christa L. McKirland, eds. *Discovering Biblical Equality: Biblical, Theological, Cultural, and Practical Perspectives.* 3rd ed. Downers Grove, IL: IVP Academic, 2021.

Piper, John, and Wayne Grudem, eds. *Recovering Biblical Manhood and Womanhood: A Response to Evangelical Feminism.* Wheaton, IL: Crossway, 2021.

Saucy, Robert L., and Judith K. TenElshof, eds. *Women and Men in Ministry: A Complementary Perspective.* Chicago: Moody, 2001.

Sax, Leonard. *Why Gender Matters.* New York: Broadway, 2005.

Spencer, Aída Besançon. *Beyond the Curse: Women Called to Ministry.* Peabody, MA: Hendrickson, 1997.

Sumner, Sarah. *Men and Women in the Church: Building Consensus on Christian Leadership.* Downers Grove, IL: InterVarsity, 2003.

Tong, Rosemarie, and Tina Fernandes Botts. *Feminist Thought: A More Comprehensive Introduction.* 5th ed. New York: Westview, 2018.

Westfall, Cynthia Long. *Paul and Gender: Reclaiming the Apostle's Vision for Men and Women in Christ.* Grand Rapids: Baker Academic, 2016.

Witt, William. *Icons of Christ: A Biblical and Systematic Theology for Women's Ordination.* Waco, TX: Baylor University Press, 2020.

Wright, N. T. "Women's Service in the Church: The Biblical Basis." N. T. Wright
    Online. September 4, 2004. https://ntwrightpage.com/2016/07/12/
    womens-service-in-the-church-the-biblical-basis.

Scripture Index

About the Authors

Sue Edwards (MA, Dallas Theological Seminary; DMin, Gordon-Conwell Theological Seminary), professor of educational ministry and leadership at Dallas Theological Seminary, has taught at DTS for more than 20 years. With over 40 years' experience as Bible teacher and overseer of ministries to women, she is the coauthor of eight leadership books and the Discover Together Bible Study Series. Visit www.discovertogetherseries.com for bible study videos, free leader's guides and more!

Kelley Mathews (ThM, Dallas Theological Seminary), a former women's ministry director, now serves on the publishing team at RightNow Media. A DMin student at Northern Seminary, she is the coauthor of *Leading Women Who Wound*. She lives with her husband, John, and their four children in Texas. Find her blog at patheos.com/blogs/theestuary.

40 QUESTIONS SERIES

40 QUESTIONS SERIES